Amy Benjamin

The Waking Dance

THE STRUGGLE TO UNLEASH A FREE SPIRIT

SterlingHouse
Publisher, Inc.

Pittsburgh, PA

ISBN 1-58501-099-5

Trade Paperback
© Copyright 2006 Amy Benjamin
All Rights Reserved
First Printing: 2006
Library of Congress #2006922171

Request for information should be addressed to:
SterlingHouse Publisher, Inc.
7436 Washington Avenue, Pittsburgh, PA 15218
www.sterlinghousepublisher.com

SterlingHouse Books
is an imprint of SterlingHouse Publisher, Inc.

SterlingHouse Publisher, Inc.
is a company of CyntoMedia Corporation.

Cover Design: Joseph Urban and Jamie Linder
Interior Design: Kathleen M. Gall
Front cover photograph by Mark Yellen
Back cover photograph by Mark Dellas

Printed in the United States of America

Amy Benjamin

The Waking Dance

THE STRUGGLE TO UNLEASH A FREE SPIRIT

Ms. Joyce —
My best to you always.
I so cherish the
friendship we enjoy.
Hope to see you soon.
Amy

Table of Contents

Dedication

To those four little beings
who help me return to that place of trust and love
and wonder and purpose
where spirits soar and magic always remains a possibility.

A Note to the Reader

This book is a work of nonfiction. Chronology is dead-on perfect. Settings are intact. Many names have not been changed, and the depictions of those tremendous people are by no means accidental. Feelings, of which there may be close to eight thousand, are exactly as they occurred, when they occurred, all victim to the rose-colored glasses I sometimes wear.

There is a point at the end of this book where truth evolves into fiction, where it is streamed atop the wings of creative license as a means of writing the future I would have liked to unwrap. In advance of this point, truth resonates profoundly, unequivocally, as the depths of this journey could have never been sought otherwise. Beyond this point, though, there are events that did happen to me, but out of the context under which they were written, and borrowed as a means of wanting them to be real. Not ironically, some of those events have emerged into reality since the completion of this book. That is a beautiful thing.

This book was written with the sole intention of giving me strength and finding me courage at a time when I had neither. It demanded some frank honesty that I didn't know I had bargained for. The thought that it has been received in the ranks of publication is the tallest measure of flattery I have ever known. Thank you to my agent Lisa for believing in it, to my editor, Megan, for her insanely accurate command of language, to my editor, Dana, for her keen insights and technical guidance, to Jason for all of his steady energies, and to SterlingHouse Publisher, Inc. for helping to give it flight.

And So It Was

 It occurred to me, after forty years of honing all of my life skills, that perhaps I had had the wrong manual, a different text, a loosely translated edition from a distant tribe with whom I shared only some DNA. Simple truths, those certain knowings that I would have never elected to challenge, suspended before me without any magnetic pull to the source of their validity. I stood still, for perhaps the first time in my life. I began examining, like a distant observer, the course my life had taken by way of the seven million decisions made up until then. It is so dynamic, the artful play of one's life, so rich with drama and lust, so motivated by fear and desire, so subject to the narrow perception one often asserts to validate those choices in our wake.

This cathartic moment of examination actually occurred over four years' time. What began as an ascending apathy in my engagement with the life I had so precisely crafted from a blueprint that had never been challenged, concluded as a volatile crescendo of confrontation that summoned a trial of accountability that humbled the heroine in me. Satisfaction felt like an empty vacuum of a promise whose offerings were neither considerable nor valid. Whirlpools of strangers could render me the voyeur, as I watched their even banter, wholly disinterested, captivated only by its utter meaninglessness. I was anesthetized, uncertain of how the luscious, divine beauty in life had been replaced by such tedious monotony. There was great darkness in the depths that were navigated on this journey. When blind faith resided as the sole remaining asset, the charge had been met and the passage began.

I can always take my temperature by the temperament of my kids. There is a synergy among us, a collective well-being whose pulse we readily tap into. We each cast a footprint, unique yet aligned, upon our symbiotic enterprise of family, and the tide moves us forward. As mothers, we scribe our signature within the hearts of our children, hoping to impart those values we feel should be carried. And when that temperature was off, I began to wake up.

Life, as I knew it, was rarely up for examination. I moved at a pace that would lend for no such opportunity. Speed was a tremendous numbing agent, a convenient vessel with a motive power of its own. The current of routine, while pleasant for its insulation from risk, often served me with a rigid, narrow interpretation of what my true desires really were. They were branded in the rut of familiarity, morphed by way of a former application. Once I gained too much distance from my own internal compass, I was rendered impotent. And when the dice landed, it seemed as though I had inherited a life by passive submission rather than active election.

With frightening clarity, by force rather than choice, I began examining everything about my life. No fantasy, no prejudice, merely an unbiased evaluation. Few things were insulated from the the harsh scrutiny I began to assert. Namely, what had motivated me, repressed me, seduced me, loved me, and discarded me. How could I simultaneously have been the most efficient and productive human being I knew as well as the most stubborn procrastinator in the free world? What had fueled that brilliant fire of productivity when I chose to engage it? What had attracted me to things that had smothered my spirit to the state of idle sedation, barely breathing? And why had the most regarded and cherished goal of my life, to find a love rooted in passion, respect, and integrity, impenetrable to the challenges that life was certain to put forward, gone utterly unmet and I felt its vacancy like a gutted animal, roadside, regrettably still conscious? This is my story.

Some history. I was brought up in the white bread, upper-middle class suburban sprawl of Western New York, mostly recognized for its state-ranked public school system, notable lack of ethnic diversity, tremendous commitment to youth, and nationally touted lack of crime. We are adjacent to the eastern shores of Great Lake Erie, and are famous for much more snowfall than actually occurs. We boast convenient thruway access to the urban metropolis of Buffalo, NY. Buffalo lived its heyday one hundred years ago, boasts a rich architectural heritage, was home to many famed national citizens, wealthy industrialists, cultural leaders, and business tycoons back in its reigning dynasty. It was highly celebrated as the 1901 gateway Pan-American City, but has sadly coasted downhill on those tired, blue-collar laurels, though the blue blood still postures some place within our roots.

Often when economies and infrastructures erode by way of the macro forces that perpetually reshape the world we live in, there is an offsetting rebirth which is ignited in the fallout of oppression, uncovered as discards in the ash of forgotten promise. Truth be told, it is absolutely the "City of Good Neighbors," and good neighbors are a highly underrated asset when times get tough.

There was a central village near my city with a rich history c. the 1800's, flavored with equal parts quaint New England charm and humble Midwestern integrity. There were hundreds of properties designated as historical landmarks. It could be almost anywhere, but it was the town where I grew up and reside today. Franchise outfits on Main St. were shunned as taboo. The business district was about eight blocks of boutique retail, specialty gourmet, and eclectic office space, each owning a unique piece of architectural history from a place in time predating automobiles, high-speed internet, big box retail, or voicemail, let alone telephone. Many of the buildings had undergone painstaking restoration out of respect for their vintage, and a venerating conscience governed all progress. There was a tall, collective pride in this village steeped in a heritage older than any of its living citizens.

One was blessed who lived within walking distance of the pulse of Main St., liberated from the necessity of a car to engage in every stitch of commerce in their life. There were six spectacular parks within the village limits, there were creeks and bridges and waterfalls and bike paths and a library and homemade ice cream. Peripheral to the village, like the area where I grew up, that intimacy and tenure got diluted somewhat, with neighborhoods from the 50's, 60's, 70's and the transiency of new construction and infant trees and flat suburban sprawl. And most specifically, the village was a nearby asset I had largely ignored in my youth as I plowed right through on my mission for bigger and better things.

It is not ironic that I presently live around the corner from where I grew up in the 1960's. I will add that I have lived in more homes in my forty years of life than anyone I know. I must have been answering some gravitational pull like a homing pigeon, not quite as the crow flies, when I moved back to this neighborhood two years ago in the throes of a crisis that threatened me hard, absent a search warrant, demanding a confrontation whose concerns could no longer be ignored.

I was born the favored child of a mother who was largely celebrated in the circles of my city. She was a working woman with a keen and sharp business aptitude, and a sales savvy that served to build her a respectable real estate empire at a time in our world when women were just on the cusp of loosening the taut apron at their waist. Few of my friends had mothers who worked outside of the home, and I was well aware at that young age that several of my friends' parents didn't encourage our friendships for that very reason.

I was also born a tomboy, forced against my will at age ten to wear a shirt outdoors when playing a neighborhood game of dodgeball. Boys were always my competition, dolls were never my fancy. It seemed to me, even at that young age, that society's imposed branding of gender assimilation, including the discussion that it even existed, was the very prejudice which diverged the sexes. It felt implausible to me that there was a ceiling on the potential in my life by way of the threat and promise in the blossom of my breasts.

I was a great student, always performing above grade-level with minimal measures of effort on my behalf. My parents were never evasive. I had three jobs: get my schoolwork done, stay out of trouble, stay out of their way. My mother's long hours and dedication to her career definitely lightened the parental influence around our home, and I didn't mind that one little bit.

My parents divorced when I was eleven, and that was an event I have very little memory of. No pain, no tears, and, I am coming to recognize, not much emotion. This was also at a time when divorce didn't quite strike the one in two it stings today, but was just beginning its ravage into the structure of family, with long term fallout still a wild card. I don't recall any pain from my youth, which seems painfully impossible to me today. No recurrent episodes of emotional torment which might have pointed to obvious shortcuts toward relief when it all began to crumble.

Perhaps my crafted recollection of my first fifteen years was a conveniently edited version of what really happened, I have no idea. Conventional psychotherapy explores this time in one's life as the kernels of all future adult dysfunction, the buried answers to the root of all personal neurosis. Perhaps this is so. I have come to realize that I know much less than I think I know.

I loved my father, but he was just not where I went when there was something I needed. When I chose to need him, he was there for the most part. Sadly, I had little expectation from that relationship, perhaps as a measure to insure little opportunity for disappointment. He met his own needs quite well, enjoyed fast cars, traveling, golf, and other fruits of the labor of the family business he was handed as an eighteen-year-old. He didn't similarly value my summer camps or private school education, so that was certainly not where I went to fill those bigger tickets. After the divorce, we visited weekly, caught up on life, shared what felt to be appropriate, and enjoyed the pleasant surface of each other's company.

I was never hit or molested or burned with an iron or locked in a closet. No complaints, all was good. I sincerely recalled all of my adolescent years with peace and happiness. One grows to realize, however, that perception has tremendous powers to shape the memory and write the future. We own that perception. No one can ever negate the version of memory we elect to tap into when answering today's problems with yesterday's lessons.

I graduated from a private girls' prep school in the top tier of my class. I mastered the art of bullshit with a refined grace that scared me silly. I certainly found my share of trouble, getting caught smoking pot, exploring the license of my sexuality, pushing boundaries of teenage restraint, but never making any headlines. I began to learn that I was more sexually provocative than some, not as provocative as others, but that indeed it was more important to me than to most.

My first love was sent to me directly from the heavens, cosigned by the Almighty himself. We found in each other a magic and passion and spirit, discovering daily the very real possibility that no one had been in love like this before us, not ever. Today, I marvel at the intimacy I was capable of at the ripe age of fifteen, and I recognize that virginity is a place where matters other than the hymen are intact. We were together just over a year, four full seasons, one full circle. Soon after he left for college, we both scurried to refill the hole we had left behind. Easier said than done. Who was I to know, way back when, that first loves die so hard?

I boarded the carousel of teen dating. I had my heart broken several times at the callous conclusion of a relationship, and sent a few hearts there in rebuttal. I fell apart, I recovered, I moved on. My girlfriends and I would cruise all of our regular haunts, strung out on free time and fast food and cheesy music. It seemed a healthy balance could be struck with responsible playing, meeting academic demands, feeding parents and teachers and coaches what they needed to hear. Show up, get it done, and stay below the radar of authority. I was always watching the radar.

Boulder, Colorado captured my heart in college. It was without question the place that fostered my love of the outdoors, my appreciation for the awesome beauty in nature, my respect for all things of simple, organic origin. Much of the value I place today on matters of clothing, diet, exercise, lighting, color, beauty, healing, and energy were all shaped in Boulder Valley. And it is the land of All Things Beautiful. If there were titles with which cities were crowned for gathering the best-looking pool of people, Boulder would clearly be King. I would swear there was a turnstile at the city limits, guarded by a panel of very shallow judges there to discern who gets in and who goes home.

The bond forged with friends similarly exploring the potential and potency of their youth and freedom was boundless. Plentiful props of acoustic music, easy clothing, illegal recreation, late-night cafes before they were vogue, abundant Grateful Dead, a la Redrocks, all while navigating a college curriculum nary missing a beat. Our only job was namely to maintain satisfactory transcripts that insured our tuition got paid and allowance got sent. We were mostly from towns and cities in the Northeast, mostly from prep schools, and few of us never met a want in our lives that went unmet. We shared dorm rooms, then apartments, shared boyfriends and shampoo. Most poignantly, we shared a remarkably blessed four-year window of our lives when we owned the world.

I survey the lives we have all gone on to live in as a measure of damage control. Among us there are a high-profile attorney in Chicago, a not-for-profit peace activist attorney in Mill Valley, an insanely successful real estate developer of strip malls in Atlanta, an interior designer in Boston, a jewelry designer in Mexico, an international commercial pilot still in Boulder, an accounts receivable manager for a large organic food company also in Boulder, a gay computer guru nestled in the vines of Napa Valley, and a business entrepreneur always seeking new endeavors with the backing of his trust fund—which never threatens to empty—never with a permanent address. There are no brain surgeons. No rocket scientists. And each of our closets are crowded with enough stashed artifacts from yesteryear that would stand in between any one of us and any future public office.

Then there is me, a real estate broker, barely borrowing the nuggets of knowledge earned in my degree. After college, I returned to Western New York, never intending to stay. My mother's real estate career was on fire. She had broken all sales records and was considered top dog in the residential sales arena. She was then in the seat of ownership of one of the largest residential firms in the state of New York, excluding The Big Apple.

I got my broker's license largely because she was intolerant of my lazy mornings while in a holding pattern gearing up for a move to Boston with a girlfriend. Real estate was a good fit, sales was a natural, the market area I knew intimately from having grown up there my whole life. I earned unprecedented rookie awards my first year out of the gate, and climbed a sales record for the next fifteen years, placing me in the top echelon of agents, every year, without interruption.

I hate blind dates. I have been on two in my life, and I married both of them. The odds of this were painfully small, except that I was apparently a magnet for dysfunction in the long-term relationships that seemed to attract me. Most everything in my life had come without pressure or force, without doubt or dilemma. Central to the crumble and crisis of my life, which began a few years ago, was the reality that I had failed to select a life partner with whom I shared interests, compatibility, intimacy, values, a whole litany of things that people usually considered when making such decisions. Didn't even come close. Not once, but twice. Logically, it seemed that there must be more at play. My luck couldn't be that bad.

My first husband was great guy and remains a very valued friend. Perhaps with the crystal clear clarity of hindsight, time may have evolved us into a great pair of life partners; one will never know. Harry and I were set up when I was six months out of college. The date was arranged by a mutual friend in real estate. It was summer, we were ripe. We came from different backgrounds and didn't have a mutual friend in common save the woman who set us up. We shared a connection that obviously spoke to me for the seven months we feverishly dated. Unplanned and pregnant, there were decisions to make about the destiny of us.

I had never been pregnant before, nor had I considered abortion to be a procedure about which I carried a moral judgment. However, there was not a single fleeting notion of doubt that this child within me was staying within me. Harry supported my feelings with kindness and compassion. There was a very cute post-coital moment where we directed the predicament to the altar of my belly, spoke to our little amoeba, hopeful for some supernatural cue on where to pivot this turn of events. We considered not marrying, but ultimately decided to give it a try to see how it fit.

We had a church wedding. I was two months pregnant in a dress too white and ornamented for the occasion. Most of my friends were puzzled by this choice I was making, though not shy about offering me recreational drugs in the bathroom at the reception. I passed, took a pause, and only then did it dawn on me that there were going to be other decisions and sacrifices ahead of me that would mark the conclusion of the "end-of-just-me" life as I knew it. I was 23 years old.

We stayed together until shortly after our second child was born, a short three years from that famed blind date. We had a son, Peter, then a daughter, Leah. Young and energetic as new parents, we shared a few happy years together, welcoming these little people into their worlds.

I felt an absence of passion, that undeniable clarity of having found a soul mate that dripped with a wet and luscious love, extracted from the pages of a fairy tale. It was very possible that I merely had the patience of my then two-year-old. There were normal shifts in body chemistry and assimilation into newfound nuclear family that needed some massaging and adjustment, mostly by trial and error. I apparently had a crystal ball that surpassed that decade and did not see us in Adirondack chairs on an expansive porch overlooking a beautiful, postcard lake. My crystal ball had directed traffic much of my life, and I was usually in tow with its suggestions. We separated comfortably, according, of course, to me. We mediated most legal matters between us, found visitation that complimented both of our schedules, and have remained good friends and parents in all our years. It was a fruitful business endeavor.

My second blind date yielded another marriage and two children, though not with the same easy onset. Peter and Leah were four and two when Alex and I met. He had never been married. I don't really know that he ever had a functional, intimate relationship before we met, as his years from age twelve until age twenty-eight were spent seduced by drugs and drinking and their ensuing dysfunction, then replaced with an addiction to money and power after he became clean.

He fell into his family business of movie theatre ownership, learning every facet of those operations while being high, but learning them intimately nonetheless. His security in business at such a young age never prompted him to finish college. I had only heard stories of the ravage of his life from those using years. Alex's personality was an interesting cocktail of obsession, compulsion, impulse, and determination. When using drugs, he must have been lethal. He went through rehab at age twenty-eight, only once against most odds, and his clean life became his new tonic. His passion for power had new fuel, no longer underground. His love of gambling was born. His life was a freebie, he often remarked, as he was pegged a dead man when he hit bottom.

We had a rocky year and a half of dating, but somehow kept returning to our relationship. We moved in together after six months, which proved a difficult dynamic with young children, then three and five. The cohabitation seemed wise before making any permanent life choices, as kids and their fabulous chaos might have been one thing for a natural parent, but a whole different story for someone unrelated. Things between us escalated to miserable.

My kids had never before been witness to lousy adult energy, and I needed to shield them, to run for cover like a mother hen. Fearful of the fallout when telling Alex this was not working out, I plotted my exit born in deceit. I bought a house he knew nothing about, reregistered my kids in a new kindergarten and preschool, retained a mover on the sly, all while living under the roof of normalcy for a period of almost a month.

On the day of my departure, the movers arrived a convenient fifteen minutes after Alex left for work. We packed all my belongings and furniture and artwork in three hours flat. I summoned a friend to pick up Peter and Leah from their schools and keep them until later that night. I sent the moving van to a storage facility. The still of the nearly vacated home that I had just emptied was deafening as I awaited Alex's return from work. I paced around the rooms, absent a single evidentiary detail of mine or my kids', chain smoked twenty-five cigarettes, wondering how the hell I was capable of orchestrating the mess of my life.

I moved into a two-story home in an older, historic part of town. The three of us found a groove that was light and fun and relieved of the pressure that had been building for months. There certainly were questions of why we seemed to move overnight, why a new school, where did Alex go, but they were delicately handled, so it seemed. I was sensitive to their fragile worlds, aggressively inserting all things familiar from family to friends to favorite restaurants, lending little regard to the chapter of yesterday.

Alex and I handled relationship fallout via telephone for the first few weeks. He was rightfully floored at the shock of my callous departure, while I stumbled with my defense on why it needed to be that way with young kids and sensitive psyches on board. It was a circular argument that only underscored my gratitude for having fled.

The following months softened him, buttered him to the point of profuse apology for behaviors that preceded the move. He rallied for another attempt at making it work, keeping separate houses and an open mind. I was assured that I would no longer be punished for having left under such drastic circumstances, for which he took full responsibility. I bought it, we gave it a try for another few months, and married on New Year's Eve, a better bride, proudly not pregnant this time around.

We bought a five bedroom house, ready to accommodate two more kids, Sam & Sophie, born two years apart. I continued on my journey of being a mother, a real estate broker, and even learned to be a wife with a tenor that was a decent fit. The blending of the kids came naturally, as I was the mother to them all and the keeper of the peace.

Alex had very little interest in the daily activities which engaged the children. He had always seemed more like a father from fifty years ago, the kind that waited in the waiting room for the good word of his child's birth, cigars on board, next plan on deck. He seemed to feel that matters of their daily lives were cordoned to the maternal arena. Diapers, baths, meals, shoelaces, first days of school, graduating to a two-wheel bike, teacher conferences, and certainly issues of emotional concern were usually my matters alone. I learned to live this doctrine, to wear it well, grateful that one of its perks was not having to run every notion I had past him for approval. As the judge and the jury, it all worked well.

I wore a thin veil of envy when I would see dads engaged in an outdoor activity with their kids, or both parents with a camcorder at the school play, but I recognized there was compromise always, and that things were not always what they seemed. We both had good jobs, we made plenty of money, the kids had great networks of stimulation both in and out of the house. There were some great years of peace and routine and happiness in that period of our lives.

My role as mother was artfully assimilated with an instinctual guidance that had rarely wavered. I would hear of friends' kid-related issues regarding teething or tantrums or social integration concerns or school bus separation anxiety. I pretended to care, even pretended to have issues of my own lest they feel as inferior as they seemed to me. This kid banter seemed to consume the whole of that young mommy social repertoire, yet I just couldn't engage. Pleasant and tolerant, but utterly bored, became my demeanor when in the presence of mommies in play groups, Tae Kwon Do lounges, soccer sidelines, or PTA-sponsored lectures on how to raise the next President. My pulse was fired separate from these necessary forums.

My job as a real estate broker was tremendously ideal for raising a family. I owned my mornings, wrote my own schedule, and appreciated being compensated for my aptitude to work smartly. I was able to respond to work demands as they arose, able to meet the bus, schlep to activities, show a house in-between, present an offer when necessary. Micromanagement was my middle name. With every passing year, my client base grew larger, I learned to work smarter, and my sales volume could go to the moon if I wanted to send it there.

I was first on board with cell phones and e-mail. First to locate fancy software capable of manipulating yesterday's same flat data into impressive presentations for clients, tall on style, short on effort. Most agents in my industry were older than I and harbored strange aversions to new technologies when they were first introduced. These technology tools propelled my business quantumly, all while I was afforded the freedoms of living without a formal sixty-minute lunch hour, forty-hour work week, or without someone giving me the once-over if I sauntered in at eleven a.m. in jeans and a cute T-shirt. If I needed to work on a weekend or a school night, there was support in place, and I welcomed the opportunity to speak something other than "kid" for a little while. Certainly there were some crowded weeks where urgent clients, school midterms, and a class play all collided, but it all got done. Because that was what I did: I got it done.

There were many silent contributions in the Temple of Home from which children extracted their essence of hope, faith, personal potential, perceived limitation, latent fear, all simultaneously integrated into the routine of an average day. The kisses and hugs, reprimands and recourse, laughter and levity, they all played their role. A parent's moral and ethical posture, on six thousand scores, passively permeated by unspoken example rather than intellectual lesson. By environmental conditioning, children adopted the manner which best suited their notion of place in the world they were growing into. It was all good, and those average days were strung together for almost ten uninterrupted years.

I imagine that if I were to die tomorrow, the undercurrent of my funeral—the eulogy, the casket-side tears, the whispered small-talk, even the private pillow talk as they returned to their lives—would be what a dedicated mother I had been to my children. Some of my measures might be obvious to my kids today; most are still resonating until the cue arrives to launch its flight. There had never been a moment of doubt, dilemma, or reserve that I had confronted as a mother where I wasn't equipped with the guided and disciplined resolve to see it through.

Until it all changed. The assault of confrontations, fired with relentless efficiency at the vulnerable core of my being, summoned an examination it was not easy to get naked for. I recognize today the sobering advice that airline personnel share regarding how to prepare oneself in the event that the plane were in distress, even fatally: Affix one's own breathing apparatus, then tend to your children's. I had always assumed they had that backwards.

My mental stability had never been a wild card, not at any of the chapters I had lived. Certainly there were times of challenge, most of which were met with clarity, focus and control. Rarely were there decisions made that were later regretted. They were simply off my plate without further reflection. Friends had always admired that about me. I'd heard it from dozens of people, unable to accept it as a compliment because I truly couldn't fathom navigating life without that compass.

I silently stood in judgment of most when I would hear of their quandaries and the self-battery they elected to assert when making decisions. The litany of potential consequence, running hog-wild as they tried to nail down what it was that they really wanted. So futile. So insecure. I recognized that I stood alone in the unwavering self-confidence that I had always put forward, happy to not feel crowded at my post. Rarely did I ever take a pause to weigh the ramifications of skirting a responsibility, neglecting a friend, or burying a problem. Was I just a kid or was I just an asshole? I think the jury is still out.

Perhaps an impartial assessment of the success of my life today, as rendered by the survey of the bystander, would lend toward a notion of borderline empathy laced with reserved judgment. I am sure there are plenty that would think I had it coming.

I have journals which span the course of my entire life. There must be a dozen, each with covers reflective of the period of life I was living. Some are tailored with style and appeal to the school-age girl I was, others of the surreal and boundless possibility in the frenzied teen years, others with sheer simplicity from the early years of mothering. As I woke to the beauty of organic things, I had one made of hemp fiber with an exotic tree sap binding, which continually needed alternative reinforcement. These books were the pulse of my life. I had not known when creating them that they would later become such a valuable resource in my spiritual rescue.

The entries were haphazard. Some were brief and hostile, some were long and fluid, some were illegible. There was never more than eighteen months between entries, but some months had twenty issues that needed that literary release.

I wrote a lot when in the volatile throes of a relationship with a man, either manic with an obsessive infatuation or depressed by heartless, callous rejection. I can tap venom from my written words of anger on issues regarding difficult adolescent relations with my mother, spanning the better part of ten years from puberty until I was a mother. There was an ever-present current of sexual frustration that my marriage had always been burdened with. I wrote a ton during my pregnancies. My journal was never far.

As it was, my life till age 36 was a charmed one. I successfully crafted an outwardly enviable life in which I bought, sold, or bartered all of the integrated players or pieces, all neatly packaged and balanced on one thin dime. A superficial inventory would net the following: happy childhood free of any of the deranged pathology one reads of too often. A loving first boyfriend; we simultaneously surrendered our virginity in a real bed with plaid sheets, a pine headboard, and an overhead cross bearing witness to our horizontal homecoming. An exclusive private school education, an impressive BA degree in the social sciences while I partied like a rockstar, a professional career that celebrated my talent by affording me a fabulous leverage vehicle to balance income and time. Four incredible children who unknowingly help me grow up every single day, and a husband whom I largely ignored as a possibility to help me at all.

Checklist:

First of my friends to lose their virginity: . . . . me
First of my friends to smoke pot: . . . . me
First of my friends to kiss a girl: . . . . me
First of my friends to get pregnant: . . . . me
First of my friends to get married: . . . . me
First of my friends to buy a cute house: . . . . me
First of my friends to earn a 6-figure income: . . . . me
First of my friends to get divorced: . . . . me
First of my friends to get remarried: . . . . me
First of my friends to have 1, 2, 3 & 4 kids: . . . . me
First of my friends to get divorced twice: . . . . almost me

Life was my racetrack. Apparently, my set of instructions included a special prize for my early arrival, with no points being deducted for actually missing the point of the journey. Where was this fire? Why was it propelling me full throttle? Was I running toward a shrouded goal or away from a veiled threat? Did I have a clue how to seek satisfaction, the kind that could not be quantified by anything that tallied? Truth be told, none of these questions even crossed my mind.

High Tide

$\mathcal{F}$ew events that set into motion a series of other events on the cusp of a downward spiral are obvious at their onset. Something in the cosmic current of energy just changes, often without warning, rarely without a blueprint. There seem to be serendipitous moments in life where ordinary events are given extraordinary opportunity to wreak havoc.

I had grown accustomed to the usual currents in life; what was reasonably possible, what was a bearable level of risk to tolerate, what spectrum of consequence certain decisions might have had. I breathed within those boundaries. Sometimes things might have fallen out of that footprint, but rarely did they alter the long haul.

People had varying tolerances for acceptable levels of risk. Some would rarely offend their own laggard shadow, others would thrive on the dangers which rode piggyback on the heels of the long shot. And there were some who just seemed to have a horseshoe up their ass.

I was the founder of the horseshoe club, and I'd held the title much of my life. There were periods of time when this privilege proved to ward off small evil things like parking tickets, could bump me up to first class, could secure me the supermarket cashier who neglected to ring up the case of beer at the bottom of my cart, could keep a fifty-year-old furnace running without a hiccup the entire time it lived under my control. I was that asshole you glared at for not returning my shopping cart to its rightful corral, even in windstorms. The same one who was certain that the convenient fire lane in any random plaza was an appropriate place to park my car for two short minutes because, well, I moved at the speed of light. I could have crossed thresholds into the chambers of CEO's offices, past security, with the saunter of a silent partner. No one stopped me. Yes, rules were for some; I did appreciate what chaos there would be if ever I were cloned. This unseemly good fortune had always graced me. Its powers were boundless, dependable, coveted.

Most notably, this privilege proved to resonate with big-ticket blessings such as four healthy kids, with forty fingers and toes, and each with spirits that inspired me always. Well aware of the sad and sorry misfortunes rampant in the world, the title was my closely held secret, tucked under my belt and never actually spoken of, lest that would oblige me to pass it on.

And so it was, September 2000, a time for surrender. Alex and I were in Manhattan for a friend's wedding over Labor Day. It was a glorious late-summer weekend, high skies, seventy degrees, no humidity, Madison Avenue shopping, and all the promise of happy nuptials. It was as good as it ever got.

A few weeks before we left for New York, I was in contact with a friend from Boulder who told me that she had recently run into one Kate Gallagher. Ms. Gallagher had been MIA from my life since college. I had heard random tidbits of her whereabouts; she was a chef at a diner in Marin County, she worked as the manager of a bicycle store in LA, she was back in Boulder living at a freethinking lesbian commune up in Nederland. Now, I heard, she was living in Manhattan and I was jotting down the phone number my friend was giving me because this girl had never had a listed number in her life.

Kate and I met in Boulder when we were nineteen. She was somewhat peripheral to my core group, but we became fast friends in a heartbeat. She and her boyfriend had just broken up and she was heartsick, brushing against the verge of crumbling. Despite his feathered hair and crowded teeth, she was certain he was her soul mate and was crushed to discover that he had moved on. I also recall that her school performance didn't make the cut and her parents back in New England weren't funding her life anymore. Her cord was cut.

I was living in a turn-of-the-century bungalow house on "The Hill," Boulder's infamous college town pulse. She needed a place to stay for a brief while, so I offered a corner of my queen-sized waterbed and three drawers in my dresser. Over the course of the next few weeks, we grew inseparable. I slowly retreated from the routine of my usual life and immersed myself into the strange whirlwind of connection that was brewing between us.

The ascension of other-than-ordinary became more than a fleeting suspicion late one night when we were lying on the bed laughing about some hysterical event I cannot recall. We had been bellowing, trying to return to normal breathing. We had come down together, slowly, guided with reciprocal eye contact that we both recognized as laced with something most unusual. There was one long, uninterrupted moment of peculiar silence, followed by an impassioned, sensual kiss. It was unfamiliar, soft, quiet and erotic, absent the frenzied steam I was used to kissing with, and also absent the brambly facial hair and testosterone tempo. They were misplaced sensations, ones I didn't assign to women. We held that embrace barely a minute, then lost ourselves in a very peaceful gaze of sated but curious well-being. We spoke no more and fell asleep with our bodies aligned with regard for this new energy, inches apart, like babies.

Around 6:30 a.m., I woke peacefully and rolled over to see Kate. She had been watching me sleep, watching me wake. That peculiar gaze returned on cue, and within seconds we were in full embrace, caressing every inch of our similar bodies. We made love for two hours, learning a native language of the homeland never before visited.

From there forward, we spent about seven months inseparable. We would shop for, prepare, consume, and clean up after insanely extravagant gourmet meals. We would hike in the mountains, bike on the trails, picnic in parks, and get naked at any suspicion that no one was watching. It was a minor miracle that I passed any of my courses that semester. My east coast "trustafarian" (a.k.a. one who loved to dance to reggae music, who also had a trust fund) friends were very straight in that way, but also very tolerant of my new diversion. I saw much less of them, but was careful to not burn any bridges. I didn't start visiting lesbian coffee houses, transforming my wardrobe, or cutting my long hair, but the strength of the connection we were forging was very much within me.

Like most things in love and war, something shifted. It seems there is an intangible component in relationships that can one day just reboot and yield an entirely different perspective. Perhaps there is a defect in my own personal hardware that a long course in psychotherapy might begin to address, but this is the equipment I have. Exact things about Kate that were once rife with charm and delight became, without reason, sources of disturbing irritation.

Exiting any intense relationship was never easy. I needed out, she needed in, and thereby was born a rift that evolved into a psychotic obsession. I took a different apartment, got an unlisted phone number, and laid as low as one could lay without leaving a city. Still, she would find me, she would stalk me, she would scare the shit out of me.

I recall one evening having returned home from a party with my best male friend I may or may not have been sleeping with. We crashed in my bed. When I woke in the morning, I went to the closet to grab some clothes and found Kate crouched on the floor. She had spent the entire night peeping though the slatted door, apparently still interested in watching me sleep. This also meant she had broken in, entered the closet, and planted herself there for twelve straight hours without stretching a leg or speaking a word.

"Hi," her only word when I discovered her.

"You freak!" I screamed, grabbed the closest sweatshirt, and closed her right back into her box. Her pain I did not wear. My sweatshirt I did.

Stranger still occurred one night at a restaurant with ten friends, eating, drinking, and being twenty. Kate approached the table, silence fell in guarded anticipation for what she had to say. She chattered on with unbridled excitement about how she had just won the lottery, which was approaching twelve million dollars that night. My friends went wild with excitement over this big jackpot, not able to fathom that psychosis could potentially run so deep that its victim might create such extravagant fantasies. While the others were reeling with the news of her windfall, my one friend looked at me with a stone-cold expression, staring me square me in the eyes, understanding the extent of the problem on my hands.

Everyone should be stalked just once in their lifetime. I truly feel that if anyone could be on the receiving end of a stalker's bizarre behaviors, it would put an end to this freaky practice, if only in the name of its utter futility and incapacity to affect a change in heart.

In due time, Kate's grip on me lessened, and I felt free to turn corners without consequence. I returned to my core friends, my usual life before this hiccup. There was no discriminating judgment, just back to business as usual, boyfriends on cue. I graduated later that year, having spent the last semester of school without even a word of her whereabouts.

It did not seem possible, but indeed it was, that from then forward I had never really thought of this woman, not made one reflective mental return to such an intense period in my life, my still-only lesbian love adventure. I had successfully buried the carnage somewhere and went on to live my happily-ever-after life. But the corpse was quickly unearthed that August afternoon when my friend told me that Kate was living in New York where I would be visiting in two short weeks.

There was maybe an hour I owned that phone number before I dialed it. I surveyed the digits, attempting an assembly into an order that I could make sense of. What insanity had invaded my life back when I shunned accountability and welcomed the whims of being alive? When did such bold deviation go on permanent hiatus? Who knew? So I dialed.

A woman answered in an aloof, "I don't sleep with men" sort of tone.

Why I considered that, I had no idea. I asked for Kate, and she informed me she was in the shower, likely having just been licked and loved, I could only surmise. I left my name and number with this woman, suspicious that the message might not be relayed.

Almost two weeks passed. Three days before my departure, Kate called. I had nearly given up on the notion of connecting with her, but alas, we were on the line. I was brief and secure, informing her that I would be in New York in a few days and was wondering if she wanted to join me and my husband for a drink and dinner, and that my four incredible kids would not be joining us, and that my tremendously successful career fortunately afforded me the opportunity for such short and whimsical stints to The Big Apple. She didn't offer nearly as much, but agreed to the drink. We exchanged cell numbers, planning on connecting once I landed.

Alex and I checked into the hotel and relaxed in the lay of the room. He could feel my anticipation and anxiety as I tried on every article of clothing I had packed, and I could feel him feeling it. I assured him that nothing was fitting right, strangely, and that my finicky pace was independent of my rendezvous in an hour. The relationship interested him, though not nearly as much as I would have thought it might have. He made a few menage-a-trois jokes, then suggested that she and I meet alone for the drink. He could get lost in the city for a while, and we could all hook up for dinner. I was all over that program.

The bar was perfect. It was a wine bar of sorts, with an impressive piano, excellent lighting, and tremendously good-looking people, including the busboy. I was purposefully early, a rare occurrence. I can count on both hands how many times it has happened in my lifetime. I needed to stand still at the bar, I needed some magic tonic at the bar, I needed the perfect seat at the bar. My hair needed to acclimate, my skin needed to flush, my heart needed to relax. Yes, I was early.

I could see her exit a cab across Madison Avenue. She paid the driver with an ease and flair unique to New Yorkers. She cast a cursory survey of the oncoming traffic and darted across the street, accommodating the rushing ebb and flow of cars. Her physique was surprisingly similar to the girl I had known from a whole different time and place. We are both 5'8," but her hair was still long and flowing and dark blonde with highlights suggestive of her love of the outdoors rather than the salon. At most she weighed 125 lbs., supported by a pelvis that had never passed four children through, and immediately I felt like a cow who had stopped caring what the other cows thought. *Suck it in. Sit straight. Do a shot.* Look as if I hadn't successfully repressed this person for the last sixteen years.

Kate took the seat at the bar which naturally had inferior lighting to the seat I had secured two drinks earlier. The hug was formal, guarded. She ordered a glass of wine, using the name of the vineyard and the year of the grape, seemingly far more composed than me. We found a groove to begin on.

I slowly felt the anxiety dissipate, thanks to a very trusty double vodka, from Sweden, which aided my return back to feeling familiar. It occurred to me upon that return that I had never felt such a peculiar anxiety, one with a physically engaging grip that it would have left marks if it could have. It was a strange feeling that couldn't be quantified.

We shared war stories of our lives, me mostly of my kids, my marriage, my stupid sales career. I learned she had been a drifter for years post-college, finding odd jobs that celebrated her love of cooking and her enthusiasm for bicycling and the outdoors. She had only one male lover since our time together—the fit wasn't right—and had lived a lesbian life of strife since then. She shared some of the difficulties she had had confronting homosexuality, even within the open arms of Manhattan. She had eventually gotten her shit together, moved back East, secured a great job with a now-successful, then-startup company, where she was apparently at the top of her game.

Alex called my cell to see if he was still invited for dinner, which he was. We all met at a restaurant in Midtown that had horrible overhead lighting and the pungent smell of seared beef fat and curry. Someone had suggested it as new and trendy and "the place" to eat, but it scared me sober walking in there. Alex was curious to take the temperature of what was flying between us. He was silent and engaged during dinner, with eyes in full volley as Kate and I threw around some of our G-rated memories. We resumed our same banter from the piano bar, which carried the ease of a great friend rather than an estranged lover. Following dinner, we all grabbed a cab to the Village, looking to move the evening outdoors, strolling with coffee while soaking up the palpable, vibrant pulse of the rightfully celebrated Greenwich Village.

It was getting late, and Alex was more tired than me. He suggested he take a cab back to the hotel, and I could follow when ready. Exit Alex. Kate and I walked for miles, casually strolling the tree-lined brownstone streets, al fresca cafes, and curbside musicians, never releasing the easy grip of our mingled hands. Our relationship, as last-lived in the mindset of nineteen year olds who owned the world, had been so intense and intimate, so emotionally accessible. It was an effortless return to the dialogue of that window in my life.

When making that transition, it occurred to me, with the volume of a flood light, the extent of the shift that my psyche had endured in that span of time. This did not feel to be about a sexual preference; instead, it was suggestive of the miles between the *me* of then and the *me* of now. I suspected that some of this rift was caused by the normal growing pains one was forced to endure when accommodating the demands associated with real jobs, real kids, real responsibilities, real life in general. But that didn't quite cover it; there was ground that was missing. This was not an issue of mere discipline or temperance, not a matter of meeting the needs of kids, husbands, clients, each presenting needs that I had grown to master while blindfolded on autopilot. There was a visceral suspicion that my perfect life, as put forward just hours earlier at the piano bar, was more than just a few degrees off course.

Kate and I stood still at the juncture of where our diverging cabs would part, surveying the evolution of our separate souls that had been collectively nourished for a snapshot in time, half a life ago. We shared a few final words, a brief silence, then embraced in a quiet kiss of connection that transcended time and space and boundary. Barely ten seconds later, we returned each other's glances, contented and peaceful. I was suspecting that the sea of emotion that was electrically buzzing through each of us was, indeed, inspired by different sources of internal vacancy. That was all right. I got a fix of a notion that my perception of life, all things big and small, inverted and juxtaposed, mandatory and optional, was, after all, just my own dwarfed perception, one that could have been afforded some reexamination, including an honest inventory of matters I had never before chosen to challenge.

I crept into the hotel room. Alex was deep in sleep. I undressed slowly, conscious of each article of clothing as I disrobed. I was dizzy with desire and happy to crawl under covers in the dark still of night. Alex's arm gently crossed that invisible barrier which usually marked our bed territory. He rolled over in an instant, apparently more awake than his slumber of minutes before suggested.

Like any man, he wanted details. He wanted to hear that we made a beeline for her apartment, got naked in a frenzy, and explored every bodily orifice with reckless abandon. He needed to hear that the hand-holding was a mere measure of placating the lust that was rising with our pulse. I shared with him the quiet street corner kiss, though he was much less interested in the birth of my considerations and far more interested in the location of my tongue.

Most people can recall their top few sexual experiences, and that night with my husband was certainly one of them. I showed up in a different way than I had ever recalled, finding a groove that guided my way to a satisfaction of the caliber I usually had difficulty achieving. I became wholly present, strangely engaged and anointed, graced among the company of the supernaturally evolved. I was every minute of there. Climax was other than physical. It was fitted with floodgates whose waters flowed uphill, abetted by spasm and shudder, ascending the apex of my arrival. There was little discussion when we finished, and we fell to sleep closer than our usual repose invited.

From that moment forward, I had embarked on a spiral into a journey of discovery where I was without a single familiar tool to navigate my way, nor a destination road map to indicate where I was going.

The Descent

The morning came without incident, other than the fact that I was still floating in bed covers after Alex had been up, showered, and almost finished packing. We were headed to Long Island for the wedding. I had always been an insanely early riser, always prodding to motivate people out of their beds before they were ready. Alex was actually *in* the wedding, role of a groomsman, and we had to get to the hotel early to allow for the professional photography session that takes place in advance of the actual ceremony, perhaps making it the first fallacy of marriage.

Alex was certainly noticing that I was still lost under the sheets, too stubborn to pull myself from their warmth. I assured him that, because I was not in the prenuptial photography session, I would have plenty of time to get ready in the hotel room there. At the very last possible moment, I gathered my things strewn about the room and managed to make my way out onto Madison Avenue while Alex hailed a cab for Long Island.

I am not sure if we were still in Manhattan when it began. My breathing became very rhythmic, from somewhere deep in my lungs I had never before been. I couldn't seem to get in enough air, no matter how much deeper I took my breath. I opened the window in an effort to rush some fresh oxygen into me, and I urged Alex to lose his cigarette because it was making me ill. This rhythm escalated slowly but powerfully, like the ascension of a plane just after takeoff. I had no idea what was happening in my body, but its pull was undeniable, its havoc inevitable.

Without warning, my left hand began to grow numb. First the fingers, then the knuckles, then my palm. The whole of my hand began to retract into itself with my thumb toward my pinkie, and the other fingers tightening around this deformed, heinous ball attached to the end of my arm. I was alarmed. I was panicked. I was certain that I was having a stroke of some sort and that this was either the last day of my life or the last day of my life as I knew it. Alex alerted the driver to find a hospital pronto, and I remember thinking that I would never have had nearly as much composure if he, or anyone else I knew, was confronting such tragedy. I was impressed...but, nonetheless, back to the last day of my life.

We were on the Long Island Expressway with apparently no hospitals on our stretch. The driver was calling his dispatcher to locate the nearest urgent care clinic, seemingly outsourced in India. The numbing began creeping up the length of my arm with the promise of a rising tide. My hand was now totally immobile in this freakish clutch. The numbness crept up my arm, my shoulder, and then to my face. I began to lose sensation in my cheek, my nose, my eyelids, these facial features retracting into themselves as though they were misplaced, silkscreened on a canvas that was not mine.

This was it, my day to bid farewell. In truth, the extent of the scope of my shallow, self-consumed existence could best be tallied by the fact that the pressing issue of concern running though my brain was what a contorted, disfigured mess my face would be and that the undertaker would never be able to restore peace in my body or beauty to my face. Those last thoughts were not about my kids, my husband, my mom, my family, nor about a God I had not yet met. It was all about me.

After what seemed much longer than fourteen minutes, we located a humble-looking hospital and approached it from what must have been its backside. I even asked the driver what the hell kind of building this was, and he assured me it was a hospital. The driver, who had nowhere near the composure of Alex, spat out some rapid, broken language indicating that this was where we needed to be, clearly certain that today was the day someone died on his shift.

This backside location was quiet and ordinary; not a big blue H, nor a gurney, ambulance, massive double sliding glass door in sight. Alex rushed out of the cab seeking help and returned with a nurse and a wheelchair, which they awkwardly pushed over grass and a curb in this less than handicap-friendly environment. They arrived at my passenger door finding me completely unable to cross the threshold out of the car as my leg was now immobile. I was hoisted with little grace into the chair. The nurse seemed to evaporate, and Alex pushed me toward the single-entry steel back door over the grass and curb with much more difficulty now that the chair was occupied.

This Twilight Zone episode of my life continued inside the hospital. Alex hollered for help, navigating our way through the narrow hallways, which could not have accommodated the gurneys and medical props that should have been there. An ornery nurse responded, seeming irritated that we were not entering from the usual entrance to the emergency room. Alex shut her up by explaining that his wife was having a stroke or something. She directed us to "triage," with no apparent regard for my contorted and deformed condition. "Triage! Are you fucking kidding?," I barked, barely able to speak because of the unusual position my mouth now held. Triage, in my limited scope of knowledge, was for band-aids and tongue depressors, not full blown strokes. This woman was unyielding, pointing her one index finger in the direction of the clinic I needed to visit before any real help would be offered to me.

Getting to triage involved a complete tour of the emergency room waiting area. There must have been sixty people of all shapes and sizes and ages, all awaiting medical attention. Many were staring into outer space or at a particular square of linoleum floor tile. Some were moaning from their ailment, others were pacing like lunatics, but together they were a collection of the most unattractive, poorly dressed, depressed-looking souls I had ever seen gathered in one room. Many of them took notice of Alex and me—contorted and deformed me—and watched with utter disregard as he wheeled me by, as though we were the next float in the revolving parade of the misfit picnic.

I was relieved to have been granted immediate access to the triage room, with all the band-aids and tongue depressors I might be needing at my disposal. A woman behind a desk kindly welcomed us, inquiring why we were visiting today, as though she were a clerk in a boutique. She asked a battery of questions from name and address to the vital insurance carrier, and I was quickly losing patience. As Alex explained what had happened in the cab and what was continuing to happen in my neurological hardware, she listened patiently, nodding, affirming she was getting all of it. I was utterly alarmed at her lack of alarm, though I did find some comfort in knowing that if I were to lose all consciousness right then and there that the real hospital with the real doctors was just down the hall.

Like a magician with a sly bag of tricks, she handed me the most unusual prop, a brown paper bag. I thought she wanted for me to throw up into it, but she told me to start breathing into it.

And I began to breathe into this low-tech paper vessel, its belly expanded and contracted under my deliberate directive. She and Alex began conversing. "Where were we going? Had this ever happened to me before? Was I nervous about something? Had something unusual recently happened in my life?" Alex's eyes immediately met mine with a peculiar curiosity. As my breath continued, I could slowly feel sensation returning to my face, my arm, my fingers. The clutch of my hand began to release, and my leg was now an appendage I recognized. It took maybe two minutes to restore all muscular function, and then I was merely mentally numb from what the hell had passed through me.

This kind and knowing nurse, now my savior, offered us the opportunity to go through ER protocol and get in line behind those lovely sixty people we had just surveyed, for the reassurance of a thorough examination. She explained that what had happened to me was an unusual version of a panic attack. Most typically, its onset would involve hyperventilation, which would escalate to passing out, at which time breathing would then be rendered back to normal. She said this syndrome was sometimes found in teens seeking some form of twisted attention.

For some reason, I apparently took the slow and steady road of full belabored awareness of my incapacitation, and what happened to me in twenty minutes more typically happened in three. We declined the offer to stay in the ER, looking for the fastest way out of the hospital. There was a bizarre urge to laugh between Alex and me, especially as we walked, full saunter, past the collection of faces that only twelve minutes earlier had pegged me as a goner. No doubt they were wondering what sort of witchcraft had happened in triage.

The cab driver shared a similar curiosity as we both returned to the car, each opening our respective car doors, as though in a New York hurry. Few words were spoken, and I stared blindly out the window for the rest of the thirty-minute drive to the hotel. We checked in, I flopped on the bed and Alex dressed in black tie for the fake photography session. Grateful for the three hours of pure solitude, I retreated under the covers for a stark naked, pitch black return to the fetal position.

I was eventually able to shower and dress for the wedding. The ceremony was lovely, and I definitely kept a lower-than-usual profile throughout the cocktail hour and dinner. I recall trying to put language to what it was I was feeling, but there was nothing remotely familiar that I could attach to it. Despite the eight-piece swing band and festive fanfare to the nines, I laid still and low, watching the gala through a newly-noticed looking glass.

For a year before this eventful weekend, Alex had been aggressively trying to relocate his business out of Buffalo and into an economic and sunny climate better suited for expansion and year-round golf. He had continually complained about what an economically depressed city

Buffalo was. The opportunity for growth was nil, the weather was lousy, and he wanted out. He had been loosely negotiating terms with several landlords for months, trying to nail down firm commitments, and equally trying to persuade me to support this decision by uprooting four well-rooted kids, departing my real estate tenure, leaving behind friends, family, doctors, dry cleaners, and life as I knew it.

I had always half-engaged in these discussions, certain that none of his energies would materialize into anything forcing a decision. That Tuesday after our return from New York, Alex got a phone call that one of the many negotiations he was flirting with had actually come to terms. A large national movie theatre chain had just filed for bankruptcy, and a dozen sites were hungry for new operators.

He confronted me that night with a tone of gravity I had never before been crowded by, since it had never before had veins of viability. He again put forward all of his usual arguments on why he must do this. He put it on the table, slammed it down hard. Without much hesitation, and certainly riding on the heels of my perceived near-death experience, I agreed to set sail on this adventure. It seemed I had never invited any legitimate risk into my perfectly crafted version of a life. The litany of my usual questions on details, including responsible business plans and school concerns and finances, all went by the wayside. My only words: "When do we leave?"

Finding Florida

The next three months were largely dedicated to practical matters of orchestrating the move. Alex had to get there immediately to secure the lease for the first theatre and commence the startup engines of his new company. He packed one piece of luggage, shipped his car, and hopped on a plane within three days of getting the green light.

Though he had been in the business of film exhibition every minute of his working life, he had never been charged with the tall task of growing a company off his native soil, negotiating such massive lease terms with seasoned property sharks, without a formal business plan of attack and with barely the resources to float one bad month.

Alex was a consummate gambler. The thrill of risk was the tonic of his life, having formally given up drugs and alcohol three years before we met. His recovery was followed to the letter of the NA law (Narcotics Anonymous), and in our early years together he often attended two meetings a week. Every arm of his social life was an extension of the program, as he devoutly believed that leftover relationships from his using days would have threatened his recovery. Alex was also an associate member of the horseshoe club; his confidence, experience, and business acumen could fast dissipate any hot water he had ever found himself in.

For the many years in advance of the move, my interest or engagement in his business affairs was negligible at best. I would certainly take advantage of all the movies and popcorn and Twizzlers I could consume, and the kids and their friends enjoyed the playground of daddy's workplace. As for having a clue about the nature of his work from film bookings to concessions to operations to management, I had none. We both made a ton of money, spent a ton of money, and never knew of any pressures related to the making of money. My erroneous assumption on going forward with this move included the notion that we would not only retain the horseshoe, but Fat City in the Land of Plenty lay ahead.

I got my Florida real estate broker's license while I was in New York that last fall. It was, of course, the most efficient way to arrive in the Sunshine State, with four kids and a monster moving van in tow. I could hit the ground running.

I gave away most things related to winter, fall, or spring. Toboggans, lawnmowers, rakes, sweaters, snow blowers—it was a free-for-all. The promise of wearing my Birkenstocks in January, capris year round, and the beach as my playground was the destination of my tunneled focus. It seemed so sensible to have kids' clothing all suited to just two seasons: hot and hotter.

We made one housing trip to Florida; home base was to be Deerfield Beach. Housing stock was much different than anything I had either lived in or sold. Neighborhoods were completely different, often with overbearing electronic gates and abrasive guards with comically tall hats asserting their inflated powers to grant or deny access to their exclusive community. Once granted entrance privileges, it was impossible to ignore the extensively designed and manicured backdrops of landscape architecture, suggestive of lush and tropical natural habitats, with little indication that every prop from palm tree to street lamp to paver driveway to Lexus LX470 SUV had been imported to this former swampland just months earlier.

Really, I saw none of that. I saw Birkenstocks, saw shorts in January, and saw an Italian-inspired Mediterranean house with marble flooring, a master bedroom miles from the kids' wing, and a granite countertop never needing protection from sizzling oven dishes. It was the American Dream: forging a new frontier in this Land of Plenty, making new friends on similar journeys, growing a business in a promising, bustling economy, all while leaving the snow shovel behind. Ka-ching ka-ching, I heard, as my mind whispered sweet suggestions of Happiness on Easy Street.

We bought the Mediterranean mansion with the nearby park and tennis court, planning on transferring equity from our present home and adding another mere two hundred thousand dollars from the sale of one of Alex's theatres back in New York. I arranged for window treatments and California Closets to be installed ten minutes after closing. I interviewed preschools, elementary schools, and middle schools, processed necessary transfer documents, located pediatricians, even found a nearby European-inspired al fresca coffee house with nightly acoustic talent, Birkenstocks welcome.

Closing shop back in Buffalo proved to be rife with different details than I was used to processing. Alex came back only once in the three-month window before our move, and the physical burden of all this closure was on my shoulders alone.

Getting to Florida proved to be a crash landing. The last two weeks in New York were loaded with urgent chaos, crowded with issues needing immediate solutions on a moment's notice.

For starters, the nailed-down-done-deal of the sold business crumbled without warning, or at least any warning that I was aware of. The convenient sum of money that was going to be transferred from that sale into the Mediterranean mansion was no longer in place. Fast arrangements needed to be made to increase our mortgage amount by a modest two hundred thousand dollars. The fact that we were approved for this mortgage in the first place was a testimony to the hearty national appetite for excessive debt and the support endorsed by our financial institutions. I was leaving behind a six-figure income and Alex was assuming a theatre at a site that had been barricaded for almost two years. No formal income to speak of, none whatsoever.

I phoned our mortgage broker requesting that she resubmit our mortgage application, almost doubling the mortgage amount. I told her we were restructuring our whole financial portfolio. What portfolio? We had none. She amended the papers, put it in front of the powers-that-be, and the loan was approved. No income. Go figure.

In the months before the move I had to confront Peter and Leah's dad, Harry, about this relocation. I presented it to him with all the business acumen of a seasoned negotiator. I understood that it would be hard for him not to have the kids living nearby, so I agreed to fly them home every other month for more focused visitation where they would not be distracted from their usual lives of school, friends, and sports. I assured him that they would be fully available to get to know on a more intimate basis. He could have a month in the summer with them. All would actually be better.

I anticipated some reluctance, but he ultimately agreed to this arrangement without my having to invite attorneys to formally amend our divorce papers. We had never had to refer to those papers on any issue in the course of our raising Peter and Leah. While there was language therein dictating who had the kids from one Christmas to the next, we had always managed to be flexible with respect and consideration without referring to the mandates of that decree.

Not all events went so smoothly. Our retained movers had seriously underestimated the scope of vacating our house. There wasn't the manpower or the cargo room to accommodate all of our belongings, and it was utter mayhem when the van was being loaded. The lead guy was phoning for an additional truck and driver while the biggest snowstorm of fifteen years was wreaking havoc outdoors. Getting our lives to the point of a broom-swept vacant house you close the door on was no easy feat. My cleaning lady happened to up and quit. My first-ever real estate deal to fall apart took place because the seller of the house had a change of heart, was not divorcing after all, and I needed to kindly explain this to the buyer. The poor seller's elated reconciliation was getting no applause from me.

A week's worth of these disturbing days fired at my psyche without reprieve. One of those days included a phone call from my attorney, who let me know that she had been contacted by Harry's attorney regarding his interest in making this move more difficult than our previous conversations had led me to believe. I felt an angry flush of betrayal that he hadn't expressed this directly to me. How callous it seemed to be hearing of it in this way. While I had always had sole custody of the kids, Harry certainly had the right to tie this issue up in the courts, proving to be both a nuisance and an expense, neither of which I had much wiggle room for.

I phoned him in an effort to come to some terms on these matters outside of the courtroom. While on the surface the situation was rectified by throwing some money at it, it was really other than that. I felt a heart-wrenching grip of sorrow as I realized that the paths of Harry and his children were diverging in this way. The quiet suspicion that I was embarking on a frontier of thinning ice was elevated to my back burner.

One of the more difficult and emotionally miscalculated pieces of closure for me was the goodbye party that was held for my oldest son, Peter, then 12, given by the parents of his best friend since first grade.

One of the boys from his baseball team, the pitcher, gave Peter, the catcher, a small but meaningful trophy thanking him for catching most of his balls. They were an intact union, along with ten other teammates, having played tournament team baseball together for six memorable seasons. These kids were all budding adolescents, just beginning to get quirky around the opposite sex. There were hugs and tears and nervous laughter, as they all experienced what seemed to be their first grown-up understanding of the power and emptiness inherent in the words of *goodbye*. I stood among them, like a thief in the night, wearing the polite and knowing smile of "mother knows best." I felt like an evil and wicked monster.

Peter had always been a golden child every single one of his days in this world. If there was an MVP, an award from his summer overnight camp, an appointment as a class officer in school, or any accolade for an activity in which he was involved, it came to him with magnetic pull. He always sported a genuine smile and wore it with no effort whatsoever. Teachers, parents and friends of mine never ignored what an unusually grounded young man he had always been, at whatever age he might have been. His capacity for compassion and sensitivity balanced by his keen academic aptitudes rendered him about as close to whole as a kid can get.

He and I have always existed in parallel thought. I think, he responds. He thinks, I respond. We shared a symbiotic connection that needed no language. Where I was strong, he was strong, probably stronger. As well, where I was weak, he also had fault lines. I was continually encouraging him not to rest too comfortably on his laurels. He was tremendously efficient and resourceful and had the same talent to invisibly manipulate as I did. At the age of seven he could have found his way home from Paris with a credit card, cell phone, Internet connection, and twenty dollars cash for incidentals not easily purchased by plastic. If I were born a boy twenty-three years later, I would have been born Peter. If I were born a girl, I would just have needed to date him. I watch those fault lines, though; I know where he is vulnerable.

So there I was. I had fended off a court battle, emotionally retrieved all my kids from their farewells, renegotiated a move at nearly twice what had been quoted, nailed down all the loose ends of my real estate matters (which had an affinity for disaster those last weeks), and signed off on a big fat mortgage we had no business entering into. We were off, having left four feet of snow and home field advantage in the rear-view mirror.

We landed in Florida intending to close on the home the very next day. Funds were to have been wired, closing papers were to have been prepared. We anticipated just one night in the lovely, low-rise motel while on deck for the Mediterranean chapter that lay ahead.

I got the call at dinner that night: The mortgage broker told me that some glitch had developed in our paperwork as it was switched from one mortgage bank to another, that the bank appraiser had neglected to reinspect the house in advance of closing, and that this would hang us up for only a day or two. She would be all over it come sunrise.

Sunrise came, sunrise set. I spent the day on the phone trying to expedite whatever outstanding issues there were. This was my business after all; I knew the language, the shortcuts, the pitfalls. I was not to be bullshitted. I went from one voicemail to the next. All my efforts proved futile. The title company's answers differed from the mortgage broker's, which differed from the attorney's. I apparently did not know this language after all.

It was ten days before Christmas and the motel was unable to secure another room. We were six people with abundant luggage on the tail end of an exhaustive move sharing two queen-sized beds and one toilet. The kids were hungry to swim in the pool, go to the beach, drive by their schools, check out the town—all normal enthusiasm for any adventure. I spent the next seven days navigating my way through all the closing issues, with all the parties involved, on my cell phone while playing cruise director visiting the pool, the beach, and the schools.

Worse than my $650 cell phone bill that month, I discovered an invisible clause in our purchase agreement that allowed the builder to assess damages to the tune of $300 a day for closing after the written contract date, a clause he was not remotely shy about slapping onto our settlement papers. I called the builder directly, certain that I would be able to strike a chord of empathy regarding these issues, which I assured him were out of our control. I couldn't even slightly soften the hard line of his mean little pencil. To boot, leaving two packed moving vans at a standstill wasn't cheap either. Their room and board and standstill fee came to another $300 per day, all on my dime. It occurred to me we were not in Kansas anymore.

The house closed at the offices of the builder one week late, largely without incident except that we learned of some highly restrictive clauses in our mortgage that had not been previously disclosed, but at what was now $800 a day I was up for stalling nothing. The builder left us with a lovely $5600 fruit basket which I tossed in the garbage outside of his offices, and we headed to meet with the moving van. That is, I headed to meet with the van and Alex left for what continues to be the journey of building his empire.

Somehow I reverted to autopilot, found my way out of downtown Boca Raton and into our new paver driveway. The movers were hostile and grumpy and sweaty, and I was relieved there wasn't a baby grand piano among our furnishings. Vans were unloaded, and I directed traffic with a surprising efficiency. As boxes and furniture and artwork were unloaded and dispersed, I could actually smell an old life dissipate into thin air. The voluminous ceilings and stone floors and expansive rooms gave all of our belongings a different emission of energy.

I wrote off the rough landing as customary bumps and bruises consistent with such a long-haul relocation. Never mind that our first week consumed nearly half of the money in our slush fund; an endless checklist of urgent needs demanded immediate attention. I needed to transfer the kids' medical records into acceptable formats for their new schools, select school curricula that most closely met their coursework midyear, and assess the support system in place for my daughter, Leah. She had always had an IEP (Individualized Educational Program), providing her with modifications to normal school curriculum for her learning disability.

Leah was an incredible young woman, and she and I were different as the day was long. She saw things that I didn't see and felt things that I didn't feel. Her interpretation on any particular matter was often ten degrees from mine, and usually her notion shed an interesting and otherwise ignored light on my own. I thought linearly, Leah thought spherically. She was always my bird's-eye view.

I had never recognized the power of perception until I was able to crawl into her head. She was born dyslexic, with God-given artistic talent. Until the age of five this went largely unnoticed, as the barometer of her aptitude had only been the expressive language put forth in either the artwork from preschool or her oral vocabulary, neither of which were suffering. Even in her earliest years, I had always suspected something unusual about her perceptions but couldn't quantify what seemed off.

Leah had the largest heart I had even seen in a human being. She had founded an entire set of compensatory life skills that she had drafted to combat her inability to read until age eight. Her capacity for unconditional love was enormous; I was Scrooge in her shadow. She was the least judgmental person I knew, yet somehow she managed to never attach herself to people, places, or things. Today a high school freshman, her life has a remarkable balance between meeting her academic demands and volunteering weekly for a youth group that assists elderly people in handling their elderly challenges. She also operates a homespun business with two girlfriends, selling their knitted scarves and purses at local craft shows, and has a personal art portfolio you need two hands to carry.

All of the interests in her life were put in motion by her own energies. She worked overtime for the grades she got in school, still inferior to those that Peter can command with negligible effort by comparison. Academics still remain a struggle for her, but she shows up and gets it done. Peter may pay the piper later while Leah is laying all of life's necessary groundwork today.

At the end of first grade, Leah was not reading. She had a teacher that year who had been hired eleven minutes before the school year began, was new to Western New York, and had never taught first grade. I was certain that this was the cornerstone in her inability to grasp written concepts of language.

I sought the support of the team leader, who offered suggestions from tutorial assistance to language screening aptitude exams. I put as many things into motion as I could, enrolled Leah at the University of Buffalo reading clinic, hired out a battery of tests to screen for any disability, and formally dedicated exorbitant amounts of our time together to read book after book after book. Little of these efforts netted much progress in her conceptual grasp of piecing one sound or phoneme with the next sound or phoneme to form a word, one word with the next word to form a sentence. It was like Greek to her.

The screening tests proved to support that she had a quantifiable learning disability, meaning that there existed at least a twenty point differential between her aptitude and her performance. This disability qualified her to receive special supports from the school system, such as 1-to-1 reading instruction, her tests in school could be read to her until she could read herself, her spelling could not be scrutinized. She would also get time and a half to take tests, she would have preferential seating in the classroom, and all while being mainstreamed in the normal curriculum. I was fortunate enough to have lived in a state-ranked public school system, and was afforded a rough sketch of the roadmap on how to get from A to B, and ultimately to Z. Once these support systems fell into place, Leah was offered a far better opportunity to learn with the cushion of her IEP, otherwise invisible to her fellow classmates.

That was Western New York. This was Florida, a whole different story. I called to schedule an appointment with the superintendent in Special Education only to learn that no such position existed. I was initially referred to the Special Needs administrator for Broward County, located in far away Plantation, FL., then forwarded six times until someone agreed to meet with us. I brought copies of all of her testing records, transcripts, and present IEP, in hopes of landing her similar supports within their framework.

The woman in charge of Special Needs was very special herself. She was a plump and happy little woman, as she waddled the halls on our tour of the school. Communicating with her demanded an unusual effort. It wasn't so much that she talked in a constant whisper as it was that, when she did talk, her eyes remained closed for inordinately long periods of time. Dialogue was not real-time. Since one could get lost as to where to look, speaking with her was similar to having a conversation with someone who had a wandering eye. There was just no central focal point, and that threw the entire exchange off kilter.

She accompanied me to the Special Needs room, which was a separately dedicated spot for the learning of people with special needs, with nothing politically correct about it. These kids were not mainstreamed at all, except for lunch, and it seemed very unlikely they were well-received in the chaos of the cafeteria. There was a vast variety of aberrations among this group, including full-scale mental retardation, blindness, cerebral palsy, and what seemed to be broad spectrum psychological/emotional disorders. Helmets had a place in this special room and walls could have been padded. Never could there have been one teacher or one lesson plan that would have met the needs of this afflicted group.

I said goodbye to the squinting woman while she was mid-sentence and began my search for a private school that might be more suitable. There were over a dozen private middle schools within a reasonable distance of our house, a seemingly excessive number. I came to realize, a little too late, that this is because there was a serious problem in the educational system throughout the state of Florida.

For starters, most school districts had three times the students that any school could accommodate, overburdening the teachers, classrooms, administration, and even the lunch ladies. There were "portables," which were makeshift classrooms, having been single-wide trailers in their past lives. These trailers surrounded the perimeter of every single school, even the brand new ones.

Next, teaching was considered the bottom-feeding rung of professional careers in the Sunshine State. National registries of average earned income for teachers showed that Florida ranked 49th lowest in the country, in front of only Louisiana. It would not be hard to be a waitress in Florida and earn more money than a teacher. Due to the pressing need for teachers in these overburdened schools, the state had effectively lowered the bar for certification requirements for new teachers. The rampant turnover among teachers spoke volumes about how committed these people were to their profession. In that first year, my son had three teachers during his course in English, some whose native tongues had not yet acclimated. Classrooms could easily have thirty-five students in elementary school, with one frazzled teacher and one less-qualified aide.

It was understandable that the infrastructure of any fast-growing municipality, blossoming at such unprecedented rates, was tremendously burdened as it tried to accommodate new demands on schools, resources, economic development, sewers, traffic, and governmental affairs. Couple that with the fact that Florida had one of the lowest school property tax rates in the nation. It was frankly very ironic that people were attracted to the state of Florida for its attractive tax structure, yet appalled when they realized that there was only a skeleton of services in place to support their civic needs. Lesson learned.

There was a brand new K-8 school nearby that had just opened that fall. Enrollment was minimal, and the teachers genuinely seemed to be a better pool of inspiring motivators. The building was beautiful and was obviously heavily funded, with extensive computer rooms, gyms, science labs, and an actual library. It was a much better fit, except, of course, for the tuition.

By no means had we budgeted for the expense of private school, and I regretfully had to call my mother for assistance to fund it. Let me first say this. My mother would go to the ends of the earth for Leah, *and* she had plenty of money. However, I had always had a stubborn and self-righteous indignation about needing any of it. I felt particularly sensitive asking for the tuition because I sensed she was paying close attention to my financial affairs. Her radar zoned in on my life, surveying how tenuous and vulnerable this move was seeming when more closely examined. Being well-aware of our last-minute mortgage nightmare, and well-tuned into the high threshold that Alex had as a risk-taker, she sure was paying close attention. I don't like being under anyone's microscope, and right then and there sprouted some new turf for my mother and I to get acquainted on.

It was day eleven when Peter came into my bathroom after school. I was busy arranging lotions, candles, and hand towels in this exquisitely appointed, marble-graced shrine to hygiene, adorned with a rain forest shower boasting no need for a door. He was quiet and demure, a disposition I had never really known him in. He found a chair and began with small talk as I continued my arranging. I awaited the details.

As he began to speak, his voice started to quiver as he struggled to continue his thoughts. I stopped my busyness to admire him seated with me in this strange and swanky bathroom. With open arms and a punctured heart, I approached him with a great big bear hug, hoping to comfort his weary ego having become an overnight nobody in a school with fifteen hundred kids grades six through eight.

The hug pulled at every seam in my body. His tears were not to be stopped, as his breathing strained to catch up with the flood of emotion that rushed through all of him. I felt such a reckless flush of responsibility for the pain he was feeling, a self-imposed injury I had no band-aid for. He shared with me how strange his school seemed. The kids were freaks and rednecks and wore heavy chain choker neck gear. The teachers commanded no respect in the classroom, there was trouble in hallways and gangs in stairwells, and even the food was lousy. I assured him that I would explore other options that would be a better fit, from all angles.

The best fit to be found was The Charter School, a new school that had been a former shopping mall just the year before. Florida was under a constant state of metamorphosis. No surprise, there was a waiting list nine miles long to get into this school. Charter Schools received their funding from the state, thus there was no tuition to enroll, thereby appealing to nearly anyone who had even a remote interest in having their child educated outside of the droves of mediocrity. I gathered every scrap of evidence I had supporting Peter as a stellar candidate for their school, from transcripts to standardized test scores to coveted awards in all shapes and sizes. I was seeking a midyear spot for him in seventh grade, which was dismal at best with the school year well under way.

I approached the administrators with a desperate plea to consider his admission given the pain and suffering he was enduring in the overpopulated droves of mediocrity. My first encounter was with a native Floridian woman, maybe fifty years old, who had likely shopped in that mall since the day it was built fifteen years earlier, her favorite stores being razed in the name of education, and still plenty grumpy about it. She had all the sympathy of a rock as I poured forth the challenges that Peter was confronting. She gave me the once-over, the look in her eyes clearly saying, "I couldn't really care less. Get in line."

I learned right then and there that any potential sympathic chord to be struck, no matter what I was looking for, was going to be from a person who had been transplanted to Florida, uprooted by relocation from their native soil elsewhere, who was still fumbling with the ropes and the language, maybe even still scared of the ubiquitous salamanders. The more resistance they fought with, the better the ally.

I found that person, a woman from Pennsylvania in her last life. I pleaded with her to consider Peter's midyear admission. Perhaps she had confronted breakdowns of her own when she first landed there, but I did manage to speak some words she could understand. She encouraged me to seek his admission based upon his accelerated academic curriculum. His standardized NYS test scores placed him in the upper percentile of students, and their accelerated classes were not nearly as crowded as the regular classrooms. He started seventh grade at The Charter School that coming Monday.

Alex had been in Florida since September, preparing to open his first theatre for the timely Christmas break. The theatre was an older 8-plex located in the heart of Deerfield Beach, adjacent to the mall. It was built in the '80's, which, by Florida's standards, made it old, outdated, and desperately in need of renovation. It had been closed for well over a year, having been vacated by a large national theatre chain that had gone belly up.

The theatre was in total disarray. Screens had been slashed, the concession area could have been condemned by even the most lenient of health departments, and projection equipment needed a complete overhaul. Besides operational issues needing immediate attention before business could begin, the lobby and bathrooms and auditoriums were tired with age, neglect, and an invisible film of year-old coke syrup everywhere. It was a bacterial breeding ground of mold and sugar. I remember Sam's excitement when he located a box of Butterfingers in the rest room, certain that his discovery was a lucky man's find. I tossed it in the waste basket, careful not to touch the clouded cellophane it was swathed in. He was floored, declaring that it was unopened and, accordingly, fair game. Sorry, Sam.

Alex was swamped for months in advance of our arrival in Florida. He lived long days accommodating the pressing demands of landlords and city permitting offices, retaining construction crews and conforming to building codes. An endless myriad of red-tape matters presented itself as different city officials often gave conflicting requirements of his burden in obtaining a Certificate of Occupancy before the doors could open. Beyond those concerns, there was a staff to hire, a concession stand to outfit, projection equipment to make operable, film accounts to establish, ads to place. No reprieves, no favors, just the perpetual chaos of urgent details, all set against a time clock.

It was apparent that he needed help, and the only area I could have assisted with was personnel, marketing, and advertising. Certainly he could have hired out that position, which in hindsight would have served both of us better. But that was not how it happened.

I took on the job of creating a company logo, formatting ads and press releases for newspapers, outfitting business cards and letterhead, creating administrative forms, and setting up exhibitor relations with the film companies. There was an infinite sea of tasks with which I was completely unfamiliar, but I managed to plod through the morass of detail, albeit with less efficiency than I was accustomed to operating with.

Alex's stresses were plenty. There were incessant fires for him to respond to, dousing obstacles with fancy footwork. I was very impressed as I watched him conduct his affairs with landlords, building inspectors, and contractors. I had never really seen him in action in the capacity of his familiar domain. His decisions were always swift, his focus always channeled. With less than four hours' legroom in obtaining the CO, he opened the theatre on Christmas Day.

There was an impressive article in the *Sun Sentinel* that next weekend about Alex, citing his tenure in the business, the relocation of his family from New York, and the hopes and dreams he had for his new life in South Florida. I felt a deep vein of pride for Alex and those dreams, reading that morning edition poolside in January. Just maybe we had a shot at living happily-ever-after. Just maybe this budding company could go to the moon by way of the palm tree.

It did not occur to me then that this would have been the very first measure in my life where I put faith in the hands of another. That the *other* was my husband, the man I slept with and the father of half my kids, didn't matter. Never before had I passed the baton of control when it came to trusting someone else to make good decisions for me. The baton was always within my grasp. Sometimes I laid it down, sometimes I would pretend to let someone hold it, but it was always within arm's reach, and I never needed to renegotiate my footing to retrieve it.

One place where I still held exclusive sway was in our new residence. Our house was very beautiful: expansive space, abundant natural light, state-of-the-art everything. I had never before lived in a house that wasn't at least older than I was. It was a virgin canvas, mine to shape. The decorators, window people, landscape artists—they would all have to wait. We had absolutely no money to accessorize a single thing.

I had grown to cast a scornful judgment on those homes whose owners had elected to screen in their lovely pools and well-coordinated outdoor furnishings. A cage of sorts, this metal and mesh contraption encapsulated their outdoor paradise, setting boundaries to who was welcome. Reasonable, yes. Friendly, no.

I didn't imagine the cage was constructed to fend off potential drowned children; rather it suggested an air of privilege if you found yourself on the better side of its boundary. I watched these protected display environments, affirming that I would never be morphed into the narrow mentality that opted for the cage. My pool and furnishings would be more present, more accessible, more welcoming. Some punks might steal my terra-cotta planter but they could never steal my gentility. Never mind that all my neighbors chose the cage; it simply competed with my sense of civility to be surrounded by a monstrous screen.

It took maybe three months for me to realize that this screened monstrosity was surely not intended to keep out kids or thieves. Instead, it was an utter necessity to keep out the swarming proliferation of bugs and insects, many species of which I had neither seen nor knew existed. They were these critters on steroids that seemed to defy laws of gravity in order to become airborne at all. They and their waste products were everywhere, a nuisance to shoo off, a nuisance to clean after. Apparently they went into hibernation for the winter months in tropical climates, but for the other nine months you most desperately needed this cage.

People that lived in Florida did believe they had seasons, each being differentiated by a mere five to eight degrees. Certainly there was that rare cold spell when arctic chills funnelled some sobering temperatures into the 50's and people wore multiple layers of their warmest clothing, generally squirming with discomfort until the chill passed through. Blood chemistry must change, must thin to a crisp, barely rendering them warm-blooded animals.

Even retail recognized these indiscernible seasons. It was nearly impossible to find bathing suits in January, except at beach-side tourist shops. Scarves, sweaters, corduroy, yes. Bathing suits and a decent pair of sandals, no. Nearly every day in January, February, and March, the kids would spend an hour swimming in the pool, our cageless, vulnerable backyard paradise, their thick, Northern, syrupy blood still having properties to sufficiently maintain internal body temperature.

They swam. They biked. They made forts and ventured to the playground, all within our gated community, which was heavily populated with families and young children. They anxiously sought out other neighborhood kids, sniffing for outdoor partners in fun and crime, enthusiastic about living the thrill of summer activities year-round. Rarely, though, were there other children outdoors doing the kinds of things that children did. Empty backyard playgrounds, glassy pools, lonely tennis courts, it all struck me as very creepy. You could watch the school buses unload hundreds of kids, but they just seemed to disperse into the vacuum of their homes, not to be sighted again until the morning shuffle.

I accompanied Sam, who was five at the time, over to a home where I knew another five-year old boy lived. The nanny answered the door, slightly disturbed having not been told in advance that the doorbell might ring. I introduced Sam and myself, explained we lived just down the street, and said that I thought maybe the boys could play together. Perhaps this overture was not well-received because she was the nanny and didn't feel fit to make such an executive social decision. Perhaps it was because this little boy just didn't have much experience playing with neighborhood kids. Even Sam felt her distance.

I returned when his mom got home, introduced myself and Sam, suggested a play date, which was only marginally better received. The mother looked to her planner in an effort to carve out a day, two weeks in advance, with a start time and an end time. An actual appointment to play. No spontaneity, no impromptu cowboy and Indian frontier to be discovered on a moment's notice. This might seem very petty, but I kept learning that this was the way of the world where I lived. No kids barefoot in the grass (fire ants & very bad grass), no running through backyards capturing any flag whatsoever, no roving pack of kids migrating from one house to the next in search of the best snacks. Planned play dates two weeks in advance. What fun.

Then I met the Swains. They were my kitty-corner backyard neighbors in this affluent portrait community. I first met Bosley Swain when he and two of his four kids were walking around the neighborhood, checking out a vacant lot where there was a house under construction. There was the initial thrill of seeing live human beings venture out from their controlled indoor environments, then the added thrill that these particular two kids seemed engaged in normal kid mischief, including the harmless disturbing of building materials and the mounting of oversized tractor equipment, under the careful supervision of their father, who was mounting the same. I stopped the car and got out to introduce myself and the two kids who were with me. I pointed out the house we lived in, and we all found instant enthusiasm in noting our shared corner boundary.

If there is such a thing as love at first sight in friendships, we certainly found it in the Swain family. They had moved to Florida two years earlier from New Jersey, and were the first pioneers to build a home in our development. Bosley's work was mostly based out of Manhattan, but he was seeking to expand his sphere of clients in his money management business, and South Florida seemed a very ripe market to tap into. He traveled to New York several times a month and maintained an office with a secretary in a nearby office building, but he was largely a dad and husband at home. He had a fully equipped den with high-speed Internet, all the technology to support his expert servicing of clients, a New York and Florida cell phone number, and a lot of fabulous down-time on his hands.

Sarah Swain and I were both born in 1964. Our four kids' ages and sexes were mingled well. Two of our kids became instant friends, skipping over all social foreplay. There was a continual foot path between our houses with kids running back and forth without any formal appointment. Our five-year-old boys would run barefoot in the terribly unfriendly crab grass, making a game out of avoiding the steeple stacks of fire ants that would invade your leg and crotch by the millions if you miscalculated your footing.

Our homes shared the same amount of disorder, washer and dryer in continuous cycle, oversized refrigerators, garages with six bikes and six garbage cans in use, thirty balls for varied sports, miscellaneous boxes yet to be unpacked. And outdoors, it seemed our kids were the only ones to play at the playground, in our pools, on the tennis courts, and out on bikes.

Once, they were officially reprimanded by a cowardly, uptight neighbor. You could never pinpoint which one; there were far too many suspects. The threat came in writing, regarding a fort that they had constructed in the center island of the cul-de-sac, built out of fallen palm tree branches and bolstered with abandoned ficus scraps. A fort. An organic chamber of cloistered fantasy, brewing the boys' warrior missions, fully equipped with playing cards, stolen snacks from their pantries, and an arsenal of sticks to poke out at any adult who dared to disturb them. They were clearly trouble in the eyes of those looking for tranquil order in this creepy, planned paradise.

Well-aware of the Twilight Zone community we lived in, we could not understand why sightings of live people playing outdoors was such an anomaly. Why kids were rarely found dirty with evidence of organic nature on their clothes. Why nannies spent their hours shuffling overscheduled kids from one controlled indoor environment to another. Or how you could live on an intimate cul-de-sac knowing none of your neighbors by name or sight. But this was all very possible in the climate of South Florida.

I can best sum up the breadth of my affection for this newly minted subdivision in one single event that left my jaw suspended open. It was an early evening hour just beyond dusk, and I was out in the garage with Leah and Sam. We were organizing boxes onto an entire wall of built-in cubicle shelving, looking to free up some floor space beneath the congested accumulation of stuff that had found no home indoors. Atop the ladder, reaching deep on the upper shelf to securely stow a box, I pushed too far. Down fell a full gallon of muriatic acid, splattering without apology over that whole quadrant of the garage. It ate a hole right through our wooden poker table, melted the rubber of a bike tire, saturated all cardboard to create a festering smoke, promising combustion if left untended.

Sometimes when there's smoke, there's just smoke, but I saw fire looming and summoned 911 to send in their troops. After I had explained what had happened, they urged me to exit the house and await the emergency crews that were being dispatched. Smoke was visibly pluming out of the garage as the kids and I stood in the distant periphery of our over-lit mansion. Within ten minutes there were three emergency vehicles, replete with a fully-dressed HAZ-MAT team in their space suits with encapsulated, muffled voices looking for directions to every access door of the house. They ran their fumigation routine, ushering in and out of all doorways with their playful, tubular vents. I watched their mission unfold, fascinated.

I also watched my million dollar neighbors, peeking from curtains, poised on porches, as they were watching me. With one kid on my hip and three at my side, the chaos of sirens flooding my address, the neighbors stood and did nothing. Absolutely nothing. Not an inquiry as to whether I needed any help, not a blanket to offer. I wasn't sure why I wanted a blanket, it was eighty degrees; it just felt like I deserved one given all this urgent intervention. The only gesture of decency extended my way was from Mr. Bosley Swain, who pulled right into the driveway, located me and the kids among the mix of relief efforts, and asked if I wanted a cocktail. He said he'd bring a tall one in a to-go cup. "A double," I said, "with a big fat lime."

This transient environment lended an air of distance between people, neighbors, and citizens. There was an enormously vast disparity in income, privilege and class among the residents of any town, sharing the same soil, breathing the same air, shopping at the same Publix. There were exclusive gated communities adjacent to open slums sporting abandoned vehicles and neglected landscapes.

The barriers went beyond money, language, and upbringing. They seemed to invade the sense of community and heritage one assigned to the place they called home. No one was native. Few were ever attending their high school reunion without getting on an airplane. Few were having backyard barbecues with Uncle Rob or Cousin Jake. Few would even host their own funeral in the town in which they lived. Even the houses had no foundations. The suffering was insidious, rendering an intangible estrangement that was difficult to quantify, streaming the collective consciousness like a vapor of cheap perfume. But it *was* sunny, I'll give you that. This conscionable and spiritual vacancy, it seemed, was strangely balanced by the privilege of wearing shorts in January while leftover relatives north of Tallahassee were braving the storms of old man winter.

Alex was reeling full force in growing his empire. His focus was channeled, his days crowded, long, and plenty strained. He took nearly every opportunity he uncovered to secure more and more theatres, collecting them like baseball cards and rarely asserting scrutiny for the sensibility of the deal. Each deal seemed to share a common footprint: an abandoned theatre in a tired strip mall with a nearby Dollar Store, painfully dated decor, inferior projection equipment from the Dark Ages, often last running sub-run films. His mission was to renovate the space to modern specs, equip state-of-the-art projection rooms, import titillating concessions with future Playboy bunnies to peddle the candy, and bring back first-run films.

There was always a time clock, with harrowing fire/building/health codes which had to be addressed and corrected. There was big rent to pay while scurrying to render the theatre operable. There were staffs to hire, images to revamp in these towns, new news media to establish. He would go on the road for weeks at a time, needing to be onsite 24/7 for contractors and permitting and deliveries. I would stay put at the lead theatre, tending to administration concerns for the theatres, to my four children in school, and to the perpetual chaos of my new life.

As part of the skeletal services one could not expect to receive, school busses were few and far between. I had the burden of dropping off and picking up four kids from four different schools, typically at the most congested traffic hours. Pickups were a dependable nightmare, as nearly all other parents were in the same line of cars, often stretching half a mile, retrieving their kids, apparently without jobs at 2:30 in the afternoon.

I would listen to the dialogue between kids in the back seat as I drove. Peter would often have friends with him and they would be discussing matters of the school day or the upcoming weekend. His crowd seemed a much faster and more slippery specimen of 13-year-old, always manipulating parents or teachers or friends to suit their teenage motives. Always a cell phone in hand, always a plan on deck, always an answer of "Why not?" I paid particularly close attention to the way these kids spoke to their mothers as they checked in after school, clueing them in with their next few hours' whereabouts. Their words were absent the baseline respect it seemed should have been present in those conversations. They never sought permission, but instead simply stated what they needed.

Their usual banter invariably included enthusiasm for whatever recent or upcoming big purchases were in their grasp, maybe the latest video game system or hand-held something or pathetically overpriced garment of clothing. Their demands were steep and nonnegotiable: "Pick me up here at 8 p.m." or "Drop me off $50, we're going out for dinner." I would drive, I would listen, and I would sense the creeping suspicion that the lives of my children were certain to be shaped differently if they were raised in South Florida.

My mind would run amok. I suspected I was becoming unglued. Here I was, land of booming economic opportunity, destination to unprecedented droves on a seeming national migration, all descending on this peninsula by their own volition. Young, old, rich, poor—they were hungry for something that obviously overrode the work-in-progress of the life they left behind. Yet I surveyed my environment, trying to assimilate into a world that was apparently attracting these droves willfully. I lived in the most beautiful house in the world and I hated the blood money that was paying for it. All I saw was dislocated communities, inverted value systems, insatiable consumption, rampant fraud, lovely palm trees.

Nowhere else were millions made and lost overnight, or houses sold fully-furnished as though one had no connection to the belongings one accumulated. There was a totally disposable mentality, from art to appliances to neighbors. South Florida was a land where top priorities were placed on suntanned sculpted bodies, Lexus love affairs, and transient commitments aimed at moving targets.

I would have needed to resign myself to surrender, in the name of my kids, all of the subtlest of childhood comings of age: no ice cream men in their decorated trucks selling frozen confections by way of their signature musical melody; no neighborhood block parties featuring potluck everything; no jobs cutting the lawn down the street; no pile of leaves to hurl into; no school plays, and no tenured coaches to dig deep for the inspiration to motivate your kid. Never a high school reunion to return to.

Most poignantly, I would have to surrender the subtle power in the network of community and its passive, integral role in shaping our children. Each man for himself. It has long been said, "It takes a village to raise a child," and never before had I felt such a gaping hole, swirling with currents of temptation, exposing the fallout of greed and consumption and hedonism like a raw nerve under a heat lamp.

The mind is a funny place to spend too much time. Its powers of perception and distortion could not be gauged by familiar boundaries. With physical ailments, there was comfort in knowing the extent of a disease or affliction as compared with others similarly stung. There was relief in knowing how others had responded, given a similar bout of whatever. A broken bone, a healing scar, a case of pneumonia—one knew what to reasonably expect from onset to departure.

Like a threshold for pain, absent a gauge of measurement, when it came to emotional and spiritual disturbance, I could only suspect how well I was tolerating the thrust of its charge. Similar to the creeping suggestions that some might attribute to normal wedding jitters, how did one discern between *normal* wedding butterflies and *wake-the-fuck-up*? Were these simply benign issues of acclimation that I was having? Was my ego wounded that I would never run into an old friend at the supermarket? Was I allergic to the freon pumped throughout all controlled indoor environments? Did I have issues that this was the first time in my working life I wasn't earning money? Was I a paralyzed control freak rendered impotent when out of the hot seat? Was I over-inflating the importance of these core values, now painfully absent, the same values I had largely ignored when they were under my wings? Was the native language really English? Did I cross a border? Oh yes, I would wander aimlessly with these queries, these unanswerable pontifications swirling into circular oblivion. No life lines. No compass. No mercy.

Matters worsened as Alex opened theatre after theatre after theatre. My hours were consumed with petty administrative demands and marketing efforts to launch a new location. After dropping kids off at school, I would go the theatre, manage necessary affairs, eat lunch on the fly, grab the kids, return to the theatre with them, let them loose to graze at the sugarcoated concession stand, watching feature film after feature film while I tied up the never-ending loose ends.

Alex was continually consumed with operational matters, with almost sixty screens under his control. There really wasn't an adequate infrastructure in place to support the scope of issues that needed management, nor was there time or money to hire and bring up to speed the help that could have relieved some of these growing pains. It seemed Alex's ass was always in a frying pan, from one to the next, as he learned to dance with deadlines and flirt with fire. He borrowed from Peter to pay Paul, all day long, and Peter didn't always get paid back. He kept money in such constant motion that a talented CPA would have been nauseous chasing its trail.

By the time the balance of that school year finished, I was overcome with fear. Its grip on me was steady and strong, often running the gamut of expression from uncontrollable tears to raging anger to irrational psychotic thought, often in the course of one single day.

I tried to confront this seeming imbalance with logic and reason, hoping to identify the core issues that were contributing to my overwhelming fear, like one would tackle an algebra problem. I would make lists of my feelings and attempt to embrace with utter honesty what it was that I was so afraid of. I would offset an ill with its corresponding upside, then attempt to reconcile them in order to attain solutions. I would describe the heavy weight of the physical manifestations I could feel, often threatening disaster, which seemed to be just around the very next corner. I tried to confront this imbalance privately at first, certain I could tackle this monkey and free myself from its grip. Me and a monkey, and I wasn't going down.

There was no reining in my emotion, no appeal to my intellect to restore control to my well-being. Alex seemed to have an utter disregard for my fragile place. He had no tolerance for discussion on the why and how and where it all seemed to be off-track. He maintained that my fears of our financial disaster were phantom phobias, that our pressures with money were just short-haul constraints typical in growing a new business.

Never before had we barely made ends meet. Never before was there just enough money to cover monthly obligations, and sometimes not quite. No cushion, no float, just expenses and burdens that were twice what had been anticipated with half the income we had ever known. The lousy mortgage we entered into had an escalating interest rate, which, when borrowing such an enormous sum of money, can be enough to sink you fast. I needed out of that mortgage, out of that house, in an effort to relieve the added pressure of the upcoming increase in payment. My crystal ball saw bankrupt fools trapped, caged, destitute. The neighborhood was weird anyway. Maybe finding some different space with less obvious affluence would have answered some of the other ills that were still so very wrong. And so began our downsizing.

I found a neighborhood that boasted lush and abundant maturity rarely found in settings outside of tropical rain forests. There were massive mangrove tree canopies gracing the winding streets, mingling in the middle, lending a very welcome reprieve from the oppressive and incessant sun glaring outside of its gates. The homes had been built in the mid-80's, and refreshingly, no two looked the same. There were, at most, one hundred properties within its gates, offering the suspicion of a more familiar network of neighborhood within. There were homeowners tending to their own landscape or straightening out their garage, there were kids out on bikes and scooters. All good signs pointing at the distinct possibility that people engaged in the living of their lives and the parenting of their kids rather than hiring the whole damn thing out.

We sold the Mediterranean mansion in two days, early summer, and I felt the familiar rush of competence streaming though my veins. Real estate was always an arena I could command like a seasoned veteran, dependable, controllable. Alex wanted no part of the physical burden of the move, refusing to pack even his toothbrush. With high hopes of relief, I closed the Mediterranean door, waved goodbye to the empty tennis courts, and left for the Swain's my forwarding address while they were on summer vacation.

It was August, hotter than hot, humid as hell, but the move was smooth sailing. The kids were confused about why we were moving, having lived in the first house only 8 months. I certainly wasn't going to share the scope of our financial crunch, lest they think me the fool that I was feeling to be. The new neighborhood was indeed very beautiful and the house was awesome, with hardwood floors and mature trees and a massive floor-to-ceiling stone fireplace central to the great room. I wrote it off as just a better place for us to be. I recall being surprised that their trust in my judgment seemed intact.

I was desperately hopeful that relieving these pressures would net me some peace. Simple math alone did not seem to address the root of my displaced self, but hope was all I had, and I had it in spades. So many ills, so many issues, so many scornful judgments on a life I was just incapable of assimilating into. This spiral of self-examination often turned into destructive self-battery, with me as chief witness to the sad and sorry turn that an otherwise rewarding life had undergone, all on my watch.

I found an interesting columnist in the local paper who put forth weekly advice on issues regarding relationships, money, sex, and other universal subjects that anyone with a pulse could get hot about. When I responded via e-mail to one of his articles on money matters between partners, he replied with bold literary fervor to the quandary I presented. We exchanged e-mails for several weeks. His writing style was simple and eloquent, and he captured tall ideas in small nutshells both with grace and humor. He was a therapist by day, a columnist by night, and I wanted this man's job. I asked if he would be interested in seeing me and my husband for marriage counseling. Our paths had never before been so divided, and this estranged new territory was looming with separate agendas. He agreed more eagerly than Alex agreed, and only after resorting to being female and fragile did Alex agree to show up and give it a shot.

Therapy was a place that neither of us entered with a very good attitude. We tried to fast track our issues in hopes of timely resolve. Our fighting was destructive, futile even, yet it had an insatiable appetite we continued to feed. He loved exactly the things about South Florida that I did not. This didn't appear to be merely an issue of geography. I truly believed that, given a different set of circumstances, which were clearly not *our* set of circumstances, things might not have eroded so rapidly the *me* as I knew it before this move. Our problems included weighty and complicated issues, ones for which neither compromise nor flexibility felt right, and each of which we viewed so differently. Best synthesized, there were three simple matters.

Number One: Raising Kids.

Risk and kids do not marry well. There was an undeniable responsibility to provide children with the best environment possible, one which most mirrored the values one strove to instill. It was always a balancing act, but one tempered the fluctuations as best as one could. There were matters of solid education, matters of material consumption that were feeling like a religion, matters of communities that were feeling spiritually impoverished, and matters of character when assessing the pool of friends who would invariably cast an imprint on their temperament. There were hosts of other irritating sub-issues well beyond the mosquitoes and the Paris Hilton trophy dogs and the crabgrass and the flea markets, and they all contributed in ways large and small to create a wanton hostility between me and a seemingly harmless, sanctioned state in this good country.

Chief of my disturbances, relative to the raising of kids, was that I recognized that the foremost obstacle compromising my maternal efficacy was the exodus of my instinctual confidence upon which children rightfully depended every waking day. I had always been a pillar of strength, maker of sound decisions, keeper of faithful temperaments. My instinct was trusted, my word respected. I was never a screamer, never a manic, flaming hormone seeking to restore an order that was more of a goal than a reality. The kids had a faith in me that I had earned, a faith that, in the face of challenge, never wavered. That was yesterday. Today, it felt more as if my life were like sand being filtered through a colander: The initial loss might have seemed negligible, but the eventual empty shell was but a matter of time.

Number Two: Risky Business.

Never before had our finances been so tenuous. Speculation on success was invading my sense of responsibility to make prudent decisions. It seemed the empire was iffy at best, perpetually behind an eight ball with many sharks at bay, even as bed partners. I had a particular pet peeve with some of Alex's newfound spending habits. It seemed, overnight, he grew a passion for sports cars, gourmet food, and fine gentlemen's accessories. He bought two Porsche sports cars, the second of which sent me into a particular orbit I never quite returned from. He always maintained that everything was under control, no threat of crumble looming near. Most notably, he had little regard for how fragile the possibility of this demise made me, and that, to me, was the the virulent root of that problem.

A big mistake was our working together in the business. I was the front line of defense when problems arose such as theft, rats, fires, lawsuits, broken air conditioners, irate landlords, absent managers, bounced checks. There was a turnstile of problems needing regular service. Yes, I was impressed with the control with which he juggled those fires. But I was paying close attention to the near misses, and never before had I felt that our future was being banked on a deck of cards in the face of a prevailing wind.

Why was the potential of a business gone bust enough to unglue me? I suppose it happened every day. People followed a dream, worked passionately to give it flight, and things just didn't work out as planned. I knew there were measures of insulation, such as bankruptcy. No one was going to jail. No one was on life support. There was just me, and four kids depending on me, and I felt like a mute spectator at a high-stakes craps table where my ego and reputation were the currency and I could only knock on wood that sevens didn't show up.

Clearly I was phobic. Clearly I was a control freak. Clearly I had no faith in anyone other than me. And surely, I would die alone.

Number Three: Our Marriage.

It was miserable. It seemed that in no time flat we were both given a never-before seen vision into who we were individually and there wasn't a common thread we shared. Trust, intimacy, laughter—not a shred of anything to reinforce our union and see us toward a finish line. Our sex life did not exist. Months would go by and he would decline my advances toward intimacy, time after time after time. He felt it was hard to feel sexual toward me when I was such a source of aggravation for him, and I argued that perhaps my displeasure was exacerbated by the fact that we hadn't had sex in months. These were the conundrums of our circular arguments. The chicken, the egg, what the hell did it matter? We weren't getting laid.

Core values seemed exposed and raw. Alex's tolerance for risk was miles from mine. His passion for material things seemed to fill him as it emptied me. He welcomed the lack of seasons and the need for an overcoat. We had polar interpretations of how we might define success, namely in ways other than financial. He had always depended on me to keep everything running in a seamless continuum, operating with high octane efficiency. Up until now, even the fumes had run dry. I was nowhere.

In my darkest of hours, I retreated to examination of my mental well-being, fearful of discovery. These three concerns would continually jockey for position in their pressing burden of priority. I could logically see that each individual concern should not have had the power of suffocation strong enough to destroy decades of earned accomplishment. Yet the monkey of the three of them had me in a mental strait jacket, with little room to breathe or wiggle.

Was I imparting my ideals of what a rightful childhood should include from a time three decades ago, which were merely a part of my own? Was I inflating the value of these sentimental rites of passage well beyond my own coming of age and transferring them into the very different world of today? Why was that noxious cocktail of freon, mold, and transiency enough to launch me into a spiral of fear and insecurity, leaving me impotent in its wake? And why did the punishment for one bad decision seem like such a wicked and ruthless spanking without the possibility for a do-over? I wanted my do-over. I had never known such darkness in all of my years.

The therapist did a lot of listening. We made it through three sessions of supervised venting with our paid referee mostly nodding and taking occasional notes, likely his reminders of things needing to be picked up on his way home. He was quick to look to Alex for validation on all that I was putting forth, as Alex was not very verbal, especially in that kind of setting. Alex agreed with the nature of the issues on our table. He concurred that nothing was being fabricated, and stoically maintained that his wife had fears and paranoias that were neither grounded nor rational. Alex offered his hope that I might resort to some pharmaceutical relief to restore some peace in his life. Alex also thought I needed to put my real estate license to use and get out of the movie business. Very valid points, both of which I had considered long before he presented them to the judge.

While therapy had not served its end by narrowing our rift, I will say that those three co-pays were money well-spent. Having aired the whole of our division to a professional stranger, he summed our issues accordingly: Alex, he said, seemed to be living a life on a death wish. He exhibited an unnatural indifference toward fear and consequence and had a flagrant disregard for showing emotional engagement when it was called for, even in relations beyond his and mine. He was flying high on the urgent rush of a good gamble, the tonic to any recovering addict. As for me, he offered without hesitation, I had a crippling fear of failure that was stunting my ability to engage in the living of my own life, even pre-dating Florida. A loaded summation. Not bad for a shopping list.

Selling real estate would certainly have relieved the lion's share of our financial pressures. Not only was it an explosive market with exorbitant sale prices, but the transient climate in this purgatory lended itself perfectly to easy penetration in finding new business. There weren't the factors of tenure and trust that were the foremost ingredients in earning clients back where I had been schooled and seasoned.

Making matters even easier, people seemed to be moving all the time, always looking for something different or newer or more expensive or less expensive. With such unbridled appreciation of property values to the conservative tune of 25% a year, no one balked at the big fat commissions they would be burdened with. I also recognized that it was an opportunity for me to buy back my ego, which had been bartered somewhere along this journey.

I placed my license with an aggressive broker. My tenured sales career, with a track record that had rendered me lead dog back home, barely earned me the private office that they kindly offered me. That office was more likely secured by my confidence and personality, which seemed miraculously restored as I walked into the pulse of that unique environment which is present in every busy real estate office in the country. There were familiar reception areas with expensive, upholstered furniture and well-dressed pretty people, duty-areas equipped with sophisticated technology in an effort to seamlessly capture prospects calling in, conference rooms with overbearing closing tables, and coffee stations complete with someone's leftover baked goods, with whittled down portions for those agents on their chronic diets. This all was a language I had been nursed on, spoon-fed its venacular cues since before I could speak.

I began working that summer, 2001, which meant little more than unpacking and arranging the two boxes marked "work" that had been stowed in the bowels of the garage, holding the nuts of my career. There wasn't a center of influence for me to tap into, not a host of attorneys or past clients I could call looking for business. Just me, a phone, a computer, and a lot of territory to learn overnight.

I found a buoyant thrill in being new to an office, as I had worked all my years in the same stale space, with all of the same faces, under the tall leadership of my mother at the helm, which brought its own set of perks and problems. It all felt brand new and familiar at the very same time, and I looked to this lifeline as owning all of the potential to restore some sanity to my shrinking world.

The Fall of Falls

The kids were all back in school, Sam started kindergarten, and September was historically a quiet time in the movie business as it recovered from a summer of blockbusters. The calendar called it fall, but not a sign of it was anywhere. I almost felt Alex's foot on the small of my back that morning I left the house to start the engines of my real estate potential. All signs pointed to GO. To the moon, Alice. Go make a lot of money. Go get out of the movie business. Go find a life.

I joined a women's yoga group in an effort to find some Chi, find some balance, find some private possibility. We met on Tuesday mornings, 8am. After that second class, feeling a disconcerting sense of uneasiness from perhaps having found too much Chi, I returned home a little frazzled. I pulled in the driveway, finding Alex standing post at the front door, top of the walkway, with the unrehearsed expression one might wear if someone had just died. I immediately looked to see that I hadn't brought my cell phone, and was certain, indeed, that someone did just die.

I got out of the car, approached his strange post with his stoic, militant stance, and he offered, stone-faced, "The country is under attack. The World Trade Center is in a fucking smolder." And, like everyone else in the world, I will forever recall where I stood at that moment I learned of this tragic assault. I felt numb and speechless and violated and frightened, certain in that one nanosecond that this particular event would serve as a vortex of life before and life after. I knew that I was breathing the very air in the kernel of that vortex, without a pulse on the direction that this pivot would yield. I was certain that the scope of life as we knew it would be shaped and changed in ways that would feel neither friendly nor familiar.

We engaged the flood of the media blitz in the face of the TV. There wasn't a channel without coverage of this fantastic drama that proved to exponentially underscore the grave reality that surrounded this event. This was not a terrorist annihilation B-grade, made-for-TV movie; this was on every possible channel in more than one language.

These tears and fears and horrors fell far outside the realm of emotion that canned drama could reach or capture. It was raw and violent, absent a single coping mechanism that I could grasp onto. I sat still, speechless, as the second tower was eviscerated. It took all of two minutes of contemplating the incalculable extent of loss sustained by that massive collapse for me to react. My only words, "I'm getting the kids. Be back soon."

I was certain that there would be utter mania surrounding the schools, with chaos and congestion eroding any order that an emergency evacuation plan could have anticipated. I pulled into the Charter School, stunned at the otherwise normal ebb and flow of school in action. No droves of parents gathering their kids, gym class as usual out in the parking lot, random people entering or exiting the front doors with no hurried agenda.

I parked like a movie star, ushered myself quickly inside, made a beeline for the attendance office, and requested that my son be called down for immediate pickup. The attendance lady was sporting a business-as-usual demeanor, which proved to further contribute to the surreal aura of the day. The woman standing next to me, sharing my apparent urgency to get her children back home, was wearing a well-tattered sweatshirt with the faded words, *Cape Cod*. I offered her a knowing smile of sympathy for being as far away from her home base as I felt from mine.

Each school proved to have that same creepy sense of nonchalance. It took a total of seventy minutes to return home with each of the kids. My interest was not to stay planted with them in front of the TV, and I wasn't even sure how much of this assault was appropriate for them to learn at this early hour of 11 a.m., just two hours after what was feeling like The Big Bang. I just knew I needed them home. It seemed that when crazy shit happened, more crazy shit happened, and I was running for cover, needing everyone under one roof.

The balance of the day was spent glued to the thrust of the inescapable media blitz. I also checked in with family and friends, taking inventory of anyone I knew who had a relation to New York, making sure that none of them had taken a job with Cantor Fitzgerald in the last week. Endless hours ensued as I made phone calls to family and friends, needing affirmations that these people weren't somehow swept away in the wayward chaos of insanity where anything seemed possible.

The phone served as conduit for exchanging overwhelming grief, mourning the unspeakable pain and fallout whose ultimate bloodshed was well beyond fathom. This patriotic injury stung the nation with an astounding and sophisticated precision that woke up an entire country in five minutes flat. That vicious dagger carved a wound in the heart of a nation at a sacred site where we had never before felt a vulnerability, a place that our ancestors had fought grueling wars for freedom and independence so that we might own this impunity and never have to surrender it. Those scenes of devastation and annihilation and rubble and panic, not in the New York I knew. Those early speculations of sketchy, disorganized terrorist groups responsible for this brilliant assault, not against against a country that I thought I knew.

It was crippling to embrace the extent of devastation on our native soil. Beyond the 2800 lives that were lost, there were the families and friends and young children whose lives would forever be shaped in the far-reaching fallout of this tragedy. Even in those early hours, when shock was the sole flooding emotion, it seemed painfully apparent that the whole of our big, beautiful country would confront a set of intrinsic challenges for which there was no durable blueprint. Our notion of union and patriotism would soon be up on trial, internally among our citizens, externally among the rest of the world. Nothing was static, nothing could be taken for granted.

I recalled having seen similar scenes of devastation and destruction and displaced urgent faces from news clips of faraway lands on the other side of the earth that I live on. Their battles for freedom had spanned centuries and somehow, sadly by proxy, they simply owned that particular forlorn landscape. It struck me as being painfully narrow and self-absorbed that this should all strike me so differently now. The same lost soul, the same aimless child looking for relief, the same destroyed building, yet it never hit home until it hit home.

My friend Sarah and I went for a long walk on September 12th. We covered probably ten miles, walking at a brisk pace in an effort to relieve some tension. We walked and talked and cried and wondered what in Hell was really happening. We watched people we passed by, tending to their lives, and yet it just seemed that life had stopped and everything needed to stand still until there were at least a few answers to what went wrong. The expansive, endless blue skies of South Florida, quiet and still, absent a single airplane in flight, were testimony to the extent of the paralysis that gripped us.

As weeks went on, it became impossible for me to shut out the inundation of fear that permeated my world. There were brand new task forces, grueling relief efforts, batteries of new intelligence factions overriding those that were apparently sleeping in advance of that doomed day, 9/11. There was the nationally instituted color-coded gradient of how much fear we should adopt for any given day. There was suspicion that there were ulterior motives and agendas in determining the transition from one color to the next. There were urgent national pleas for answers to matters I had never thought to question. Nothing was familiar or friendly. That was all I knew.

It seemed that any responsible mother might start to take matters into her own hands. Fear was rampant throughout the nation, from threats of shoe bombers to anthrax scares to water supply contamination to terrorist cells living matriculated lives in our very neighborhoods. When I learned that one of the Logan Airport hijackers lived but five streets from where I lived, I needed Plan B because Plan A was clearly not looking out for me.

Sarah and I went to local stores to procure supplies that one might need in a nuclear war or national Holocaust. We purchased the essentials of self-sustainability, packed neatly in two oversized Tupperware storage totes, kept at all times in the back of our oversized SUVs, including but not limited to:

- batteries of every size
- tarps & space blankets & tents
- waterproof matches, lanterns, flashlights
- rain ponchos which fold up to the size of playing cards
- playing cards
- knives of all kinds
- Sterno, siphons, flares, and duct tape
- emergency radio
- fat wood fire starters
- set of fine outdoor cookware
- vitamins, aloe, Advil, baby wipes, peroxide
- fully-equipped toiletry needs
- fully-equipped first aid needs including iodine tablets
- maps of the country
- books on survival
- $1000 cash
- 14-day supply of Cipro
- change of clothes for 6 people for 4 days

This was fear in a box. Two boxes, actually, which were with me at all times. Never mind that in the event of dire emergency, I would be presented with insurmountable difficulty retrieving kids, filling my gas tank, finding a road out of the state of Florida that wasn't bumper to bumper cars going nowhere. Surely I would have been the best prepared nut-case in that traffic jam.

Alex had no patience for my insecurity. He had unwavering faith in our good leader and his cabinet of ulterior interests. While he watched the testosterone-laden football-style coverage on Fox News, I found these underground networks disseminating information on the issues it seemed the conventional networks weren't covering. Alex discounted any covert conspiracy theory I might have stumbled upon and found folly in my fear. Partaking in pillow talk on the gravity of this unprecedented global assault might have served to bolster our private connection amid a sea of public mania, but he would offer no such forum. It felt as though any concern of mine became an anti-concern of his. He wore the conviction that, when the last of the rubble was carted offsite, people might return to their usual appetite for movies and popcorn. Waiting for this moment seemed to be his only complaint.

I know next to nothing about the furtive agendas of foreign policy. I had never been much of a politically engaged, flag-waving citizen, nor had I ever been comfortable having dialogue on matters with which I was not reasonably familiar. I knew that there was not a crash course to be had in understanding the complicated and dynamic truths that were fueling this war, nor was it likely that any lay energies spent seeking its intellectual synthesis would have proved anything but futile. Born then and there was a powerlessness, a private-citizen vacuum of acceptance that those in the seat of making decisions for the rest of us would need to be trusted, though it was likely that the better part of the national bell curve was not the primary agenda. Accountability may come later. It may never come at all. I felt smaller and more insignificant than I ever recalled having felt, a peon among the masses, awaiting my allotted handful of government-issue updates and heavily-censored propaganda. A national orphan, only porridge for dinner.

There was a particular sadness when the time came that network news began their evening editions with stories other than 9/11 concerns. Wounds were still festering, still bleeding even. It was reasonable, I supposed, that other incidental events were still happening in the world, but I was grateful not to be sharing the room with the wife of a fallen fireman as the story about breast-augmentation advances was aired with more enthusiasm than seemed appropriate. Life does go on and survivors do move forward. If matter is neither created nor destroyed, we can assume that our collective suffering moves forward with us as well.

I wore this veil of passive acceptance as I attempted to reengage in life, either going to my office listening to the same petty banter, or going to the theatres to learn of the same problems with clogged soda machines or broken air conditioners. The hardest questions to answer were those from my children. They were well aware of the shift in national security. They were also used to hard and fast answers to most of their questions.

I had a very vague pulse on where to be with them, in their minds and hearts, on the full scope of what likely lay ahead. The fallout was enormous. While it didn't seem right to insulate them from the sincere and grave threats that were being waged against our nation, nor did it seem right to insert a canned patriotism of Uncle Sam on steroids, ready to squash the evildoers, a mentality that obviously had landed us there in the first place.

The time came for me to take my first flight since that famed day. Peter and Leah flew to Buffalo every other month to visit their dad, and while I did harbor a newfound fear of flying, it didn't seem right to confound my fears with those visits. They were in the 6th and 8th grades and usually flew alone, but in the week before their scheduled flight the vigilant powers-that-be elected to raise the threat level from yellow to orange, a spike that called for me to accompany them in all good conscience.

The airport experience seemed out of a militant movie, cast with stone-faced soldiers sporting massive rifles and strange little berets that didn't suit their gear. They were trained to respond to nothing other than valid threats to life. A kid could throw a hot dog at them and they would not move. A milkshake, nothing. I imagine some lesser-ranked orderly might appear and do away with the little trickster, but it wouldn't be the man in the beret unless the kid happened to admire his nifty rifle, the size of his thigh, curious as to whose team he was actually playing for.

Carry-on luggage would get rifled through with utter disregard to the order in which things had been arranged. The special task administrator would be subpoenaed for any borderline weapon, such as a nail file, sharpened pencil, or versatile compact mirror. This *specialist*, casting a scornful eye of surveillance right into its owner, would fondle the item in their hand, feeling it for suspicious inconsistencies. There were all these new jobs, new appointments, new task forces. What were all of these people doing for work before this insanity, and how qualified could these new recruits really be? These strange and stupid questions always volleyed for answers in my mind.

The actual flight was otherwise uneventful. I spent three days visiting with friends while the kids caught up with their dad. I was immediately aware upon exiting the airport that I was far closer to Ground Zero than I was in South Florida. There were still flags flying high on cars, discussion everywhere on the daily discoveries of pursuits of answers, a collective pain and mourning that felt far more appropriate than where I had been. Retail was still standing still, unlike in Florida, where it barely missed a beat. For all three nights, evening news still considered the top order of business to be matters on issues relative to the continuing hemorrhage of 9/11. I felt far less alone, and I appreciated that feeling as passive evidence that perhaps I wasn't as unglued as I was growing to feel.

When we returned from New York, I was startled by Sam's urgent confrontation. "Mommy," he'd been waiting to ask for three days, "what would have happened if those bad guys came for us while you were gone?" Fear within me had its level of tolerability. Fear within my child was a whole different story. I held him close to me, as though I could extract its grip within him and discard it like spent ash.

Sam was born the smallest of my kids, weighing in at just 8 pounds. He was born laughing, and rarely takes a reprieve from laughing today. He has always had a humor far more refined than his years. He finds levity in everything he is engaged in, including his schoolwork, which is really not funny at all. Farting is hilarious, and trick jokes are always in open season.

Sometimes when I watched Sam bellow with laughter, I was regrettably able to chart the miles between me and my childhood, back when hilarity was a reigning player. I wished I could borrow his disposition once in a while, wear it like a frisky fashion accessory. If I were feeling unusually permissive, he would craft insanely elaborate forts out of blankets & pillows & duct tape & broomsticks. He was a cowboy and an Indian.

Yet this little boy had a set of fears to balance that laughter. He was perpetually worried about tornadoes, hurricanes, tsunamis—just about every natural disaster known to mankind. He had long considered the many potential pitfalls an airplane could endure at 30,000 feet, even before the threat of terrorists. I was always very careful to keep my fears off his radar screen, knowing all too well that he had less ability to synthesize gloom and doom than I did.

He is presently nine years old, which is a particularly magical time in the life of a boy. He owns fragments of new autonomy, is not yet encumbered with the burdens of puberty, and still thinks hanging out with his mom is cool beans. He loves a good cuddle, a game of checkers, and a backyard bonfire with G-rated ghost stories. He's got a wild mane of curly hair in a deep shade of red that invariably invites comment from anyone looking in his direction.

Riding bikes with buddies, catching frogs with bare hands, and roasting a marshmallow on a stick are the potluck of his perfect day. He makes friends with strangers in doctor's waiting rooms, is never at a loss on how to entertain himself, and owns a healthy appreciation for the value of an ally in his world. Sam is all boy. He is simple and predictable and fends off excessive emotional engagement like one avoids the flu. My recent appreciation of the profound genetic differences in men and women, differences which no course in communication therapy could begin to bridge, are founded in Sam. He has taught me to pick my battles more wisely.

Christmas came that year, and that unbridled trolley of consumption stung me hard. I had never been one for the mall scene, but that particular year I found the holiday music, the litany of garbage for sale, the canned wishes for good tidings, the urgency to own what was hot, all beyond being tolerable. The illuminated lawn ornaments sporting Santa and his reindeer, backdrop palm tree, felt blasphemous and borrowed. Even the cookies felt counterfeit. I knew my kilter was more than off when I was at a store, waiting in a line an inordinate amount of time, and was greeted by a cheery clerk with an ear to ear smile who offered no apology for my wait. I offered "Go fuck yourself," stone-cold and sober. I summoned all efforts to get to January when people returned to their usual grumpy selves.

January brought a new set of issues that gave legs to my paranoia of Alex and the movie empire. He had always operated with a silent partner, more of a private bank, who was no longer so silent. They had a business relationship of over fifteen years from back in New York, conforming deals mostly by handshake. Two of the eight theatres in the circuit proved to be economic losers, and there were significant investments made there with threatened hope of recovery. The partners began paying closer attention to details on the mechanics of each operation. They were determined to recover lost funds, and were driven to be whole by all standards. If the microscope on me netted some irritating insect bites to manage, the scope on Alex, with a swarm of vermin crawling up his ass, paved the road to a violent conclusion of their courtship. A million dollars on the line makes people funny that way.

Alex's philosophy was this: Annex the losers—two of eight not such a bad loss—and move forward. Especially considering the steep learning curve that first year, six of eight were worth celebrating. Accordingly, his and his partners' agendas parted ways. They attempted to assert financial burdens on those theatres that were thriving, compromising their continued profitability. It was hard to watch the erosion of that tenured relationship that had weathered many rough seasons and recovered, and it appeared as if Alex was confronted with what was seeming like insurmountable obstacles.

They each retained attorneys and engaged the legal arena to find the resolve to suit their divided ends. Know this: In battles of love and business, attorneys are the only sure winners. I have tremendous respect for a brilliant attorney whose expert advice and guided direction are his or her stock in trade, and their energies should be applauded with fat sums of money. Many, however, operate on the low road, mired in trumped-up conflicts, feeding adversarial appetites, all while the meter is running, confident that they will be the last man standing.

What began as friendly dialogue between two parties attempting to meet minds escalated into full-scale warfare that was threatening to throw a well-positioned monkey wrench into the flow of operations. Exorbitant energies and sums of money were expended to defend positions and propel separate interests, never with solutions on the near horizon. Alex had an uncanny ability to jockey plans A-F at all times, yet never did he remotely consider that a dissolution of that relationship would jeopardize his post as king of the castle.

Money was king. Money lended control, control lended power, power lended privilege. Alex was always one to put privilege in front of money, sort of similar to having a big, beautiful sail boat without the prevalence of wind to launch it forward. I loved his capacity to dream, still do. I found his visions bold and daring. He held a reckless edge in his demeanor that had always captivated me, but it was easier to get lost in the folly of fantasy when I had a six figure income to rest my laurels on.

There was increasing reluctance for him to share with me the gory details of those battles, as he was dead-on right that I was paying close attention to the financial stability of our life. We argued incessantly about matters from his business to kids' schools to my frustrations with can-

celed little league games because the coach didn't show up. There wasn't
an argument to be won or lost. Alex and I fought like twin sisters with red
hair. We both kept score, seeing the same set of circumstances from polar
perspectives, clearly never moving forward on any of our issues.

I tried to enter the quiet of my inner sanctum (no roadmap available) in hopes of hearing some guidance. With no voice to hear, I began
reading my horoscope in the newspaper and online. I even consulted
Sam's Magic 8 Ball when no one was watching, sometimes going for two
out of three if my answers weren't coming through with profound conviction. The only kernel of peace I found was in knowing that, whatever
it was that was blinding my sight on how to best relieve the mess of my
life, its spell would have to lift at some point because nothing, absolutely
nothing, stood still for long.

One of my college girlfriends, Daniela, responded to an e-mail I
wrote her regarding the chaotic state of my affairs. She, like most of my
friends, had never seen me in such a desolate place of uncertainty, which
was evolving into a self-battery of sorts. Daniela lived in Mexico, lived a
life very other than the rigid Western way that I had always known. Her
e-mail expressed concern for me in the type of spiral I was enduring. A
compass off course and under pressure, for extended lengths of time,
could not escape consequence.

She urged me to take special care of my body and to listen to its subtle whispers. She recommended a book, *Anatomy of the Spirit*, by Carolyn
Myss, which I promptly bought and parked on my nightstand amid the
dozen other self-help books I seemed to have a newfound knack for collecting. I was no stranger to that section of the bookstore. The author was
a nationally recognized, acclaimed medical intuitive, with great tenure
steeped in spirituality. It was an excellent work written with tremendous
clarity and wisdom on the integral relationship of mind and body,
respecting the powers one can harness in honoring that balance, as well
as create by ignoring it. I challenged most things unfamiliar to me, especially on issues related to the intangible, yet this book spoke concepts to
me that I already knew in the bowels of my physical body. It made such
astounding sense to me that I grew fearful that my infirmed mind and
spirit had a body not far behind.

My confidence in my ability to make good, sound decisions continued to erode. Logically, it appeared that there was an overwhelming presence of uphill battles, ones for which I had neither the passion nor the
ammunition to fight. Beyond the streaming freon, the endless strip malls

of equal parts pink and concrete, the inferior education, the Prada goddesses, the retail religion, I felt paralyzed and mute even in the privacy of myself. I wasn't totally certain that it wasn't an internal battle of my own, irrespective of these external inputs, that was the real war I was fighting. Was it convenient to direct all of the ills I was feeling to an extraneous environment rather than nailing down my inner struggle for control no longer in my grasp? I was pleading with the Universe to simply realign itself and return to me my bearings.

Streaming within each of these lofty questions was a common, recurrent suspicion. It seemed to originate from a place that demanded an honesty and humility one would never invite when all was going well. Certainly, my trio of valid dilemmas was not fabricated to mask a sinister agenda. They were real and their grip was firm. But underscoring each of them was a question from a higher summit: What was my core motive? A motive. Seemed simple and sounded like murder, but everyone had one whether they knew it or not. Yet why had most of my measures to satisfy that thirst not furnished an answer with any staying power to speak of?

Exit Line

$\mathcal{D}$riving on I-95 with a seasoned familiarity I was not proud of, on a balmy eighty-seven degree day in February, a light bulb went off. I was retrieving Peter and Leah from the Lauderdale airport after returning from a visit north to see their dad. Peter shared with me the events of his weekend, including skiing, downtime, and the lowdown of a party hosted by best friends, old girlfriends, and familiar rituals.

Peter was fourteen at the time, and he and his friends were a quirky collection of budding and budded hormones. They had all grown up together since grade school. He was very forthcoming in recognizing the quality of those friendships as compared with his friends in Florida. Naturally, those tenured souls would have carved a post of righteousness in his heart that new friends couldn't touch, but he remarked that it was other than that. There was an intangible component of reality that was somehow short-circuited in the Land of Plenty, he actually noted to me. The dagger twisted, contorted further into my sizeable gut of guilt. Leah shared with me her pleasures in just having some downtime with her dad. A nice relationship between them had begun brewing after we left New York, and the distance ironically seemed to bring them closer. Peter was to start high school that fall, and I became determined to get back on track by then, come Hell or high water.

I began to champion the plan of relief. Yes, relief, from all counts. The sky cleared, the sea parted, the fog lifted from my humid, two-ton, eighty-seven degree perspective. I'm outta here.

Alex was on the road throughout the state at least every other week, and when he was actually home, he was anything but home, sporting his Nextel walkie-talkie in one hand, cell phone in the other. There were the usual fires of operation that needed regular stoking, and now the decline of his financial backing, all to still fit in the same business day. Every day was a business day. Even on Christmas, you can always find Chinese food and a good movie.

I underwrote a plan and presented it to Alex. I move back to Buffalo with the kids, restore my job and income, and get the kids back into the schools that undoubtedly better served them. I return to the kids the sanity of the mother they once knew. The cost of living was more reasonable without the palm trees. Throw in Alex's twice-monthly flights and we were still ahead of the game. And, the coup-de-gras, when Alex came north, he could enjoy a much-needed four-day reprieve from the incessant chaos of his world. While this seemed like more of a necessity than a vacation to me, Alex didn't share in my solution. He felt that I was responding with dire alarm to issues that were all under complete control.

I tried to impress upon him that this was really a gift to him. He could put on the boxing gloves, fight those sharks with reckless abandon, alleviate the pressures from our marital nightmare, and it was his own personal get-out-of-jail-free card if all went bust. I neatly packaged it as a four-year plan: Get Peter through high school, get Sam and Sophie some stronger years of early elementary education, get his business affairs in fiscal order, restore my income, all while giving some space and distance to our rapidly eroding sense of commitment to each other given the heavy burdens we were wearing like wet, day-old clothing. If all endured, we could return to Florida with perhaps some of the structure and stability we should have arrived there with in the first place.

I always assumed that the more comfortable Alex got with the plan of us returning north, the more insurmountable the affairs of his business had become, though I would never have been so stupid as to seek that validation. I flew to Buffalo in April to look at a few houses, none of which were particularly suitable. I sent mailings to that particular neighborhood in the village that I had always loved, sent them to each and every house that spoke to me. If I was going to do this, I wanted it done right.

My letters netted nothing, so I made some phone calls. One of those calls was a big score. While the kind woman on the phone did share with me that she would not be moving in her entire lifetime, she did tell me her neighbor was trying to sell her house, without the assistance of a broker, dwarfing any exposure she could have had. I was online daily at that point, and I also had some key agents in my familiar marketplace looking out for that right house. This little gem, however, was off of everyone's radar except mine.

And little it was. It was a gingerbread house c. 1905, original clapboard in the finest condition I had ever seen. Moldings nearly 12" tall, with vintage hardware and fixtures intact. Floors were solid cherry and had never seen a dog or a two-year old. The kitchen was renovated with light hickory cabinets, a gorgeous slab of granite, and a kick-ass Viking stove I never knew I couldn't live without. There was a storybook front porch within a stone's throw of the village's sweetest little park.

The reason that this Victorian gem was not on my original mailing was now obvious to me; it was teeny. Gorgeous yes, but teeny. There were three bedrooms, with the smallest of them larger than many walk-in closets. There was not a place to sit with a piece of toast in the state-of-the-art kitchen. All meals would be had in the dining room, lending an air of civility, I supposed. There was one bathroom, which meant one toilet, and a shower barely big enough to accommodate people's particular fancies for favorite shampoos and shower gels. And there was a living room in which all living was to be done, because there were no other rooms to be found.

This modest little home had a strange appeal to me. One hundred years ago it was spacious enough for any size family. Why not mine today? I made her an offer, she accepted, and I told myself that the little house would be a perfect temporary landing pad until the right home in this neighborhood became available. Closing was set for June, and I felt a particular enthusiasm that the front porch weather that lay ahead would lend at least another 80 square feet to our living space.

Closing shop in Florida brought a new bounce to my step. Selling our house was effortless. Packing the house, which would be the third time in eighteen months, was almost effortless. Understandably, Alex wanted nothing to do with these energies, but I was plenty used to that by then. I packed boxes for him to include a complete setup for a new apartment. We split up kitchen wares, linens, artwork. We split the proceeds from the sale of the house. Movers were booked. We would be leaving the day after the last day of school.

Sam was excited to return to seasons, to snow, to friends, and especially to escape that year's upcoming hurricane season, which, gratefully, a buddy of his had told him was going to be a really, really bad one. Peter would be starting South High School, exactly the place he ought to have been. Leah was even, though I suspect she wanted her mom to know some peace that did not seem to be available for her on the peninsula. I think that girl could live in any environment and never stand in judgment of what it was or was not. Sophie, however, was a whole different story.

Sophie didn't like me. This didn't start as a response to my pulling her away from Florida and her daddy. There had always been subtle cues to this effect since the day she was born. I loved her tirelessly, wished I could penetrate her the way that had come so naturally to me with my other children, but I hadn't yet found that key. I would swear she was switched in the hospital if it weren't for the truth that she was the spitting image of her father. She and I didn't even look related.

Her daddy was her compass, always had been. She had the same passion for consumption that he did, as well as the same disregard for simple measures of conservation that he had. Without a stitch of uncertainty, she wanted to grow up to be a movie theatre popcorn maker, scooping the corn with expert efficiency into its vessel. "Would you like a Coke with that?" she practiced saying in the mirror.

Not without irony, her urgency for him grew into borderline obsession once he was not living under her roof. When we all lived together, she offered him the same indifferent regard that I get today. Few of her daily needs were actually met by him, since Alex was never one for mundane household duty. When in his presence, she reverted to baby talk, exhibited behaviors less mature than her years should have allowed for, and put her foot down at any energy that might have involved a little growing up. She had a passion for plastic as large as a landfill that I just couldn't get cozy with. Daddy was Disneyland and fast food. Mommy was broccoli and homework. As this homemade handiwork was further bolstered by my election to leave, I can censure only myself. I prayed this phase would pass, I loved this little girl. Until then, she would just go on not liking me.

Making matters worse, youngest children were further challenged by being last in line. Mothering any pack of kids took tremendous energy, with little reprieve from the get-go. Keeping them all engaged in their worlds, from school to friends to sports to clothing, season in, season out, could tire anyone. The older kids were entrenched in activities, and the youngest got dragged into things that were invariably not about them. With time the tightest resource, it was much easier to just tie their shoe than to craft a fun lesson teaching them how to do it for themselves. They were witness to the privileges of older siblings, sidelined from their fun, freedom, and later bedtimes. Even my enthusiasm could seem like a hand-me-down. I understood this was a hard place to be. By the time Sophie was geared up to ride a two-wheeler, my diluted energy didn't demand that I search for my camcorder to capture the big event. Shame on me.

Every once in a while, Sophie had moments when she was not such an angry girl. Those windows came without warning and left without reason, but I welcomed witnessing the possibility of peace that could exist within her. I most certainly took note that the challenge of her recovery was the tallest order of business on my plate. I knew from minute one that the greatest fallout from our move would be Sophie. However, one well-being could not have tipped the scale; it barely even budged it.

The weeks preceding the move weighed heavily on my weary bones. After eighteen months of extraordinary challenge, I had woken up to the fact that for the first time in my life I was not the pillar of strength I had always known, and my husband was nowhere to catch me. It is comforting to believe that, if need be, a safety net exists when we are down. It is shattering to realize that it may only exist in our mind. I did not, however, wake up to that. I carried that fallacy with me even further. *Adios*, Florida.

Re-Entry

As any good astronaut might confirm, the pressures, tensions and strains are never more challenged than at the moment of that final surge. I summoned all my strength to gather myself and the kids, and returned to the place I had discarded just eighteen months earlier, kicked to the curb like a flattened soda can.

I had lost close to ten pounds in those final four weeks. The only upside of stress was the weight that seemed to effortlessly evaporate. Put that on an infomercial and sell it, sadly, all day long. I felt like a shadow of the self that had departed, having nothing to do with the ten pounds. I felt unsure of how to resume the role I had left behind, and I felt slightly more naked having been stripped of the confidence that had layered my ego with abundant insulation. It had been whittled down to a scant memory, obvious to me only after my return when the loss seemed more calculable.

The climate was perfect. I hadn't realized how much the humidity had fogged my thinking until it was no longer humid. In any northern climate, there was that sheer rush of being outdoors, liberated from layers of clothing those early days of summer. It's funny: While seventy degrees was shedding everyone else's clothes, I was rummaging for a sweater with blood so thin I felt transparent.

Beyond garments, there was a palpable energy streaming in people that was invigorating. One might think that this rush can be found year-round in southern climates. Think again. Seasons were the means of charting growth and progress, a yardstick of checks and balances. They were not cesspools of stagnation, ripe for mold and decay.

I did have some concern for what the kids would think of the sweet little house, as we had lived in homes easily three times its size. With great relief, it was a perfect fit. A mental fit, not a physical one. Half our belongings went straight for the garage, to be revisited at a later time and place. The two boys shared a bedroom that barely held the bunk beds. The two girls had twin beds, opposite corners, with a distinct invisible line marking their territories. Closets were stuffed. They were each allowed only one favorite shampoo, and their toiletries had to go to and from the bathroom with them. It was like summer camp, and it was awesome.

The simplicity had great appeal for me. The slow speed of summer was a welcome reprieve. We hung out at the park and walked into town for dinner and ice cream. There were reunions with old friends and backyard barbecues. The kids would bike to the convenience store, to the town library, to wherever they could pedal to. There was no school agenda to adhere to, just long summer days and warm summer nights. There were baseball games, outdoor concerts, neighborhood block parties, the very rites of passage that contribute in the subtlest of ways to the whole of a soul.

Peter's tenured baseball coach applauded his return. He found him a spot on the diamond in a heated season that was well underway. This coach was one of the most extraordinary inspirers to youth I had ever known. His dedication and commitment to this team of boys went well beyond baseball. He was a character coach. He imparted values on sportsmanship, teamwork, stepping up to a challenge, as well as on all baseball technicalities.

It was motivators like him that helped kids stay out of trouble, helped to reinforce what parents worked to instill. There was good fortune and good timing when such a person entered the life of a kid. The coach was an attorney by day. His entire law practice went on hold during baseball season, no doubt his favorite four months of the year. His paralegals managed the phone tree, his secretaries shopped for Gatorade, and his opposing counsel must have loved baseball as much as he did. He was the tallest of Braves. Atlanta knows not of this Little League Leader who moved forward the reigning spirit of their ball club.

Beyond the ball team with its strong leadership there were the families of these boys, and we had all grown up together on these diamonds over the many seasons of their play. We had weathered hail storms in May, had served our sentences grilling burgers for boys, and had seen our younger kids graduate from babies in strollers to being little ballpark rascals, harmlessly disturbing the order that those damned adults kept insisting on.

The moms and I had watched our young men evolve from daisy pickers in the outfield to being disciplined athletes requiring deodorant, razors, and their girlfriends in the bleachers. They commanded an impressive talent to show up and win a game, and watching that talent was engaging beyond the reason that your kid was playing in it. The dads were tremendous. They were attorneys, dentists, bankers, and teachers by day. They were baseball by heart. They were heroes by way of thirteen young men who had grown up under their wings. I realized then and there how much I loved baseball.

There were some aggressive energies I needed to assert to kick-start my abandoned career. With my mother's interest now dissolved in the office where I had worked before my departure, I decided to move my broker's license over to a different firm, its biggest competitor. I geared up with new personal brochures, marketing materials, press releases. I excavated my list of past transactions, forging ahead with an enthusiastic campaign seeking tomorrow's business from yesterday's forgotten client base.

My mother's leadership role in her firm was unparalleled. Our office, back in the years before she sold the company, was the top producing office in Upstate New York for over a decade. She worked an uninterrupted thirty years with a passion and enthusiasm that never waned. She was both pioneer and anchor in the world of real estate, her opinion considered expert among most. When she stepped down from her throne, new management stepped in, and slowly the agents migrated elsewhere. Many of the key players from my old office went to the new office that I was moving to. It was a great homecoming to be back in that pulse.

There were, however, always those that thrived on others' miseries, and many of the people that I ran into were desperately wanting to ask, "What the hell went wrong? Who moves from Florida back to Buffalo? Where is your husband? Why are you so thin?," but refrained from doing so. I had always found great power in offering few words. Explanations were folly for fools, and I was playing no part in contributing to the gossip of their circles. I just went about my way in the same private fashion that explains why most people consider me to be inaccessible at best, and it goes downhill from there.

Alex came north about five days of every three weeks. He spent that time relaxing, enjoying doing a lot of nothing, including playing golf which he managed to do just once in the eighteen months we were living in the golf capital of the world. He even put forth some words suggesting that this might not have been such a bad plan after all. Few words, vague words, but the sentiment was conveyed by way of his detached cell phone, hammock downtime, and eager return to the throne of the barbecue.

Work began to take shape. I readied the kids for enrollment in the fall, married the Florida school transcripts and medical records, and especially enjoyed the arrival of fall clothing on the retail scene. It was time to relax and celebrate standing still for the first time in a long while.

The Fall of Falls, Part Two

Fall had always been my favorite time of year. Days were still long and warm, nights called for favorite sweaters and cozy pajamas. It seemed that the shift to autumn was discernible first by scent, then later by sight. All the magnificent, organic colors found in nature peaked to their unique octaves in a chorus of breathtaking beauty; it was marvelous. There was football and apple cider. There was homecoming and pumpkins. And there was my birthday.

October had always found me happy. I entered this one with a particular sense of peace, having been through the war and back. In a routine visit to my primary care doctor for an annual physical, that peace evaporated.

I lay on my back and underwent a gentle, tactile physical exam from my doctor of many years. Familiar voice, familiar touch, but not so familiar a look on his face when he examined an area on my breast with unusual scrutiny. He told me he felt something suspicious. I went to feel it, and, indeed, suspicious was the right word. It felt like I had swallowed a BB and it had lodged in my right breast, planted itself in a fixed position, and was stubborn to any effort to move its post. Yes, I felt it. How had I missed it? Perhaps if my beautiful breasts had gotten any attention in the last several years of my life the BB might not have been so palpable today. Damn my husband. That was my first thought.

My doctor qualified his suspicion by noting that he was not a breast specialist, and wrote a script for a mammogram. Before handing me that paper, he made a quick phone call, told me that he just secured an appointment, conveniently across the hall from his office, in just fifteen minutes. His urgency spoke volumes. I recall thanking him for his thorough breast exam as I left his office.

I made no phone calls between those two appointments, though I had plenty of time because the mammo wait was exhaustive. It was a private hour of contemplation I was not ready to share. I paged through some magazines, read the wall plaques, and reviewed the oversized poster on how to give yourself a good breast exam. I had considered myself an efficient examiner before today. My regimen included self breast exams monthly, missing maybe two a year. I had honed a technique from my gynecologist, seeking diligent proficiency just after my mother got breast cancer two years earlier. I may have been diligent, but I sure wasn't good. So much for that technique.

The technician wanted ten images of my squashed breast, which fell far outside of the amount of radiation my body needed in a day. The rigid compression of tissue did not seem to be a friendly way to confront this little BB, but I took the directives and did what I was told. I dressed, I waited, I still made no phone calls.

I met with the radiologist, my ten images like illuminated concert posters on his sterile white wall. He pointed to the area in question, kindly noting that its particular shading with spiked boundaries made it suspicious for malignancy. I surmised that this man reviewed films all day long and had a clue which films warranted the sharing of that careful word, "malignancy."

I was then ushered into a room where I underwent a sonogram. My only other medical experience with sonograms were when pregnant and vibrant, awaiting visions into the magic of the womb that cradled the private world of my mysterious baby. Not today. This technician was kind and clinical, not shy to communicate the delineation of how the sound was behaving on my little BB. Fat-based and water-based masses responded to sound waves differently than did malignant tumors, where the waves crashed right back at you, impenetrable to current, with a nasty ricochet. Another suspicious test result.

That should have been enough to validate the likelihood this was no benign cyst. But alas, I was ushered into another room for one more test. This was called a Large Core Needle Biopsy. Different than a fine-needle aspiration, it was explained to me as follows: "We numb your breast, thereby making it as comfortable as possible. Then we fire this appliance into the side of your breast and a large needle is ejected at 72 mph directly into the tumor and extracts cells from its core. We do this five times just to be sure." So no one had a heart attack, they then fired the gun at the ceiling so that the sound of it was familiar. Its noise was deafening, a hostile cross between Navy Seal rifle and sophisticated medical appliance. It didn't feel right.

I sat up, confirming by my vertical position that I didn't want this test. I didn't know why, I just knew I didn't want it. The doctor responded to my concern with an assertive and confident delivery of a speech about the safety and dire necessity of this exam to confirm the presence of cancer in my breast, inserting language one only learned in medical school, passively reminding me that she was one hundred times smarter than I was. I guess she was in sales, too, because I lay right back down.

After the gun fired twice, I was done. Its violation to my breast felt more unbearable than the acrimony I would receive from the good doctor. She read my body language in a way that opened no door for further discussion on the matter. I explained that she had her two samples, and would have to do the best she could with both of them.

I will offer this to anyone reading my story, hopefully to be shared with a mother, daughter, sister, friend, or neighbor who may one day be confronted with this drama. I am no doctor, no kidding, but in my lay opinion, this test is not indicated. I argue that it is contraindicated when the suspicion of malignancy exists. When there is a mammogram netting a suspicious image with peculiar boundaries and edges, and a sonogram netting the same with the attenuation of the sound waves, what sane woman would elect to disturb this potentially cancerous tumor, peacefully planted, with an assault powerful enough to disrupt it and risk scattering its lethal cells? The tumor should just be surgically excised, then sent out for due pathology. If it were to prove not to be cancerous, I can't imagine there are many who would wish that this benign suspicion were still with them. If it were to prove to be cancerous, leaving it as undisturbed as possible until that swift excision is unequivocally the wisest measure to stave off further spread of disease.

Strangely, my body knew this when I first lay down on that table, but my mind had not yet caught up. Bodies are born survivors, whereas sometimes an appeal to intellect can smolder that instinct. That particular lesson I will own the rest of my life.

I left the medical facility about four hours after arriving for my routine physical, and I was clearly in a fog. They told me they would have the pathology results in four days, but I didn't need those results to respect the road in front of me. It was time to make phone calls.

My first was to my mother. This was a particularly charged one because she and I shared an intimate connection on so many levels. She was like a best friend and a mother and a teacher, conveniently packaged. Its extra potency was because she had been touched by the same stroke of misfortune just two years earlier. It was very painful for her to see and feel my trials of the past year and a half. It was hard for her during that time to watch my suffering. It would not be easy to share with her that there was a new set of challenges on my next horizon.

My mother and Alex had always had miles of distance between them, on many counts. Central to each count was the truth that I had always felt a constant pull between each of their strongholds, and that had not been healthy for either relationship. I had known it for so long that I no longer recognized it as a pollutant. It was a dance I had learned to tango to. So be it. I called her first.

Her own breast cancer did not scare or startle her. She wanted no fanfare whatsoever in getting though it. It came, ironically, in the month before her scheduled retirement, and she confronted it with the same dispassionate, decisive execution as any of the business challenges that preceded it. My brother, my sister, and I thought it was very unusual, but supposed it was a very personal thing and chose not to compete with how she elected to process the situation. She was very quiet about who she wanted to know. She had surgery, she had radiation, she took the script for Tamoxifen, and she was through with it, a tedious memory in her rear view mirror.

She didn't share the same indifference when learning that her daughter was stung by the same disease. She demanded all of the particulars of what I knew, namely why I was calling after such lengthy escapades of the day. I reminded her that she waited two days before she even spoke the word *cancer* out loud. She insisted on driving to my house, drinking wine with a purpose, and mapping out what needed to get done.

My next call was to Alex. He was at work, amid a dependable crisis that was consuming his day. He was brief and unapproachable, but I shared that it was important that he call me back soon. As I stood still, call disconnected, I considered why I was being so coy, not insisting that we have that discussion then and there, why it was tolerable to discuss the matter at a later, more convenient time.

There were so many things to reckon with. My mind was a live neuron entertaining countless fleeting considerations, from surgery to hair loss, from life insurance I didn't have to motherless children I maybe had. I couldn't tie down a topic for more than an instant. It was a freak slide show:

1) Me with no hair at the grocery store, having lost it in Aisle 7

2) A birds' eye view of my funeral where I was noting what people were wearing. It was winter.

3) My four children holding hands in a place I was unfamiliar with, in clothing I had not bought them

4) Me as an old woman looking very happy

5) My father and mother hugging

6) Me jogging, having found that runner's rhythm I never really knew. Whether I was running away from something or toward something else was unclear.

7) Alex at the theatre ordering catered food from his favorite Jewish deli

8) My tombstone, but I did not like the stone or its shape. I wondered who had selected it.

9) My sister and I when we were 7 and 8 years old at summer camp in Algonquin Park, Canada

10) My father holding me as a newborn

11) My brother and I playing a game of witchy-poo when I was seven and topless, against my mother's wishes

12) Most of the men I ever slept with gathered in one room, with me singing into a microphone, very well-dressed

13) The scene of a decadent party, with friends from many different chapters, lots of paraphernalia

14) Sophie in a school play

15) Me again as an old woman, still happy

16) My mother holding my hand at my bedside, never letting go, whispering repeatedly, "My little Pie."

At most, the slideshow was thirty seconds long, and I recall, when snapping out of it, being left with an utter respect for the power of the brain that it could produce, edit, and air such a collection of visions on a moment's notice. The phone rang. It was Alex.

His voice was still as I spoke. He definitely heard what I had said, but he was uncertain how to respond to it. I explained that test results wouldn't be back for a few days, but he didn't need them either. It's a strange funk you find when you enter such a place. Words are few, feelings are many, familiarity is none. Sometimes silence works just as well.

My mom was in the driveway when I pulled in. I was grateful to see that she wasn't wearing doom and gloom, but was instead carrying her portfolio and two bottles of white wine. Without speaking, I grabbed two wine glasses and an opener. She located a pen and some chocolate. We convened on the porch on this glorious October day, with an hour to spare before the kids descended from school.

One might think that the experience of having been through challenges relative to her same disease might have brought some clarity to this situation, but I swear she had completely forgotten she had had breast cancer. Perhaps not forgot, but went through all the motions of getting rid of it without a stitch of emotional engagement that would have aided in her recall. It was much like what one would go through in six different lines at the Department of Motor Vehicles: getting the application, then the picture, the eye test, then the cashier, but one really couldn't retrace their steps. My mother just did what they said, no questions, no concerns, no emotion.

We discussed some of the immediate procedural matters such as surgery and recovery. In truth, there is very little to discuss in those early hours of devastating news. One just has no clue what lies ahead, and there's not a book or a doctor or an Internet search engine that can take you there.

Next call, my girlfriend Laurie. Laurie and I were famed friends for having met just six years ago. We had a profound affinity of connection for each other with telepathic understandings that were never challenged. We share an unspoken language that transcended the need for words or explanation.

I met Laurie when she became a client of mine. Her husband had been relocated to Buffalo, and she came in tow, kicking and screaming. When we were out looking for houses, driving on an expansive stretch of country road, I ran out of gas. No joke, the car just stopped without apology. I would have been utterly mortified with any other client, but we got out, continued our incessant talking, and walked along the quiet road, sure to find assistance when it found us.

They had a boy and a girl. Her only job was caring for her kids, husband, house, and affairs, a job which was perhaps the most under-celebrated energy going, and she did it remarkably well. Our boys became excellent friends, and we had enjoyed many moments peripherally entertaining them while postulating on what we were going to do with our lives when we grew up.

We shared an appreciation for simplicity, an art too often ignored in the chaos of our world. We exchanged herbal remedies, applauded most organic alternatives, and harbored the same suspicion for mommies in stylish socks with Pottery Barn living rooms whose lives appeared perfect. We were sisters with secrets, dreamers with vision, and mothers in sweatpants. I will also add that her mother died of breast cancer.

I called Laurie and told her to come over. I knew I could not have shared this over the phone, as she had a healthy capacity to shed emotion and should not have been alone when we hung up. I had never forced such a demand, and not surprisingly she showed up ten minutes later, even though she lived fifteen minutes away. We were seated across the room, facing each other, an unusual distance I elected to assert. I explained that I had been to the doctor, that he had a concern.

She broke the silence. "You have breast cancer," she simply said. Neither of us know where that came from, but she hit home. She cried, I held her close to my heart, her tears opened flood gates of grief and fear, passing the torch from her mother to her best friend. The loss of her mother was with her every waking day. Laurie was her only daughter. They shared a loving and intimate connection always, one which was forged only deeper through her illness and Laurie's care of her during that ten year decline. There was a vacancy there for no one to fill. She protects it in honor of her memory.

Laurie sat beside me as I called my father, that delivery being controlled and confident. For some reason not apparent to me at that time, I shunned being weak in the face of a man. I had a game face or I had no face at all. I phoned another girlfriend, my sister, my brother, my mother-in-law, and that concluded my early inner circle. My immediate burden of notification was almost complete. I didn't have a single piece of language in my arsenal of words to aid me in confronting my kids.

The surgery was set to take place in nine days, three days after my birthday. Alex was going to fly up, and we decided to tell the kids together, I being most relieved to have put it off as long as possible. If all went well, the surgery was a same-day, drive-through variety, and recovery at home no more than a few days of downtime.

This was all I knew in those early days: I had a tumor, invasive ductal carcinoma, just over 1 cm in diameter. Scheduled lumpectomy with a sentinel node biopsy to determine the extent of the spread of disease. If sentinel nodes looked clear, only the first few would have been sacrificed. If they showed any signs of disease, all of the nodes in the armpit would be removed. I knew my mother had had it, she seemed fine, and that was good. I knew Laurie's mother had had it, God rest her soul, and that was bad.

I felt ready to tackle the threat. I spent strange amounts of time palpating this little BB. I needed to feel its lines, its boundaries, its nearby landscape. I needed to know it intimately, lest it leave any cousins behind. I needed to make friends with it and tell it that I heard its message loud and clear. I needed to say goodbye. Alex thought I was from Mars, having interrupted one of my little sessions on the eve of my surgery. I assured him I was from Mars.

In my signature last minute style, Alex and I sat with the kids the night before the surgery. I explained that there was something *funny* they found in my breast, and they wanted to get rid of it. It didn't seem to be a matter of great concern, but I had a very conservative doctor. I should be home that very night, so what did they want for dinner? Yes, I would be able to help finish that project with them. Never was the "C" word even spoken. I thought I was so smart.

The surgery was unremarkable, business as usual in the hands of an expert breast surgeon. With utter gratitude, I learned that my lymph nodes were clear, that the tumor was excised with clean margins, and that it would be a week before I would receive the histology report on the unique pathology of my particular BB. At that point, I was uncertain what else there was in that report that was material to me. Cancer is such a learning curve. That day, it was all I needed to know. Only time could lend the appetite to learn more when I was ready to learn more.

I had never been confronted by a disease for which there was no cure. One entered this medical arena with the same notion of trust and confidence that had always been in place, intact from the cures and relief that it had dependably put forth when called upon. Cancer was very different. Solutions were not hard and fast. Solutions were speculative. They offered a suggestion of how others had behaved before you, given a similar set of circumstances, which was an impossible playing field to ever level. Second opinions only further confirmed the reality that these were merely opinions, especially when they were not in concert with each other. "The practice of medicine" seemed to be an appropriate term here: Go practice on everyone else, and call me when there's a consensus.

One has but one pathology report, netting lots of data concerning the tumor's size, location, clear margins, over-expression of particular genes, responsiveness to particular hormones, presence of certain biomarkers. The unique characteristics of a particular tumor are important in the prediction of how aggressively it might behave, thus material to the prescription of the best therapy that should follow. Yet two very esteemed oncologists will interpret the meaning of this report differently.

One might prescribe a certain chemotherapy drug, the other will favor a different one. One will suggest that breast irradiation be done while chemo was being administered, the other believes they should not be done concurrently. One feels a final adjuvant hormonal drug, Tamoxifin, should be taken for five years following the other regimens, another feels the drug has limited efficacy in the arena of premenopausal estrogen-sensitive breast cancer, plus its own set of ill side effects. The conflict was dizzying.

Furthermore, it was frightening to recognize that this choice of doctor, of regimen, would most certainly have net a consequence in its outcome. Which regimen would result in remission? That guess is as good as mine. But the choice of how one chooses to attack the disease becomes a very loaded decision, offering only one pull of the trigger. Live with it. Die with it. Synthesize an oncologist's 10-year education in the three weeks it takes to plan the attack, then make your peace with it.

I can massage my intellect all day long. I had always assigned a level of control in my world when I knew all there was to know and had exhausted all realms of possibility in its path. I immersed myself in reading and reading, research and more reading. I found no comfort in learning that there were far worse prognostic outcomes for women with breast cancer in their 20's and 30's, that the disease tended to behave far more aggressively and with less predictability. There were separate mortality charts for women who had not yet been through menopause and were confronted with breast cancer. There were very few large randomized trials for this age group, which represented only around 8% of all cases. And there were certainly not as many long-term studies on enough different treatments to net an obvious path to best combat its potential progression into metastatic demise.

If one got kissed by this disease five years ago, treatment options would have been different. What was common protocol and practice today was often malpractice tomorrow. If one got kissed in Europe today, a society more socialized in its approach to medicine, chemotherapy would likely not be offered at all, as they more universally supported hormonal therapies. If one got kissed five years from now…that's where I wanted to be. I was sure if I could decode all of the stats in front of me that I could logically arrive at the place that the others where struggling to get to today.

I incepted subscriptions to hardcore oncology magazines. I joined online web sites geared to medical professionals offering research capabilities that could take me much further than Google could. I paid real money and got a password, a big feat for me. I was a regular visitor at three of the best websites on breast cancer, "Young Survivors Coalition (YSC, youngsurvival.org)", "The Website For Women" (Susan Love, MD., susanlovemd.org, author of *Dr. Susan Love's Breast Book*, the most complete bound resource I have ever found, and very well written), and "National Breast Cancer Coalition (natlbcc.org)". In learning of the anomaly of this disease in my particular age group, I began to realize that this was not my mother's breast cancer, nor could I depend on the same smooth course of therapy, behavior, or outcome that she had.

No matter how much you learn or how extensively you exhaust what is available to know, no matter how many esteemed specialists you seek opinions from in aiding that direction, the decision on how you elect to have your body treated becomes a very personal one. There are many variables that play a role in the course of therapy. The drug, which drug, how it was administered (or not), presents nine or more variables alone. The radiation and when it was administered (or not), three variables there, the hormonal therapy (or not), just two there. Not to discount the option of doing nothing at all save the surgical excision. So many possibilities, too many, especially when you insert the support from the increasingly recognized *complementary* therapies, ranging from visualization to yoga to juicing.

I was desperately without the conviction to make this decision. Both oncologists I saw suggested a different regimen. There is presently much debate surrounding one particular component of tumor histology; lymphatic vascular invasion. The quandary is whether or not it served as an independent prognostic component when determining how aggressively a tumor might behave, thus shaping the course of adjuvant therapy. I did have this particular, unfavorable element on my tumor pathology report, meaning that individual cancer cells were sited in the surrounding lymphatic vessels, outside of the boundary of the tumor, thus mobilizing their opportunity for travel. It is postulated that vascular invasion can result from the Large Core Needle biopsy procedure, blasting the poor tumor into shattered oblivion. Pass it on.

I couldn't uncover any hidden truths to tip the scale. I decided to climb out of middle-America, onto the highest mountain I could reach, and tapped right into the internationally recognized arsenal of knowledge within the red brick walls of Memorial Sloan Kettering Cancer Institute in New York City. I gathered all of my films and slides and reports and blood work and opinions of the two other doctors, and flew to Manhattan with my mother, with the intent of putting this baby to bed one way or another. Looking for the tiebreaker, I found a third opinion altogether.

The oncologist at Sloan Kettering was female and African-American and frighteningly clinical. This appointment, which took weeks to obtain and exhaustive energies to prepare for, took all of eleven minutes. There was no hand-holding or compassion, no empathy for the lack of clear direction that her chosen field of expertise could provide me. And notably, no apology for the four-hour wait in the waiting room. "Go fuck yourself" didn't even cross my mind.

Her opinion suggested that either of the chemotherapy drugs *should* prove adequate, but the mode of drug administration for patients at Sloan Kettering was other than what either of the doctors back home had offered, essentially putting forth a new set of variables, which I was certain produced a new dynamic of consequence. Put all that in the pipe of variables and smoke it. It was a mess to synthesize the myriad of these possibilities, and I most poignantly did not want to over-treat my body out of fear or ignorance. Control was clearly not within my reach.

My whole foundation felt shaky. The rock of our nation still seemed so fractured, from post 9/11 fallout to Iraqi war agendas with a rubric of catchy-named operations, as though the blueprint had long before been drafted. Modern medicine in the land of cancer felt like a wild card, a disjointed game of witchcraft offering no collective consensus. Different regimens, pick one, good luck. While the world didn't owe me a cure for cancer, it sure seemed to owe me more than this.

It was November and getting chilly. Doctors were urgently reminding me that treatment decisions needed to be made. At the conclusion of this overwhelming mental and emotional digestion, I decided to proceed with the doctor, not the regimen. I could only pray that the consequence was negligible, and that either therapy would prove adequate.

The decision came to me when I least expected it. Laurie came over after my return from the esteemed cancer institute. She knew that this third variable would have found me a new orbit to oscillate in, and she knew I needed to put this to rest. When in doubt, go see a Reiki Master.

Reiki is an ancient alternative healing art with which I was completely unfamiliar and borderline suspicious of. Rarely had I offered much credence to matters of service exempt from calculable inputs. It seemed likely that the masters of these trades where not necessarily swindlers; rather they were a breed of drifters who were not required to offer valid evidence of having performed any explicit service that could be proved or negated.

One could be assured, however, that this mysterious service would be performed in a setting which was peaceful, with peripheral music that was pleasant, with a scent suggestive of yesteryear's aroma of incense long forgotten until its smoke was revisited. I'd spent the same amount of money on massage, but at least then I had been afforded the opportunity to pay by debit card rather than cash. However, in the alternative treatment underworld, cash was king, and I was a peasant begging for the clarity to start making some good decisions.

Reiki can be described as an energy healing force that enables a body to access a vibrational channel of energy that has great capacity to restore one to a place of peace and well-being, both in a physical and spiritual sense. No two people would describe either its merits or powers in the same fashion. Its origin was born of Eastern influence, thousands of years ago, with its early history mostly cultivated in Japan. Its Japanese name translates as "Universal Life Force Energy," and there is an interesting similarity in study between Reiki and metaphysics, which both look to examine the vibrational forces that surround all matter and seek to understand the relationship of that vibration and its capacity to affect a desired outcome.

Unchallenged, Reiki accepted that a higher frequency of vibration, one with marginal means to quantify, surrounded the state of all things animate and inanimate alike. When this force was disrupted, it got congested, and the resulting chaos would manifest as imbalance somewhere in the physical body or mind. The goal of a Reiki practitioner was to free these blockages and restore one to a state of free-flowing energy so that the body could take care of itself and stave off the ills that threatened it. Sounded good to me.

I arrived at the mystical palace of the energy guru hopeful and hungry for relief. Laurie and I entered the unassuming neighborhood, discreetly concealed in a '50's development of modest, low-rise ranch homes with single-car attached garages, conveniently located beneath the flight pattern of the nearby airport. Surely this woman's neighbors had no clue about the alternative hocus-pocus that emanated from her innocuous address.

We pulled into the driveway, exited the car, and Laurie moved to approach the doorbell as a natural course of our journey. I found myself standing still, immobile, as if paralyzed from the ability to further negotiate my footing, braced at a crossroads surveying the whole of my emotional landscape. I stood for six minutes, silent, deaf to the weather, the overhead planes, the chaos of the world as it plodded forward.

My horizon was a sphere. There were countless destinations possible within the scope of its boundary, each affording a separate and distinct journey, as well as a unique set of ultimate triumphs. Shrouded like the rough of a diamond, the conclusion of each destiny was but a suspicion of the roads one must take, decisions one must make in a measure to find home. I saw many roads in front of me, and I saw the dust on the roads I had been on.

Descending upon me with a passive force of awakening, there in that strange driveway, was the suspicion that I had been looking in the wrong direction. If not the wrong direction, then maybe on a plane of a different consciousness, usually clouded by the errata of the moment. I had continually answered my life with a cerebral engagement that had been both relative and subjective, mirrored by the distortion of the relativity and subjectivity of those in my presence, simultaneously managing their version of the drama at hand. There was always a drama at hand. Count on it. It occurred to me that the drama was superfluous, immaterial. I suspected there was a greater application of its meaning that was worthy of my attention.

The idea flashed, then vanished. That brief illumination put forward a question rather than an answer. In that question, I knew that the set of controls that I had mastered with seamless proficiency were of little value to me. It was like owning a doctorate in English literature and being airlifted to an Iranian slum with no translator in attendance.

The question suspended before me seemed to originate from a place I rarely chose to access, one guided by feeling rather than logic. Though without the comfort of an obvious answer, there was a sheer lack of fear in that examination because I knew I was looking in the right direction. I felt blind and enlightened equally. Somehow, it also liberated my footing as I moved forward with eyes and mind open and vulnerable.

She seemed nice enough, Michelle the Reiki guru, discreetly assimilated in her tract of suburbia. She offered water and some strange tea as beverage choices. Her apartment was sparsely furnished, adorned with nothing particularly expensive. There were easy colors and decent natural light, and I always appreciated the absence of fluorescence. Her hair was longer and straighter than most women kept it, and very neatly tended. The particular shade of ice blue in her eyes made it uncomfortable to keep her glance for any longer than necessary. We visited briefly, and the small talk seemed to cheapen the moment of mystical anticipation that lay ahead of me. I finished my water in one fell swallow, indicating I was ready for the business for which I had come.

Her initial oration was a layman's introduction to the world of Reiki reserved for the newcomer. She was confident and studied, quick to tackle any question I put in front of her. I got a dime store education on the meaning of the chakra system and its role in the balance of the body. She offered the names of several authors and particular books that she considered a great beginning that wouldn't impart a feeling of voodoo among the Freshmen.

She began with a lesson in breathing. Certainly, I thought I was born knowing how to confront that task. These exercises were other than any effort I had ever practiced. There were unusual and visceral animal sounds that were generated from this exercise, and I knew immediately that I would have been prevented from mastering this controlled energy had there been a man in the room. Any man. Maybe not a very old man who was seated in a chair minding his own business, maybe not an infant boy grabbing at his dancing feet in the air.

However, any penis in between, present to witness the release of the grunting necessary to find my truest rhythm, would have sorely compromised my ability to engage. That thought struck me as odd, uncovering the reality of a sexual tension that surrounded every single male/female integration with which I was familiar. That particular vanity I had worn as a veil, akin to my skin, ever-present in its unspoken assumptions long before this breathing lesson. I affirmed that I would pay close attention, ignore no detail, and relearn a practice I had never officially learned.

It was exhaustive, the art of breathing as practiced by a pro. It felt miles from a natural energy. I learned of separate chambers in which one can accept breath, and found new muscles with which one expels it. I couldn't quite make the connection between this mastery and the answers I was seeking, but that was all right, unchallenged in its own right.

I then lay down on a bed similar to a massage table, though lower to the ground. The faint music in the background seemed from a distant hillside cathedral of versed, chanting monks dating one thousand years ago. It was pleasant and repetitive, and before long I was mentally transfixed by the distant language. Michelle's hands scanned my body like some medieval MRI, and I noticed the intent with which every movement of hers was calculated. She had no concern whether my eyes were open or closed, but, of course, they remained open.

She began by cradling my head for a period of time longer than my head had ever been held. It was elevated slightly, and it felt like an examination of my alignment with subtle corrective measures being painlessly asserted. She often paused to attain the posture of prayer, and spoke language that made it seem as though she were a channel of administration from a source higher than the room we were in.

Her hands were her instrument as they surveyed every inch of my body, levitating about twelve inches above my being. I watched her intently. She was consumed in the work of her hands, as though the rest of her were not present at all. Those hands appeared to be in synchronous movement with the chanting monks and my emanating energy in a chorus of unfettered harmony. Her hands abruptly ceased their methodic movement with the sober stunting of a brick wall, dead center on my right breast. My eyes opened a bit wider as our eyes collided in that understanding.

My left brain must put forward that this appointment was secured without disclosure of a particular problem I was having. I was not shy about sharing that I had a medical concern about which I needed to make some complicated treatment decisions. Just because I had breasts did not mean they had cancer. My goal that day was to seek some clarity in restoring the focus that had been painfully absent in allowing me to move forward with these decisions. Having been confronted by conflicting Western medicine approaches to tackling this threat, I was on borrowed time, and sought swift resolve in this quandary.

But there she was, hands fixated above my breast as if by a magnetic pull that was apparently drawing them. She was quiet for some time, then summoned the words, "I see black." I looked into her eyes, and I confirmed that black was me, and that she had isolated the site where a malignant tumor had been excised just four weeks earlier. It was all feeling a little creepy, and I had difficulty returning to the rhythm of the monks, as though their foreign melody were offering me suggestions I did not want to hear. She began her familiar movements above my breast, altered slightly as though she were paving a clearing in my lymphatic vessels.

Her next focus was my axillary cavity of lymph nodes, nestled just below the armpit. "Black" was not her color of choice to describe the state of affairs in my nodes; rather she concluded they were a taxed bunch of grapes working overtime to answer the threat of an enemy that had invaded the homeland, poised on the front line of defense. She did not quite speak those words, but that was what I heard.

I lay still on my back. I surveyed the ceiling, the walls, the quality of late-afternoon lighting that was gracing the room. The music seemed to simultaneously conclude its dramatic ascension just as Michelle had finished her handwork. The stillness was palpable. What began as a lone and token tear running past my temple swelled into a salted, even current of release that was pooling in my ears. There were none of the usual spasms one associates with a hearty cry, nor were there the quickened efforts to catch one's breath. Just a steady flood of anger and tension and guilt and fear in its tangible wetness demanding its way out of me.

Concluding my climax, breaking the silence, Michelle asked an unusual request: "Pick a color, red or blue." Unaware of the direction her quiz was going, I was stymied. Was there a right and wrong answer? I was clueless as to the meaning of her request, but I knew the answer because I felt it. "Red," I said, though for a reason unknown to me I wanted it to be blue. But it was not. It was all red. She found my answer curious in a way that I wished I had owned the color blue.

Red, she told me, carried the weight and symbolism inherent in the traditional disciplines of Western Medicine. It was the road I had metaphorically chosen to take to confront my threats. Blue, however, carried meanings more consistent with Eastern philosophies in processing the truer nature of disease and seeking a healing modality that looked to the core of its origin. What I found most interesting in her exercise was not my choice of red, but rather that there was an alternative choice that was whispering for my attentions, but I knew it did not yet belong to me.

Laurie and I said little on the drive home. There was no language I could find to sum up the scope of the session, but she could visibly see that I was wearing some relief. There were issues mounting in front of me that demanded my total presence. I needed to start eating this elephant one bite at a time.

In the course of the very next business day, with a particular clarity I hadn't known for some time, I began to move forward. It seemed reasonable to me that if I were going to go through a six-month course of chemotherapy with potential side effects including nausea, hair loss, exhaustion, probable chemically induced menopause, and just general malaise, that this darling little Victorian summer cottage with one bathroom was going to get very crowded for me and four kids. It was already almost Thanksgiving. The changing season seemed to underscore the actual size of 1200 square feet, with the front porch, fenced gardens, and nearby park not as welcome as one began to button down for winter. It was all closing in on me. I had hoped to find a larger, more suitable home in that storybook neighborhood within a year or so, and naturally there were none to buy at the moment I needed one.

There were never many homes for sale in our market here that would have been suitable. There were boundaried school districts that needed to be respected, a necessity (and I hate to use that word) for five bedrooms, given the sexes and ages of the kids and their lifestyles that were not in sync, plus my own personal affinity for mature trees and hardwood floors that could not be ignored. But there was one.

The house was built in the late '60's and had never been updated in any capacity. The kitchen and bathrooms and wallpapers were just awful, and the major systems were all approaching the end of their usable lives. There were five bedrooms, with the master bedroom conveniently set apart from the others and offering its own bathroom.

The property, however, offered a mature setting with extensive gardens, hundreds of perennials, and three massive oak trees climbing almost a hundred feet toward infinity. It was located just outside of the village, nestled in the neighborhood in which I grew up. I felt as if I were returning to the backyard where I used to play dodge ball when I was eight. The house had been listed just one day. I walked through, surveyed the space, and negotiated the purchase contract with a fool for a client, negotiating for nothing.

I needed to find the language to share all of this with the kids. This would have been the fourth move in less than two years, which felt to me like a branding stamp of instability that their mother was teetering on. This move also demanded an explanation of the kinds of things that I would be going through with the therapy ahead, and that the breathing room for all of us would be a good thing. I knew how much the kids had loved that vintage front porch neighborhood, and that a digression to suburbia, just one long mile away, would feel like a demotion, despite the five bedrooms and a backyard to play regulation football in. But it needed to be.

Kids amaze me, particularly at times when my reserves seem to be fully tapped and my strength feels more like a memory than an attribute. If the flexibility, fearlessness, and optimism of a child could somehow not erode as life's necessary confrontations took their passive toll, perhaps this world could better invite events of true, forward progress. They each packed their bedrooms like a football team hitting the road, recognizing that home field advantage knows no address.

I didn't imagine that Alex would have cared much. He was flying in every three weeks or so, staying a few days, and I didn't feel he needed to sign my permission slip. He would have never given me three dollars to assist in the move, nor would I have ever thought to ask him. He seemed to feel that I had a proclivity for moving and a talent for packing boxes, and accordingly, he never accepted that cancer and the potential need for a little more personal space was a consideration. His business affairs were escalating into threatening wars between him and his partners, as the battle of their egos approached an impasse and his energies were concentrated on fitting his arsenal. I was growing to not depend on his support, so fortunately there was little disappointment when it didn't come. Worse than disapproval, it was his indifference that was most remarkable.

In advance of closing, I secured permission to begin the work. Time was not my friend, and I was determined to get this house in relative order before descending with the kids and the abundance of trappings and furniture and gear with which we travel, modern chattel, as it were, which was beginning to feel like its burden exceeded its intrinsic value. Nonetheless, I know the exact cubic feet of a moving van that holds the nuts of our lives.

I had three weeks' time to complete what should have taken ten weeks or better. My urgency was largely motivated by the fact that I would have already begun chemo before the moving date Mid-December, and was uncertain of my tolerance for living among contractors once we moved in. It was a whirlwind of chaos navigating the contractors and vendors, picking out cabinets, appliances, carpeting, paint colors. Any sane person would have never embarked on such a project. I had four children in school, a job, a household to keep on track, and a scant-at-best husband. I think a lobotomy might have served me better.

If I could tap into the sentiment that motivated my mission, which only hindsight affords me, I would offer this: Fear was my motive. Fear of the kids with cabin fever accented by the shortage of living space. Fear of being ill in the only bathroom in the house and their being witness to more than I would have preferred. Fear that the cosmetic distaste rampant in the new house would have been offensive. Fear that Alex thought the little house was too little and would visit less often. Fear that, in the event of my death, there wasn't the opportunity to restore proper order to my affairs, because most of what I had was still in boxes in the garage that I couldn't access. So I chose to move the muscles and get it done, because that is what I did. No other option had a fighting chance in Hell.

The Napalm Bath

Friends have grown to assume a central and celebrated place in my world. I have networks of friends from all chapters of my life. If there is one resonating truth that speaks volumes of life's foremost achievements, it is the collection of friends we keep. They hold a different candle than family does, as their role in the continued prosperity of the relationship is not forged by guilt or obligation.

Like a collection of gems or fine art, we can return at any moment to the time and place where we first found them, the vacancy that they first filled, the evolution of that found union. There are friends who we take only to certain depths, and there are those who can be taken anywhere, unconditionally, absent an ounce of judgment. Each tenured relationship serves a soul with the sustenance that any rewarding life thrives on. It is with the support of this network that we are most capable of navigating the trials of our lives. And the trials are plenty.

Dr. Dave and I had our first official meeting in the living room of his home. I had put to bed the sea of variables under consideration, and wanted to meet with him in a less clinical setting to go over what lay ahead in the course of chemo, radiation, recovery. My decision to work with Dr. Dave was largely inspired because I liked him, hardly the cornerstone tipping the scale when choosing an oncologist. He was associated with a large and reputable oncology group in my city, but clearly not the top dog within the practice.

By this time I was six weeks immersed in the world of breast cancer, and armed with significantly more knowledge than any lay person should ever have. Dr. Dave was the only doctor who would engage me in analytical discussions on cancer, answering questions with an intellectual and technical respect for all that I had learned. It was not his intellectual validation I was seeking; rather, I needed someone who could stroke my appetite for an understanding that would make me feel less vulnerable. He sensed this was part of my therapy.

Many doctors were quick to explain, vague to commit, reluctant to extrapolate, and stubborn regarding the stance of their ego. Dr. Dave stood still. He listened. He reined me in when I would wander into theory I had no business having an opinion on. He was also the one doctor in his practice that was willing to administer the chemo via infusion, as it was done at Sloan Kettering, rather than by intramuscular injection, which was at that time the protocol for administration in his practice. Perhaps it was the same drug at the end of the day and its channel was irrelevant, but no one was willing to go there but him.

I was to start my first round of six treatments on the Wednesday before Thanksgiving. After completing the baseline round of scans, blood work, weight checks, vitals, I was given a detailed, reasonable set of expectations/side effects, including:

- I may or may not lose my hair, but it would suffer somehow.
- I would likely go into menopause as a result of the drugs.
- I could expect decent nausea relief from the anti-nausea medications.
- I should sleep when I was tired, preferably before I was tired.
- I needed to get a needle draw of blood before every infusion appointment to insure adequate white blood cell counts.
- My skin would change, not for the better.
- I may lose 20 pounds.
- I may gain 20 pounds.
- Chemo Brain. Don't ask. It was exempt from being deemed an official side effect, as there was not a gauge of measurement to quantify its toll. Thus it surely must not exist.

Nothing was definitive. There were two hundred other possible side effects laid out on ten pages of paper. My signature was required, on many lines, indemnifying their practice and the pharmaceutical companies in the event that anything whatsoever plagued me during the course of my treatment until the day of my death. I offered my informed consent to start their Western engines.

Dr. Dave took a special time-out to share with me a concern he had. There was no message other than this: "Slow down. You could afford to lower the bar a few notches. Relax a little. Give yourself a break." He offered this in a demeanor that I suspected was not part of his routine delivery. I assured him I would give it my very best shot.

Dr. Dave was well-aware of my out-of-state husband, though uncertain how this dynamic might change that arrangement. He knew that I had four children. He knew I had a job that I couldn't afford to quit. And, he knew me. His chief concern was that I would be run ragged at a time when my body needed to stand up and fight. I welcomed his concern, notably not dismissing it as an imposing arm of restraint issued for its own sake.

Not ironically, he was also the only doctor to lend some credence toward organic measures I wanted to assert during the course of the chemical assault. He was by all standards a doctor of Western medicine in all of its rigid applications, but offered some space in his intellect to recognize that efforts such as diet, exercise, visualization, meditation, prayer, mental focusing, and herbs could play an integral role in the whole of healing, as well as bolstering an environment more prone to long-term remission. Many doctors ignored the efficacy of these potent measures, discounting them for their impotence and their folly.

I was bold enough to approach Alex on what kind of expectations might be reasonable for his supportive role during treatment. He thought he'd be able to come north a little more often, spend a little more time, and be able to lighten my load during the visits. I recall choosing to express my disappointment to him in body language rather than verbal language, imagining that my sentiment was still bleeding through. I was female after all; these two were one and the same. I respected that his business affairs were insanely consuming, it was not possible to up and leave for an extended period of time. This was not a matter I was going to plead for. I was just happy not to be in Florida.

Laurie and I devised a game plan, like in any famous female pow-wow. We mapped out the course of therapy with a specially dedicated calendar. Treatments were three weeks apart, and there were a total of six. They took place in an infusion clinic where many others received treatments for their particular cancer. Each infusion would take approximately two and a half hours. The course was typically completed in five months, as there were likely to be times when blood chemistry was too low to accept another dose and the body needed more time to recover. She was able to be present for each treatment. Treatment days would be very civilized, including some form of special indulgence, and we would outfit them as follows:

- Tea was a must. We explored certain blends, paying perhaps more respect for the promise on the package than was intended.

- There would be one visitor, a different visitor, for each session, with no one invited twice.
- We would each bring one interesting item to share, in a sort of show-and-tell style format.
- There would be one new book or article that either of us could have located, from which we would read brief excerpts aloud and discuss if we felt like it.
- I picked Wednesdays for treatment. I was supposed to feel lousy for two days following. Monday and Tuesday were busy work days for me, and Friday would have trashed the weekend when kids were home from school.
- A candle and an aromatherapy atomizer and my 32 oz. blue Nalgene water bottle would accompany each session.
- We would begin and conclude each session with a moment of prayer and a moment of silence.

There was an unspoken understanding that if Alex were in town Laurie would be ousted without question, but that was not how it worked out. He was, indeed, one of the six guests. Laurie remained my guest-host, my Ed McMahon if you will, throughout the entire course of treatment. I was Johnny Carson, with an entire revolving cast of actors for our amusement at each of the episodes.

The Chemo Pit was circular, each notch of the radius dedicated like a medical cubicle. There was a fabric curtain as a token measure of privacy, a suspended TV, a bed, a chair, and a window. There were some additional areas for infusion not as private as the cubicles, placed wherever there was available floor space when there was an abundance of patients receiving treatment. These floater chairs were less than ideal, as there was the perpetual bustle of doctors, nurses, patients, in chaotic, clinical motion. I did check if one might be able to make a reservation for the private lairs, like one might make at the Hyatt, and the woman didn't even think I was serious.

Session One. I was lucky enough to secure a lair. I immediately extinguished the flood of fluorescent lighting that doused the room. Each patient was assigned a nurse who largely oversaw the course of that day's treatment. My nurse, day one, turned out to be my very favorite one, and I was grateful that she was sent to me for my indoctrination.

Your weight needed to be established. I thought it was curious that it was taken on your word, as few women ever exactly hit that target when cornered. She explained that the precise calculation of the chemicals, unique to me, having been shipped via FedEx from some pharmaceutical lab in Iowa, was critically balanced against my weight. This left little room for me to bury the last five pounds I otherwise didn't bother accounting for.

This cocktail was mixed onsite in an apparatus which resembled the incubation chamber that insulated a one-pound baby in an hermetically sealed environment until it was stronger. There were astronaut glove inserts, exacting temperature calibrations, and instruments for penetrating vessels that no one apparently wanted to get too close to. I asked her if I could witness the amalgamation, only to learn that she had never been asked that request in her modest fifteen-year career as an oncology nurse. She checked. I couldn't. And I was certain that my request was noted on my thick chart in that special area reserved for nurses' behavioral comments that doctors peruse before entering the exam room.

While the chemicals were synthesized, Laurie and I prepped the room. Lights off, window shades slightly drawn, a plastic makeshift toilet-on-the-fly moved elsewhere. Laurie sprayed an atomizing pump to clear the air, of what, I'm not sure. We planted the chairs, respecting the distance between them. We located a stool to serve as an end table, drew the fabric curtain closed, cracked the window open. And we said a prayer.

The nurse returned with a considerable plastic pouch containing about one quart of a liquid which would undoubtedly glow in the dark for days. Its chemical components were Cytoxan, Methotrexate, and 5FU; CMF, for short. The color could best be described as the marriage of neon yellow with neon pink, not to be found organically anywhere on this planet. There was another, smaller vessel with an inert-looking clear liquid, Anzamet, which was to be dripped in advance of chemo to stave off the effects of nausea. She kindly asked if we wanted to know how to operate the TV remote. In chorus we turned to her, "No," spoken with our eyes louder than our voices.

The intravenous needle was inserted with an expert single attempt, most appreciated given its amplified size. The bags were hung. She said that I might feel a cool sensation, or a warm sensation, and I again wondered why there was such an unpredictable component to every step of this journey. My job was clear. That liquid was to be inside of me. I had two hours. Now go away.

The initial sensation was warming. There was a metallic taste resembling foil that slowly dissipated, gratefully, as it was communicating adversely with the silver fillings in my teeth. The warmth was replaced by a chill that I couldn't shake. My hands needed gloves, my body needed a down comforter. Laurie went to fetch my gloves from the car, and was able to locate a tissue-thin polyester blanket from the nurses, which felt as cozy as cuddling with a square of Kleenex.

As I eased into quieting all of the stimulation, from noises to scents to tastes, the only language I could summon for the feeling of this drug flowing through my virgin network of veins was that there was a *buzz*. It was an electrical charge that was subtle and of a low vibration. Had the TV and the fluorescent lights been on it could have gone unnoticed. But I was there to notice everything, certain there were cues and impulses that demanded my full attention, and that this was how I was to empower myself.

Visualization is an amazing journey. Like Reiki, there is no right or wrong, no set of instructions to defer to. When I think of visualization, I think of the mind being given artistic license to dance without judgment and fly without boundary. I recall a quote I have heard, uncertain of its origin, which best sums up my feeling about this practice.

"No one told me that, when I lost my mind, it would be so much fun."

Aiding in my efforts to hone this technique involved tapping into my reservoir of life experience. The only thing I could recall as being a similar energy were from events that occurred during some of my highly debauched hallucinogenic trips, while reeling on mushrooms or ecstasy. Naturally, all were filmed in Boulder, Colorado. I could be a forty-year-old parent and warn children that these drugs were much safer way back then before they underwent their commercialized metamorphosis steeped with tall profits and ugly drug lords, but I dared not go there. I haven't taken any recreational drugs since those years in college, and had never really considered anything about my use of them until that very moment.

I began with retrieving my journals from those years. There were a handful of times in the course of my college years that included hallucinogens as the front liner.

Sometimes there was a large crowd of players, such as when ten of us went to an outdoor water park outside of Denver, high on mushrooms, and found a home in the water we had not known since in the womb.

That quality of laughter, originating in the mind of a child but executed in the body of an adult, can sadly not be replicated without such stimulus.

One time four of us took some ecstasy and resigned to stay in the apartment in an otherwise familiar routine. There was nothing familiar about anything that occurred that evening. We listened to vinyl music, business as usual, and heard secret messages in the lyrics which we replayed and replayed for confirmation. We then got charged to clean the apartment, employing vacuums, cleansers and long feather wands, all set to the tempo of Crosby, Stills, and Nash, with Young still on board. We found this dancing/cleaning rhythm that lent an enthusiasm to the art of cleaning that it rarely ever gets. We hit this groove for over an hour, four of us, having simply run out of things to buff. In the morning, I assure you, there was a caliber of clean no college apartment was ever touched by.

I recalled one event that most particularly awoke me to the power of the mind. Three of us were brushing each other's hair (I recognize this would not happen outside of a drug-induced setting). We were seated Indian style on the floor, in a line rather than a circle, each with a brush in hand. We would brush the hair of the person in front of us, then turn around so the one in front wasn't the beneficiary of an undue free ride. Seems simple enough.

The sheer joy and pleasure and satisfaction that can be captured from the contact of brush to scalp, the pull of the root, the tension of the strand, the folly of the fall, in rhythmic repetition, was, beyond fathom, an approach to euphoria. A big leap, indeed, but then and there it held the most satisfying expression of peace and love, sisterhood and sensuality. It celebrated simplicity and equality and enlightened elevation equally.

People often refer to ecstasy as the "love drug," supposing that it might be incredible to fuck like monkeys while high on it. I imagine that anyone who has ever tried the drug has experimented in this arena. That sexual expression has not worked for me personally other than generating some giggles when fumbling with funny body parts. I can harness more of its magic in the art of touch than in the aggression of pelvic thrust.

It was that harnessing that gave me the guidance and direction for visualization. In the still of my mind, I knew that somewhere I owned the power to enter a place in my brain where creativity and possibility ran free, unrestrained by imposing judgment. There was a guard that went to sleep when I had taken that drug, and I had free rein to play there for hours on end. I needed the roadmap to access that place, pushing my private property line and reclaiming the fruit that grew there.

It was a buzz that I felt. I imagined that buzz to be similar to what a laser might feel like when directed with a purpose. The laser was in my veins, illuminating all vascular tunnels, seeking the stray, lone cancer cell hiding behind a tricky turn. Zap. It was discovered and annihilated in a seamless emission. When a rebel was exposed, I swear I could feel a charge in its destruction. Arm hairs would stand alert, saluting its sorry-ass demise. The laser continued its superhero journey throughout my body. This was how I visualized the process, and it worked for me.

Every treatment tended toward a different feeling. I would listen to that feeling with an ear I never before used. I learned to locate the key to access this fantasy while permitting myself to invite the intangible.

The guest at session one was my brother, Jon. He entered my drawing room looking as if he had apparently been lost on a regrettable tour of the entire Chemo Pit, seeing far more than he cared to let in. He entered, closed the curtain behind him, and stood still. He wore a startled look of implausibility, hidden behind a supportive smile, seeing me in that chair with an IV set up and a bag of electric Kool-Aid suspended overhead. He sat down.

We discussed topics mostly related to family, work, and Thanksgiving the very next day. Notably no dialogue on the business surrounding us, mostly by my own design. Our mother was already in Florida for the winter season. Our father lived in Florida permanently. My brother was spending the day with his wife and her extended family, the sum of them all being the intact holiday postcard, unsplintered by divorce, fortified by tradition, rich by tenure. How happy for him that he had found a place, unfractured, to grow his own family.

Feeling slightly like an orphan, I had planned on going to Laurie's for the holiday dinner. Together we would create as traditional a gesture for this screwed up Thanksgiving as my spirits would allow. Alex was flying in Thursday morning. Our husbands could recline and watch televised football, our kids could disperse their bedlam throughout the house, and she and I could retreat to what happens naturally with women and a kitchen and a tall bottle of wine.

Jon and I are three years apart, I being older. As kids, we were very playful, very light and witty. We covered each other's asses constantly, each having different talents to avert the powers-that-be who threatened our fun. We spent our teens and twenties consumed in our own disorder, and I embarked in the wayward world of babies long before he did. Now that our kids are growing and we have exited those consuming early years with infants, I am hopeful that we can find new terrain not defined solely by our children or our parents, and return to the spirit of some of those early antics. He was a fabulous brother, and I was blessed by his unwavering presence in my life.

He stayed for the whole of the session. By the time the bag was emptied, I was hungry for fresh air. An extra thirty seconds of sitting still after my job was done was enough to start my pulse accelerating. I prompted Laurie to start walking the Pit in search of my nurse, as she was far less aggressive and far more pleasant than I was. The needle came out, the band-aid went on, and I promised that I would stay seated for ten minutes while I acclimated. Jon looked to his watch, as if I might have respected that directive. Yeah, right.

When I returned home, I felt an urgency to walk. The air was brisk and damp, but it called for my dedicated pace as though there were a destination in mind and I was late. There was two hours before the kids returned from school. I walked alone for almost three miles, engaging every mental gear I had to the uncensored truth of my world as I knew it: I was on chemotherapy. My husband and I were at serious risk for divorce. I had to move in two weeks. I needed to restore my past income, 100%-commission based, and maintain that necessary focus. I had four children, none for whom I've provided a live-in father. Though I felt an utter gratitude for those in my life whose love and support were ever-present, I felt alone and seriously misunderstood, wondering how the hell the State of my Union had escalated to this fury.

Unsummoned, the chemo angel landed in my life. There was no invitation, no expectation. Rather it was an offering originating from a whole different land. She was a woman who I had worked with in real estate most of my life, knowing her mostly within a polite, professional context. She was also a good friend to my mother, as well as a wife and a mother of two grown children. She had always owned a genuine kind heart and an unbridled desire to help random people, an energy which I never really understood. Curiously, she also had a religious lifeline in the Catholic church from where she tapped endless pools of faith and compassion that never overflowed where they were not welcome. My mother had spoken to her from Florida a few weeks earlier and shared with her how bad she felt for the road that lay ahead of me. No dates, no schedules, no particulars were conveyed other than her saddened sentiment.

Like from a movie, background snow swirling on a late-November evening, dusk at 5 p.m. on the eve of Thanksgiving when I couldn't even think about cooking, this woman barreled her Volvo into my driveway, flooding my garage with her xenon headlights. I stood at the door, watching the backside of her fur coat while she gathered things from in her car. She stood erect, carrying enough trays and bags and boxes that she could not see beyond her load. I sent Peter out to relieve her, and saw the face of an angel walking toward me. Her name is JoFrances.

She brought dinner, cooked by her and her 78-year-old Italian mother, Dolores, who I would swear was a saint from the heavens. She brought cookies from the best bakery in town. She brought toys for the kids and brought expensive shampoo I never buy for myself. She brought a candle the color of the ocean and an arrangement of cut flowers and a box of Italian dark chocolate. She could have had no idea of the weight I had worn on that particular day. But somehow she knew.

She stayed only briefly, emptied her arms, hugged my kids, and was off. The toys were thoughtful and not frivolous, a hard chord to strike. Leah processed the gifts, assembled the plates, and discarded the packaging. We arranged the flowers, lit the candle, and enjoyed a dinner sent from a place that I did not know existed.

When I spoke with my mother later that evening, certain that she had shared details with JoFrances about the event of my day, she assured me she had not. It seemed reasonable that in her absence she would send someone over with such kindness to share, but she had not. It was an unsolicited act of love, awakening in me the suspicion that I needed to rediscover a world I thought I had figured out, to start paying attention to concerns I was accustomed to plowing right through.

The move was sheer pandemonium. Boxes were stuffed with little respect for order. Breakable items weren't treated with much better regard than were board games. I had some friends helping, but I was feeling naked and vulnerable at the thought that my affairs could have had such a sense of utter disarray about them. The new house still had a laundry list of improvements not yet complete, but I was grateful that wallpapers had been stripped, paint colors were applied, and new carpeting was down. It seemed my bar of expectation for everything, from contractor's attention to detail to the order in my life, was getting lowered by the day. I had a week to restore a household while gearing up for round two.

Alex was supposed to be in town for this treatment. The official legal dissolve of him and his partners was well under way, attorneys were actively engaged, a bankruptcy was looming as the answer, and he wasn't able to be there.

Session Two. Private room again. I came equipped for this round with a pair of gloves and a down lap blanket, in addition to our usual props. It was mid-December, 2002. Garlands of Christmas rope surrounded the perimeter of the Chemo Pit, tacked up with love by the evening custodian. There was an artificial tree with artificial presents beneath it, hollering the artificial message to have a happy fucking holiday. There was an oversized token Hanukkah dreidle, and a Kwanzaa poster dragged out of storage, taped where weak with medical band-aids. In its broad spectrum political intention not to offend, it was an offensive affirmative action display from the seasonal aisle at WalMart, devoid of any bona-fide spirit, recycled year after year, heavily diluted. The most genuine expression in the room was a generous plate of handmade cutout cookies at the coffee station, iced by hand, made by the woman in my next cubicle with no hair or no visitors. I grabbed four cookies, filled my water bottle, and thanked her with a walking smile.

We killed the lights, drew the curtain, and moved the chairs like seasoned veterans. This nurse was not so nice, barely making our acquaintance, barely making eye contact. She retreated to the amalgamation chamber while Laurie and I readied the room.

Same warming sensation, same flood of a chill following. (Cashmere gloves are worth every dime they cost). Trailing the Anzamet, the neon drugs ascended in the plastic tubing, approaching the site of entry at my vein. Crossing that threshold, I waited to see what I felt. Session two, I felt Arctic.

There was a polar sting that was fierce and not friendly. I exhaled to see if I could see my breath. The top of my shoulder blades felt brittle and hollow as they drew closer together. I asked the nurse for hot water with lemon, five of them if she only had the little 8 oz. styrofoam cups. I grew the suspicion that the Kool-Aid wasn't mixed properly. Perhaps it was the formula for a 280 lb. man. Perhaps it was the formula for full-blown liver cancer. Even the neon shade in the bag seemed different. There was a mistake somewhere. I needed the nurse back.

When she returned with one hot water in one baby styrofoam cup, I asked her if it was possible that the drugs were intended for someone other than me, careful not to suggest that it was her screw-up (which was, of course, very possible). She assured me it was not possible. I then asked if she knew what I weighed, curious as to why she hadn't inquired. I could have been nursing Ben and Jerry's for the past three weeks. This all got me nowhere but frustrated. When she left the cubicle, she took a moment to jot down some notes on my chart.

If there were a notion to visualize in this frigid environment, it was crystals. Ice crystals masquerading among sultry dancers in the warm pulsing flow of my blood, gliding in a whimsical waltz seeking the predator, flash-freezing him into a vapor, and returning to the artful tempo with the finesse of a matador. The warmth of my blood helped to temper each vessel from freezing over, sometimes just barely. And the beat went on.

I jockeyed the visitor's positions, thus the guest at session two was my sister, Karen. She lived in Ithaca, NY, a three-hour drive in the best of weather. She was a Spanish teacher to seventy middle schoolers in relentless puberty. She took a personal day and left at sunrise to join me in the Pit. I love her very much.

Consistent with the roots in Ithaca, she was a child of the earth. She applauded all measures of conservation, preferred simplicity to abundance, and only wore clothing of natural fibers. Not surprisingly, she wore the same look of startle that my brother wore when entering the room. Her first comment was regarding the overwhelming inorganic smell of the whole of the Pit.

She surveyed my quiet space, taking notice of the candle, the lighting, the book on sacred chakra energy, and the lavender atomizer. She smiled peacefully. No language could have better summed up her approval of my attempt to tolerate all of this. Karen and I are physically very different. She is 5'2" on tippy toes, has wavy, long strawberry hair that never gets blow-dried. She considers my measures of vanity slightly ludicrous, but I don't live in Ithaca, I assure her, and this demands that I pay closer attention to those shallow details. Our affinity to engage more meaningful connections with each other gets elevated every year, and I have recently grown to recognize how blessed we both are to share our parallel yet unique journeys by each other's side.

Karen had very little curiosity of the IV or the fluids it yielded. We caught up on life, kids, work. She brought me a book on Greek mythology, imagining I needed a reprieve from the oncology journals I was buried in. Very weird and random. I hadn't read any mythology since I was in high school, at a time when it was probably homework as well as a burden. It seemed a curious selection, but the gesture was appreciated.

She stayed for the balance of the session. We grabbed some famous cutout cookies on our way out and went to a nearby cafe for lunch. Warm soup, quiet music, easy company, it was simply perfect. She dropped me off at home and set out for her return drive with just enough daylight to get home before dusk.

All else was going well. I felt all right, looked all right, all things considered. The new house was finding an order I could live with. My contractor was always filled with hot air and talked way too much, but there was moderate progress in the right direction. My daily regime included half an hour of stretching, which began as an effort to maintain flexibility but quickly escalated into a meditative journey I had never before been on.

It started with music. I visited my very dated collection of CDs that hadn't been improved much for over a decade, probably two. It largely included my favorite artists, mostly peace-loving, tree-hugging, politically-left acoustic talent inspired by a love and spirit that did not feel as prevalent in this millennium. As I strolled through the titles of these groups, I realized that I hadn't really listened to music in a very long time. Really listened. Music had once been such a central part of my life, the backdrop to nearly every event worth remembering. First dances, college road trips, copious numbers of parties and concerts, even nursing a Sunday morning hangover. It was the score to my life back when I knew how to have fun. It had been replaced by diapers and never reinserted when the diapers were done. I grabbed some perennial favorites.

There was an oriental rug in the center of my sparsely furnished living room, a perfect forum for me to extend my limbs on. After the kids were dispersed on their morning buses, I would put on a disk and begin with some basic stretching movements. The music whispered a tangible reminiscence into my foreground, capturing a part of me that had long ago been abandoned. I would expand the depths of the stretch, very slightly at first, then escalate to a pose that pushed a boundary, almost lengthening limbs in the process.

The music was played loudly. At home it was just me and the dog, neither of us objecting to the swollen volume that filled the room and vibrated the crystal. These familiar chords were a vehicle of release for my thoughts. They presented an opening for me to explore long forgotten feelings from a time in my life when I owned the world with all of its infinite possibility at my sails, camouflaged in the journey of song. I would take the pose deeper, I would hold the pose in respect for its message. It seemed some sort of morphed pilates, yoga, and meditation movement, not to be found on any late night infomercial. But for me, it worked very well. The music enabled me to override my unfortunately brief attention span for formal exercise. I did this every morning with an enthusiasm that had no interest in ever entertaining an excuse for why I couldn't get it done.

I had a 32-oz. bottle of water that accompanied me everywhere. It was filled three or four times a day; I couldn't seem to get enough. My diet was strictly fruits, raw vegetables, low-fat proteins, no refined sugars, no preservatives, all whole foods. I was drinking so much water that the portions of what I did eat were small though frequent. Most notably, there was not the familiar sense of sacrifice or deprivation that I had usually assigned to the dread of dieting.

I called Dr. Dave to tell him I was going to Florida for Christmas, namely to see if there were any concerns I should have. He told me that I shouldn't fly or travel during the window of time 12 days after a treatment, as that would be the nadir of the hit that my white blood cells took from the assault. There would be concerns of poor airplane ventilation as well as concerns about being in a different part of the country where strains of flus were foreign, especially come winter. It seemed unnecessary to compromise an already taxed immune system.

I asked Alex if he would come north instead. He said it was hard to leave in the busy movie week during the holidays. He didn't seem to have the same respect for Dr. Dave's advice, asserting that our flight on day 11 was other than day 12. He thought the kids needed some Disneyland in their life. One of our friends agreed to fly down with the kids instead of me. I stayed in New York for the holiday, and I definitely enjoyed some time to look after no one but me, probably more than the kids enjoyed Disneyland.

In January it became official that Alex and the movies were filing bankruptcy in an effort to reorganize. Months of litigation and astronomical attorney bills later, no minds could be met, no roads could be bridged. His mounting burden to keep all moving forward now included new demands from the courts, petitions to conform to, regulations to follow within the letter of the law, as bankruptcy court had little tolerance for slack. He was regrettably not able to make session three, but would try to fly up soon after when the chaos subsided.

My mother extended her trip north by a few days so she could be there. She had not been through chemo in the course of her breast cancer, so she was green to the setting in the Pit. She spent the night at my house before the morning treatment.

Watching my morning stretching routine invited far more comment from my mom than I wanted to hear. She had never seen me apply myself so diligently to a diet and exercise regimen. While she did recognize that these were noble measures toward feeling good, she thought I was pushing hard. I assured her it was all under control and well within the energy level I had to expend in a given day. She was well-known for having candy bars for breakfast, forgetting about lunch, and ordering dinner at 8:00 p.m. She was not my role model in this arena.

Session Three. No private room available. I was relegated to a chair, central to the bustle of the pulse of the Pit. My finger stick passed again with flying colors, and the technician even noted how strong some of my counts were. Every third treatment required a brief physical with the doctor, and my mother was very interested in meeting Dr. Dave, who she was always quick to remind me had the letters DO trailing his name rather than MD, which caused her great concern.

Dr. Dave had a concern of his own. He was a very personable guy with a very hearty smile. He greeted my mother and we briefly exchanged smalltalk. Perusing my chart, he appeared to read the nurse's notations but had enough class to slide over them without comment. He had concern that I had lost nine pounds in six weeks. Not what my mother needed to hear.

Let me first say this. I have passively struggled with weight my whole life, including in the womb, after which time I was born nine pounds and ready for a diet. I had never been the kind of fat that would incite someone to formally describe me as such, but fat enough to have kept me out of the trendiest clothes, out of bikinis, off-limits to football captains, and a second choice date more often than I enjoyed. I had always wanted to have a sculpted body to strut, but apparently I wanted it less than I enjoyed eating. I had always been active, and there were enough sports I had natural talent in. But I had always carried an extra twenty pounds that seemed happy enough distributed evenly throughout my body. Sacrifice was for sissies.

As I grew into a sexual being craving the attentions from the objects of my desires, it rarely stood in my way. I rationalized that it was a good measure to weed out the shallow dwarfs and elevate the pool of possibilities. I had always considered myself beautiful, probably in the same way that everyone was captured by their own unique essence. The beholder, the self, always a good fit. Never had I felt that my formidable arsenal of seduction tools couldn't get me where I needed to go. Its powers rarely proved to disappoint.

I was selective regarding when to engage it, but I could wield it at will when I found a motive. I was uncertain of its potency, scared of it even, never wanting to learn of a ceiling that it might have had. It was a better ace in my hole, a secret suspicion, one I could go to the moon with if I needed to play the card. Skinny girls had nothing on me.

I explained to Dr. Dave how committed I had been to the healthiest of diets, that my morning stretching routine was borderline aerobic, and that I drank enough water in a day to fill an aquarium. He wanted to know about the water. I roughly summed up my daily consumption, and he suggested I cut it in half. He warned me of stories he had heard of monks who lived on a monastery who consumed excessive amounts of water until they were driven to a state of mental insanity. Duly noted, I assured him I would cut back. It was a short drive anyway.

His concern was largely that cancer was considered a "wasting" disease, and oncologists paid close attention to weight as a barometer for other threatening, metastatic concerns. They encouraged comfort foods and sedentary sitcoms. It was not usually the time that patients elected to treat their body like a holy temple for the first time in their lives. Exit Dr. Dave.

The chair arrangement in the Chemo Pit provided overabundant visual diversions. There was naturally less privacy, more hustle, more sadness. This inner-circle perspective of the Pit portrayed the truth about cancer that I was not willing to invite into my private chamber.

Even worse than the Pit was the waiting room. People composed themselves in their chairs, gathered in the privacy of their thoughts, and waited. They waited for their turn in the Pit, they waited for results from space-age tests that suggested to them how grave their outlook was. They waited for a companion who was detained, they waited and wondered if they were appropriately enlightened enough to handle this expedited curtain call, so fiercely out of the natural order of things. Waiting sucks. There is far too much to reckon with.

There were many hard truths to witness. Seeing patients receiving their treatment with no one at their side brought a grief beyond language. Their reserved patience as they sat, being infused by a similar pollution to mine, seemed tenfold as daunting without company to occupy them and diffuse the toxicity. Few elected to draw their curtain closed, perhaps just desperate for noise and distraction to absorb their senses. There were six peripheral TV shows I could hear, all colliding into a state of vapid static. Some patients had TVs turned on but stared into outer space nowhere in its sight line. I was sorry my mother was there for this one.

My mother tolerated the IV insertion routine, though I could see her queasiness by way of her body language as she retracted inward. She noted that I had an ease with it she thought I would never find. The nice nurse was appointed to my chair station. Laurie ushered herself into the Pit, happy to see my mother, saddened to see me in the chair. She found a flimsy chair and collapsed with our bag of props. The Kool-Aid arrived.

Much of our Pit time was spent discussing what type of measures we could put in place to make my life easier. Rather, my mother was discussing it and I was listening. She was always quick to offer live-in help that she would pay for, or at least a sitter who could come during dinner and homework crunch times.

I had always been stupidly stubborn about admitting that I needed help, but I really didn't think that I needed it. The kids were 14, 12, 7, and 5. My home-office set up was fully streamlined with all the hardware and software and Tupperware I could ever need. And there was plenty of time to tend to affairs while the kids were at school. Leveraged yes, all gears in constant motion, but it was working.

It seemed that if the kids saw me retaining help in the house they would be sure I wasn't being straight with them about the breezy course of therapy I was in. I had one regular sitter who I had had for years, and I assured my mother I would hire her more often, even if I was home at the same time doing nothing other than paying her. Stupid program, now please be quiet.

These conversations invariably ended up being about my marriage, or lack thereof. She was sick over the lack of support I was getting. I explained to her six hundred times that Alex was in career crisis and reminded her that it was me that left Florida. Still, it all bothered her well beyond my ability to massage it with defensive justifications. She knew I was working, and was grateful that a job like real estate afforded such flexibility. She knew what a tall order single parenting was, but still…. The dialogue never ended.

There was not a visualization to be had in the battery of discussion we shared. The background congestion stunted all inspiration for creativity, the foreground dialogue leveled the rest. Episode three, by way of the front and center Barcalounger hot seat, could not have ended soon enough.

I began to take notice that these last two years of my life had lended a different dynamic toward my relationship with my mother. We were as tight as we had ever been, undeniably. Her support always remained intact, but we had issues between us that were visited too often without the necessary resolve to move beyond.

I was without question the child she was emotionally closest to, the one who understood her humor and motivations and complex intricacies better than anyone. Unlike my two siblings, who nobly both entered professions whose rewards were not celebrated with fat salaries, I never needed her money to maintain my life. I earned two times their salaries, my husband earned three times their spouses'. Not needing someone's money translated into not needing their permission, either. I had always felt that this leveled our field and enabled our relationship to be free of the passive constraints that the transfer of money vicariously carried. Strings, they are called.

But things were different, or at least were threatening to be different in the near horizon. She was always wise that way. I was as entrenched in my career as my life could allow, having resurrected it from a holding pattern and jump-started it to the best of my ability. I was almost earning half the income I had left behind. I knew, however, that I had somewhere grown a newfound lack of interest in servicing clients who irritated me, a sentiment I really couldn't afford to put into action but elected to anyway. This privilege was to be found nowhere in Sales 101.

I would pass on business where it seemed apparent that the client would become my next seething migraine. Sometimes I would refer it out, sometimes I would just let it go. But after sixteen years of doing the same job, I could smell these headaches a mile away. The work ethic I left behind before going to Florida included this annoying client and all of his cousins, but the one I returned with had no interest in them.

The clients I did choose to work with, however, I enjoyed more than I ever recalled enjoying before. I loved working with first-time home buyers, giving flight to their dream of starting a life together, and aiding in the process of getting them there. I loved working with elderly people who might be scaling down into different property more suitable to their saddened, shrinking needs. I would listen and pay attention. I would survey their home and all of their belongings, considering the lifetime of memories that contributed to the collection of their wares. I would appreciate the burden entailed in packing and allocating and boxing their things, and I would inquire if they had adequate assistance in meeting that burden. I don't think I had ever asked that question or thought that thought before.

Death, divorce, relocation, bankruptcy: These events often forced the sale of a house in the wake of change. There were many attorneys who fortunately provided me with a consistent stream of referral business to meet that end. I showed up at the property with a smile, a camera, and a lawn sign, there to clean up the brick and mortar carnage of a life that had passed, a love that had died, a dream that had gone bust. The ghosts were everywhere.

All heartstrings aside, this newfound emotional engagement with my job was a luxury I couldn't afford. Alex's income was significantly compromised with his extensive litigation. Some failing theatres were weighing heavy on those that were prospering, which translated into limited funds on his end. Even with half my income, I could just make ends meet with no fat to spare. I was happy to spare the fat. The fluff was of no interest to me in my present way. Alex was quick to cite that his expenses were barely lightened since our departure, as though all that kids really cost were a loaf of white bread and a gallon of milk. His car, his house, his necessary living expenses left little surplus to pass along. No, I wasn't aggressive about collecting support.

So, when my mother offered me money, my hands were open. She had always been insanely generous and elected to gift to her children healthy chunks of money the IRS had no problem with. In the past, the money was incidental; it was either invested or spent frivolously without much regard for the sacrifice. I couldn't have cared less whether it came or it didn't.

It was my indifference toward that offering that permitted my mother and me to really be friends. But I was growing to feel crowded when that indifference shifted to necessity. It seemed to simultaneously insert a passive obligation that I couldn't quite identify, but one I needed to humbly wear in quiet reservation, often stifling my voice when it needed to be heard.

January in the northeast always brought a frigid chill. I was growing resentful that Alex was dependably so self-consumed. Our daily phone calls more often than not concluded with heated outbursts of our individual dissatisfactions. When he would come north, I needed him to hold me, to stroke my hair and face and ego and tell me that he missed me. I needed someone to lie next to me in silence and lighten my load with unspoken levity. I needed someone in the house over the age of fourteen to talk to. And without question, I needed focused physical affection expressed with a lusty, visceral desire to satisfy. None of these measures of honoring intimacy were being answered. Alex would lie next to me in bed, spent from the turmoil in his own world, tired from romping with kids in his otherwise kidless life. I was hungry for the warmth of his body next to mine, for the familiar rhythm of his breath in repose, but he would fall asleep. I would touch my body, stroking my aching desires to my own private crescendo of satisfaction, tapping solely into the comfort of his slumber as validation that I was not alone.

Alex assured me he would make session four. He was arriving on a Tuesday, leaving on a Friday, just in time to join his friends at the Superbowl. He had never been. He was very excited.

Session Four. I was so relieved when there was an opening for the private lair in the Chemo Pit. Alex definitely had an aversion to public places, largely for the presence of people that occupied them.

Some common ground that Alex and my mother shared was their blatant disregard for all concerns born in the world of the freethinking hippie. They respected nothing that that world celebrated. Beyond Bohemian melodrama, they considered National Parks wasted space, did not own a recycling receptacle or a pair of sneakers, and could only do business at the top of their food chain. Details were for those at the desks downstream. They were hard and fast. They built empires. They were blind to minutiae, open to the negotiability of property and people alike. They would have had no use or no imagination for anything that was in our bag of props, which was as central to my recovery as the Kool-Aid. They were twins in this way.

Alex and I entered the Pit. The finger stick passed. I waved hello to some nurses and patients I had befriended during my stays, with a slanted agenda to emphasize his distance from this domain. I filled my personal mug with hot water, tossed in my personal wedge of lemon, and sauntered to my room with the tenor of a rock star. Alex followed behind me, taking notice of my demeanor but wearing none of it.

We were seated among the medical paraphernalia as he surveyed the set up. Within seconds we found quirky things to laugh at. The floating portable toilet invited much humor into our space. Alex and I laughed very well together, we had always owned that. Laurie arrived shortly after, props in hand. As she unloaded our wares, Alex gave negligible consideration to the spirited tokens that we carted around, seeming to feel they were a burden to account for and a folly to value.

With the startling volume of a megaphone, the TV suddenly was on. Alex reclined in the chair, more comfortably than the scene should have permitted, surfing channels and landing the surf at a special broadcast for the upcoming Superbowl. Laurie and I looked at each other with the curious awareness that we had not yet turned on that big box. The Kool-Aid arrived.

Seamless entry. Toxic countdown. T minus 4, 3, 2…approaching threshold…. It appeared Tampa Bay was the favored team that year. Oakland was a long shot, but their quarterback was a wild card who just might tip the scales and hail an upset. I was actually watching these commentators air their enthusiasm in anticipation of the upcoming Superbowl XXXVII.

I summoned the remote and lowered the volume, imagining that any perceptible human being might perceive this as a cue to turn it off. Unnoticed. Alex did ask some questions about the feeling of the drugs in their encircling vascular journey, worded a little differently. He lended some sensitivity to our space that did not go unnoticed.

I had a frightening capacity to forget our physical and emotional distance when we were together. I would find a small place to crawl into where I could see no evidence of the barriers between us. In that space, there was the suspended possibility of bridging this madness and landing this rocket, against the barrage of constraints that seemed Hell-bent against it. It would dangle in front of me with temptation. Its shrapnel could blind me for not wearing my goggles. I would grasp its essence, only to feel its vacancy. It was borderline delusional, but that delusion seemed better than having no delusions at all.

I visualized a flooding. The pressure and force of the current was breathtaking and not frightful. The swell of its surge could rise with my breath, and be released with a discipline under my measured and guided control. Its pulse was born a thousand years ago, its promise was timeless. In those waters there was no resistance, no futile effort to shift its currents, just the glory of surrender. Good and evil were one and the same, neutralized in the synthesis, benign in its threat. I was a part of that energy, for that brief moment in time, used and discarded with my grateful permission.

As the nurse was dismantling the IV set up and gathering her goods, there was a strained silence among us demanding intervention. I introduced her to my husband, certain that she had considered the possibility that I was only married in my mind. She seemed to have a curiosity that needed to put a face to the band on my finger, which never quite matched up. They met, and I proved something more to me than to her.

Session four was over. 66% was a passing grade last time I was in school.

It was February and time for any good real estate agent to kick-start the spring market. I spent more hours than usual in my office. I sent out a few mailings to my client base, made some connections with the usual sources of business, and managed the transactions I had underway. There weren't many in my office that I shared my present trials with, except for three very close associates and my office manager, all of whom assured me that there was a confidence that needed no sanction.

Cancer, however, spreads like wildfire. It overrode the usual decorum under which people normally operated and rendered them unfit for idle conversation. I was a veteran in my office. People remembered me from long before I had children, some even remembered me as a three-year old coloring at an available desk while my mother parked me in favor of business that needed tending to. It was strange enough that I returned from Florida, the land they were soon to retire to, now even stranger with buzzing suspicions that I had cancer. Those suspicions were never confirmed by anything other than hearsay.

I would have answered anyone honestly that had approached me. But people became mute and quirky when they held hearsay knowledge that had not been confirmed. Add the missing twelve pounds and the radiance that raw vegetables bring, and they were stumbling in their footsteps. I often stayed longer than usual in casual conversation at the copy machine just to incite some questions to that effect. Nothing. I looked great and people just couldn't handle the conflict of doomed destiny vs. complacent well-being without official validation. All I got were polite exchanges of the superficial happenings in our worlds. I wore my cashmere gloves at all times, certainly a behavior that would invite comment, but I received nothing. The creepy stillness of nothing.

Until something. That something irritated me beyond reason. An attorney whom I had a professional and personal relationship with, spanning well over a decade, called me, but not about business. I tolerated the initial small talk, and then he asked me how I was doing in a fashion that surpassed that usual inquiry. He was a friend, and promptly disclosed his concern over what he had heard. His compassion was genuine, and the standup guy that I had always considered him to be was upgraded three strokes by the balls it took him to call me. My irritation, however, was seething in that he had heard of my trials from one of the agents in my office who had engaged me in their bullshit, weather-related small talk one too many times.

I later learned that another comrade propelled this spread of gossip to another friend and long time client, who also called with concern. This client had been relocated out-of-state, was at a cocktail party in a relaxed social setting, and was talking with another one of these agents. Without recourse or apology, she feigned her saccharin sorrow for my looming decline into oblivion, hungry for nothing other than the listing on this man's home. This is sales and it sucks. Rather, this is people and that sucks harder.

I needed a breather. I decided to get away for the weekend to tap into some Swain energy. Sarah had championed a successful argument out of the state of Florida three months after we left. She and I shared many similar frustrations with the world as we knew it in our time there together. Half were forged in the inverted sense of social values and spiritual poverty that we felt, half arose from the plague of fear that ensued post 9/11. Each struck us where we felt a non-negotiable vulnerability, questioning our posture both as chiefs of a family and citizens of a country. Owning control only in the family, our exodus was the only voice we could carry.

They moved to Ithaca, NY, having found the makings of what *might* be a good fit during a trip north the summer after I left. I knew Sarah was in search of something other than what she had going in Florida, and I suggested that they explore Ithaca. It was a unique, not-so-sleepy little town in central New York that captured a spirit borne outside the status quo. One might think that, as a comical gag at a drunken party, they had hung up a map of the country, threw some darts at it, then checked to see what stuck where. But Ithaca fit. It was reasonably close to Manhattan for Bosley's weekly sojourns, situated at the southern tip of Cayuga Lake, and located in the colorful heart of three excellent universities. College towns were the ticket to an enriching life well beyond the diploma.

I imagine that any bystander would cast scornful judgment in her direction, and in mine as well. My exodus was partly fueled by economic necessity, and partly by an eroding marriage. Hers was not fueled out of any necessity, just her resounding desire to cosign her children's childhood with a different set of values than those she found in the Tropics. Her motive was inspired by far more courage than was mine, especially because she up and moved her family to a city where they had no friends, no connections, and no networks other than a suspicion she might find some.

Her move was also different than mine in that her husband joined her. Bosley arranged his same home/office, only in a different state. Give

Bosley his kids, 62" of plasma, a satellite dish, and no neighbors in eye-shot and he could probably live anywhere in this country.

They bought a log home, which Sam calls a cabin. Their cabin was over 4000 square feet of the most artfully crafted and organically inspired testimony to civilized living I had ever seen. It was located in a beautiful neighborhood of far more modest homes, fortunately offering a discreet access road that meandered into a 120-acre piece of property boasting forests and creeks and nature as it happened all by itself, all bordering a protected State park.

I packed up the kids and hit the road. The kids loved getting lost in Swain space, either outdoors or in. There was never an abundance of plastic, and there were plenty of kid-friendly diversions from Play Station to musical instruments to six household pets indoors, to ATVs, trails, trampolines, and a spirited creek with native critters outdoors.

Adult downtime was equally fun. We caught up on life, their move, my cancer, our kids. With the kids relatively dispersed throughout the house, we snuck down to the basement and smoked a joint. I didn't have much practice as a consumer of recreational drugs outside of the college setting, perhaps just a handful of times since those dedicated years of deliberate debauchery, each of which felt a little awkward and borrowed.

Those years just seemed to end with the granting of my diploma. Outside of being a mother, maintaining a career, and probably not having a clue where to locate it, I was married to a man who had no tolerance for such behavior in others, let alone in me. I truly had not given my abstinence any thought; it was never a sacrifice to manage. Strangely, this also included drinking alcohol. There were maybe three occasions in my entire marriage when I drank for the sheer fun of drinking and wore a buzz that could have put me on a dance floor.

Smoking a joint was a ton of fun. It was a flashback. Not to a particular event, but to a frame of mind that had been long ago discarded as being impractical. Once the initial rush subsided, I seemed to get out of my own way and let go of something I hadn't realized I was clutching. I couldn't imagine why I had ever chosen to exclude recreational fun, or had extradited it from possibility on my social calendar. Where was the evidence that everything was to be taken so damned seriously? And how, above all things, had I ignored the inherent value in humor to lighten a load?

I felt much smarter way back then when I trusted more and worried less. This reprieve was feeling pretty practical indeed. Therapy Cannabis. It was knocking on my door seeking my coy attentions like an old flame that never died. Masquerading as an ex-lover who aged exquisitely with a character only time can lend, Clint Eastwood was at my door. I could definitely let this in once in a while.

We enjoyed it all. We were eventually located by the kids and their homing devices, and returned to playing some board games with an enthusiasm I rarely brought to Trivial Pursuit. We listened to music and hung out doing a lot of nothing in particular. Though brisk and February, Sarah and I took a long walk in the morning. The trails on the property invited a clearing of most of life's mental congestions as we navigated our way over and around fallen brush, careful to avoid pitfalls, seeking the best footpath to get from A to B. Very simple. Us and the deer. Go find that in Florida.

On returning from Ithaca, there was an oversized shopping bag at the side of the garage. It was filled with over twenty frozen dinners. Not the Swanson variety, but the "made over the stove of an Italian woman and individually portioned and frozen in expensive Tupperware" variety. This angel of JoFrances landed over ten times throughout that year, never with warning or obligation, merely offering unconditional gestures of uncluttered kindness. Not a single hidden agenda.

Session Five. Very few people get closer to their mother-in-law as the strength of their marriage loses steam. Not so with me and Nancy. We had always enjoyed a connection which was other than the polite tolerance which the in-law deal usually got. However, she and I found a new frontier when the trials between me and her son began to escalate.

Also a Florida snowbird, she felt a grief for my burdens exacerbated by her own seasonal absence and her son's proclivity for emotional absence. Many mothers might have hidden behind the veil of blood that bound family, but not Nancy. I didn't feel in any way that her support to me was an affront to him; rather it was inspired in a love for him that overrode conventional judgment of whose side one should take in love and war. There are no sides in real love. One shows up or they do not. She showed up in a big way that transcended convention.

Nancy and I shared many things. Namely, we fell in love with the same man, and will likely carry that love with us for all of our days. Alex's father and she divorced when their four kids were relatively young, shortly after she discovered that he was sleeping with her very best friend. Once the shock subsided, it was he that chose to pursue divorce, not her demanding any recourse for such a betrayal. Having lost a husband and a best friend, living in a strange city to which they had relocated just the year before, and a newly single mother to confused young children, this woman was a survivor.

She was not afraid of tough love, and she did not keep her head in the sand on matters related to her kids. She did remarry several years after her divorce, but she had always bore a burden of pain that I knew weighed heavy on her, contrary to what she would ever admit to. Alex's father died early in his life, and left behind four children and an ex-wife who had a big vacancy for no one to fill, perhaps bigger for his elusive presence. Salting that wound, she still sees this woman socially quite often, as any small city becomes more of a large living room once you've lived there long enough. There may be alcoves you can hide in, but eventually you have to make it to the middle to get what you need. There is a focal country club where their crossed paths are inevitable, and their allegiance impossible. This was many, many years ago but it stings like yesterday.

Alex and his father were not the same man on all counts, but quite similar on many. Alex was the oldest, and was probably best able to tap the temperament of his father when it was most abundant in those early years. He learned the ropes of the movie business under his father's loose watch since he was able to walk. Most learned behaviors people have were acquired through passive observance rather than formal lesson. I got the same loving disregard from Alex that Nancy got from his father. It could be as simple as we were each married to the wrong man whose desires for us never peaked, but it could be as complicated as the notion that we desired that subordination. Yes, we were friends.

She flew in expressly to accompany me to one of the treatments, which seemed utterly unnecessary, but she would hear of nothing else. The private lair was not available, but it didn't feel like such a curse that day because there was barely any bustle about the inner ring of The Pit. I surmised that all had either been cured or died. I did learn that the Christmas cookie woman with the warm smile had been transferred to Hospice and that she was very "comfortable." I wondered if she would have used that very word.

I passed the finger stick with flying colors. The technician remarked that it was impressive at the tail end of therapy that my blood levels had not yet been compromised. I felt like Superwoman. It was almost the end of February, and I saw tulips in my future.

This mother-in-law of mine is Jewish *and* a grandmother, thirteen times. She removes schmutz, she shleps, and boy did she kibitz her entire way through a two hour course of Kool Aid while needlepointing with expert precision. The IV's, the fluids, the visual aversions—they were nothing for her. She'd been to the war, and she knew that some battles just get ugly. She honors and protects a strong bond of sisterhood, a shared female oppression mirrored in her own life, betrayed but only once.

Laurie was in awe of Nancy's apparent disregard for the setting, and thought she might start knitting herself. Nancy refilled my hot water four times like any good Jewish mother would, and even tried to push dough-nuts on me, insisting that they were healthy. We closed up shop like women finishing a routine chore, and the three of us went out for lunch and some take-home matzo ball chicken soup.

That last leg was the longest. They warned me from the get-go that the tail end tires hard. Just as the last three weeks of a pregnancy can feel like an eon, so was the anticipation of making it to the final round of chemo. I was ready to move beyond this chapter, close that book, and start reading a different one. It seemed I couldn't recall not being under the spell of those drugs, but then it seemed that the whole whirlwind of change that had descended on my life was just an evening's phantom nightmare I would wake from at any moment.

I worked overtime to keep my hair intact. It was washed with a love that scalps were rarely offered, lathered with gentle soaps whose botani-cal derivatives held mystical promises. Then it was combed gingerly so as not to offend any brittle rebels, and massaged with a touch reserved only for the touch of a baby's face. I had always carried a strange attachment to my hair. The cut, the style, the color: always a difficult trio to score in perfect chorus. When all three were in sync, I had a guaranteed good day, and no other concern could rob me of it. And if all were unruly, the win-ning lottery couldn't beat my funk. So when I signed up for the chemo program, that particular concern was always looming near. But my hair fared all right. It was a little tired and lacked some shine, but that was due more to my mood than anything else.

I had read an article once, early in my cancer journey, that brought tears to my heart. The story was one on the courage and compassion and love that one discovered when faced with extraordinary challenge. The woman was also in her thirties, but presented with a rare form of aggres-sive liver cancer. Her doctors brought out every weapon in the arsenal to confront this enemy. I could only imagine the color of her Kool-Aid.

On the morning of her first round of treatment, she descended her staircase, preparing to leave with her husband. Standing at the foot of the stairs were her husband and three kids, silent and holding hands, all with heads shaved in the most loving testimony to their mother that they could have expressed. The art of miracle speaks many languages when a silent, powerful testimony of love is offered.

The promise of spring was palpable. Suspicions of its arrival can be found in the particular quality of sunlight that changes in late winter. I had not seen the birth of a spring in three years, and this one was all mine. Late March brought an astonishing early garden of lily of the valley in my backyard, which had been under a foot of snow since we moved in. I clipped a dozen sprays and headed to the Chemo Pit for my final farewell.

Session Six. My oldest and best girlfriend in the world was my very last guest. Wendy and I carried truckloads of secrets and memories, borne in a time when our only job was making them. Though we went to a girls' prep school, our collection of flashbacks was very coed. She was born the last of five children, and I was the product of a working mother, so there was ample permissiveness whenever we played. Because we shared an academic aptitude in math and science, we were seated next to each other in those accelerated honors classes. We were undoubtedly the only two in those halls with IQ's less than 150 and a social life that had any legs.

She went to college at the University of Vermont, and our intentions post college were to convene back in Buffalo and move together to Boston in search of jobs, loves, and lives. It was during that brief post-college stint while saving some money freeloading in Buffalo that Peter found his way into my belly. She found a boyfriend she never married, then found one she did. They had three kids.

Where there is great tenure in a friendship, there is no trial that can't be weathered. You show up, you get it done. No questions asked, no one keeps score. There is no petty banter inserted to fill empty spaces, there is no fear of silence. In truth, Wendy and I are very different, perhaps more so than most of my other friends, making us excellent devil's advocates for that very reason. I can count on nothing other than her good judgment and her confidence, neither of which ever need to be qualified. Wendy was a great lifeline for me when I was in Florida and fighting those trials. We talked often, and she always offered the simplest, most uncluttered advice: "Get home, but give it eighteen months."

I offered the lily of the valley bouquet to the station nurse, then took my post with a very pensive resignation. My finger stick was gorgeous, but that was beginning to bore me. I had an internal silence that found no words through the entire course of IV insertion as I prepared for the final round. When Laurie arrived, just before take off, she noted the silence, lit the candle, and seated herself. There was a theme of exhaustion that was weighing heavy.

There was no denying the burn as it entered my veins. It had a cauterizing singe that I was relieved not to have felt before. My breath was abbreviated because I was afraid that my lungs and veins might rupture at contact. The pain was urging me to apologize to my body for inflicting it so willingly, to beg forgiveness for waging this war. Laurie disappeared, then returned with the nurse, who dripped something clear into the IV, which took just the hard edge of the pain away.

Wendy found few words; she wasn't one to hunger for her own voice. I was sure she was thinking that the burn was familiar to me, and I assured her it was not. Girlfriends will go anywhere with you. They will hold your hair over a toilet, they will hold your secrets until eternity, they will hold your faults as treasures, and they will help you set up a new house like a Polish cleaning lady. As seasons move forward, it seems that life's trials and burdens that continually revolve, as certain as death and taxes, get far more diluted in their dire urgency when you are fortified with such gems as genuine friendship.

I visualized a slumber. It was not a death nor the grip of one, just a complete physical and mental fatigue that would rise to nothing. There was a somber darkness that needed no answers and posed no questions. It just needed to resonate within itself, undisturbed, unchallenged until it needed that no longer. This was the first treatment during which I slept briefly, drank nothing, and quietly left the building with the slow drag of a dull razor. Not quite the rock star, but I did bid a few convenient farewells only to the nurses on my immediate footpath out of there. *Sayonara*.

The conclusion of chemo unfortunately brought with it the burden of finding a radiation oncologist. This burden was far more pressing in the eyes of my doctor than in my own. I wanted nothing more than to decompress outside of their sterile walls and clinical regimens. I needed Mother Earth to bathe me in her dirt, rock me in her arms, dry me in her luminous light. That was the extent of radiation my soul could invite. And I also wanted to run, shouting, "Come get me, Dr. Death, come fucking find me." But no, after two weeks of hibernation, their threats loomed and I summoned all I had to take their last noxious hit.

Finding the right doctor, again, was not easy. I did not hide behind the truth that I must have been a hard medical fit. I was front and center with my concerns at consultation meetings with two of these specimens.

The first one I saw, Dr. Radar, was just plain evil. I had no concern that he was clearly younger than me or that his English was broken at best, but he was a man with the bedside manner of an arrogant sultan who was relegated to a day's work against his will. While he came highly recommended, I knew I was not able to look at his face for thirty daily sessions of enough radiation to sear meat in an instant.

I did find a loving veteran teddy bear who had practiced radiation oncology since before I was born, and was relieved to see that his equipment had been updated since then. The fit was much better. He asked questions that suggested he was paying attention to matters that could not be discerned from my chart, and that went appreciated. He reminded me of my grandfather, who, ironically, was also a radiologist but died many years ago, an occupational hazard, I could only surmise.

My first meeting with Dr. Teddy Bear brought tremendous disappointment; he regretfully shared that he couldn't give me what I was looking for. All the reading and research one lay person could find pointed one long arrow at the next frontier in radiation oncology: IMRT (Intensity Modulated Radiation Therapy), providing more targeted emissions that better isolated the desired field, thus producing less scatter of harmful rays to nearby sites. IMRT had become standard protocol for therapy in the prostate, and the breast appeared to be close behind.

This new frontier promised a different bed upon which one received the radiation, inverted on purpose. This bed allowed a woman to lie on her belly, breast suspended to the floor with the aid of gravity and clamps (leave your humility at home), as the radiation was emitted at her hanging orb. Most desirably, this mode of emission almost completely eradicated the exposure to the nearby lungs, heart, and chest wall, which the standard positioning could not wholly avoid.

When I was researching breast irradiation mid-2003, there were maybe a dozen of these beds in the country, mostly at the top cancer institutes and universities. Undoubtedly, these sophisticated beds were insanely expensive and would slowly filter down to the rest of Middle-America, at which time the older protocol would be ousted in the name of future malpractice.

Tantalizing my frustration further, I was eventually able to locate a practice that had recently purchased one of these sophisticated beds in conjunction with using IMRT, in Rochester, NY. The therapy course was approximately six weeks. I could have committed to the three hours of daily driving for the opportunity to suspend my breast away from my body, but alas, their equipment was new, their training was underway, and they were only accepting prostate patients for the first twelve months. The sad and sorry truth was that this was not the first time in my life I had penis envy. No penis, get in line.

I laid aside my efforts and frustrations being marooned where I was in location and time and gender. I signed up with Dr. Teddy Bear. My chest was tattooed with their markings, measurements were calculated, and fields of radiation were road mapped with their exacting trajectories. After signing their twenty pages of disclosures, including my awareness that radiation also caused cancer, I entered their chamber of 18" thick lead walls on all four sides.

There was a challenging embrace of the truth of solitude as the technicians arranged my reclined body, naked breast and nipple paying homage, awaiting their painless, invisible punishment. The technicians orchestrated all exacting calculations, then scurried like church mice out of the shelter, vacuum-sealed the lead door, and left me poised to take the blow, solo and missionary style.

The most notable side-effect they informed me of was the fatigue that ensued post-therapy, namely because this was the first side-effect one could possibly notice. Most patients were entering their therapies having come off the heels of another course of taxing trials, so few were beginning with their best foot forward. Long-term effects will find you later. Their mission was to give you something long-term to worry about. Their motive was fending short-term threats.

Taking Inventory

$\mathcal{I}$ slept for days. I hired my usual sitter to come after school and stay until bedtime, three nights in a row. If I managed a shower and some basic hair care, I didn't scare the kids too much. I geared up as much as I could for morning routines, feigning an enthusiasm for whatever events were on board for them. One might tell me a story from their day, with far too many concerns in it, and I wouldn't even recognize when the point was made. Book bags got rifled through as one might sift through garbage looking for a token thing of value. There was a fog that just wouldn't lift in those early weeks.

I asked my oldest son to look me square in the eyes while holding my shoulders when he was telling me something that was important for me to know, to ensure that I was duly receiving the data. I also asked him to be my eyes and ears around the house for obvious concerns that I might be overlooking. To me, my home felt like a very safe place to stand still under no scrutiny or pressure. I resigned myself to put my Type A personality on hiatus and elected to take the advice of my doctor to slow down a little, though I imagined that advice was intended for during treatment, not for the brick wall I would hit right after.

In the still of my thoughts, I began to take inventory. I would survey the house, room by room, perusing the tangible things that were still standing in my life, as one might saunter through a gallery. I would consider how many different arrangements those items had known in the last several years. I would recognize that with each sequential move, there were things that just didn't make the cut. Their use to me had been exhausted, as only the most dire needs of mine and the kids became those to be answered. I would examine these weary warriors, still among my things, and I would pay them respect. Then, I would wonder why the hell I was paying attention to these thoughts, so rife with weird sentiment, and I began to pay attention to the stability of my mental faculties.

I lowered the bar. I permitted myself to let in only what was invited, to cast wayside all the rest. The business I would take would only be with clients that I enjoyed and with clients that were motivated. The friends I got together with were my inner-circle chiefs, not the peripheral "friends" often sporting private agendas, sapping my energies to feed their own curiosity or need to pass time. The extracurricular activities that obliged my kids were only going to be those that they had a greater motivation for than I had.

I wrote a note to each of their teachers. I explained that I had been inordinately taxed with medical concerns, and that my usual engagements in their class work and school activities were going to be compromised. I requested that they send home reminders for matters that were important to communicate, and that they use discretion when evaluating the importance of these issues. I would help, where able, to ready them for quizzes, spelling tests, and projects, but to expect very little in this arena. As well, I appreciated any support they could show to my children, given these present constraints. I had a child in preschool, elementary school, middle school, and high school, and revisiting any of their rudimentary curriculum, in support of helping them study, was beyond where I was going. Plain and simple, I was not in school.

The visits north were still happening. Alex would come for a breather of his own, still writhing with the discord while trying to lure new investors to recover it from bankruptcy. I didn't doubt that his hours weren't long, nor that his trials weren't necessary to defend. I marveled at how his rigid focus seemed to be crafting a tough and chiseled negotiator out of him as he fought those battles. I felt hungry for just a fraction of the attention that was cast in all directions but mine. But he was still coming north, and that airplane validated the continued survival of my marriage.

As heavy as the charge of running my daily life could weigh, there was one sole stroke of fortune that could swathe my spirits in those dark hours. If ever there was a silver lining, this was it: I had sheer and utter relief that I was planted just where I was, nesting in peace with the war in surround. Beyond having doctors I was familiar with, beyond having friends and family whose support was priceless, beyond the tenuous movie empire, and beyond the sheer luck that we would have had no health insurance coverage outside of New York State, there was a restored measure of control back within my reign.

I recognized my slippery slope was directed downhill. I was certain there was no soul who would have cast a hint of envy in my direction. And it was very apparent that things weren't going to get much easier on my near horizon, but one good decision in my wake, scant at best, seemed something to build upon.

On paper, it looked dismal at best. Declining income, questionable health, compromised marriage, four children so ever-dependent on my need to show up every damned day. I was on the heels of a long, dark winter, which was on the heels of a long, dark journey of its own, and I was trembling. I was cast in the wake of that eerie solitude, post Kool-Aid and doctors and finger sticks and exotic X-rays. Strong arms of support retracted, much like the sober quietude following a funeral blitz when the manic droves descend, ambush-style, with their urgent sympathies and tangible offerings. Soon they disperse, exposing the gutted vacancy for your own private viewing. I stood still and began to take a different inventory, namely of things that I had never before considered to be among my assets.

My concerns, however, were not borne in fear. I wore no regret for my departure, and guilt for me had rendered suffocation in the past. I could not have plotted my way out of these million broken pieces strewn about me. I owned every one of them, and could not have manipulated the pieces or players in any short cut to relief. But so long as they were broken I had a better shot at rebuilding them with a more suitable order.

My breathing room was made possible by where I lived. Exorbitant, perpetual energies were required in the raising of children. These efforts could not be ignored or sidelined for periods of time much longer than the span of a movie with a hired sitter awaiting your return. Sometimes the demands were steep and pressing; sometimes they were as small as helping a child with a short-order art project. But they were always present and that energy was appreciable.

My particular demands, however, seemed exponentially challenged in my role as parent, as most of my physical and emotional stores of energy were nearly tapped. I was a firm believer that the whole of one's world, including life outside of the home, played a measurable role in the shaping of a child. Like in a game of tug-of-war where a team pulled toward a common goal, I was afforded the opportunity to lessen my grip with negligible consequence, as there were still coaches and teachers and friends and neighbors, sporting similar values, still pulling toward that end. There, in the kernel of that nutshell, was the sum total of why we moved. And I let go a little.

When summer arrived, my first stroke of enthusiasm was executed in the abandoned book bags, which were hurled in the basement at the speed of light. Morning bus routines were renounced for morning Sponge Bob, which I had never really watched and actually found quite funny. My energy level began to rise with the temperature.

Longer days resulted in lesser pressures, as though one day's work had an extended grace period. Dinner hour became flexible, and sometimes dinner became optional. We built by hand a fire pit in the backyard. We found some abandoned bricks and slate at the rear of the property, along with some crushed marble for its foundation. We crafted a thing of beauty that has withstood two winters since. Smores brought smiles, and the kids would covet their perfect roasting twigs. We bought a trampoline, which was my first capital purchase in forever. I was once capable of impressive tramp acrobatics when I was seven and thought I might be able to recapture that form, preserved intact, accessible merely through my desire to retrieve it. I dug my roller blades out of hiding, shined them up, and hit the bike path in a daily eight-mile routine. From the buried back yard mystery gardens emerged hundreds of perennials, growing and blooming without any opportunity for me to stand in their way. There was not a summer vacation in all of my school years that was more welcome than that one.

I found a great groove between real estate, housework, kid's fun, my fun. Two kids were in day camp, and two were happy just laying low. Peter and Sam's baseball brought us many evenings to the veteran ball park, catching up with familiar faces and coaches. Five dollars could cover six trips to the concession stand, and the kids had free rein to play and get dirty and negotiate their ice cream purchases all by themselves.

I sought out every opportunity I could to see live music. I looked long and hard to locate nearby shows by musicians whose talents I admired. Some were played in outdoor open air venues, some were at weekend-long festivals where people came by pilgrimage with camping gear, their children, and a hearty appetite for a three-day party. The vendors at these festivals had booths of their handmade wares, displaying very beautiful things inspired more by passion than profit. There was a children's area where parents could drop off their kids in a supervised setting that offered workshops in everything from puppet making to belly dancing, as well as hay rides and games of capture the flag, all operated by a staff who clearly wanted to be there.

I bought my first hippie garment of twenty years at one of these events. It was a skirt made of a light, happy cotton with a flowing drape hitting well above the knee. As I tried it on, surveying the fit in the mirror, I took a long hard look at the nice pair of legs I had. I shifted my pose, finding a different angle which then accented the flat of my belly. I admired the girl in that mirror; I hadn't seen her since I was last as light as I felt on that day. My favorite band was taking the stage and I was admiring the way in which they were tuning their seasoned instruments with an easy presence they probably didn't bring to their day jobs. I paid the woman the $16 for the skirt, gave her 8-year-old daughter $4 for the matching headband, which she declared she made all by herself, and ran to the stage to help bring rise to the second set.

The way in which my kids looked at me that weekend, and much of that summer, lended me the mirrored reflection that I had not carried an ounce of levity or laughter in longer than I was willing to admit. I saw in their eyes and their enthusiasm that they welcomed my departure from the rigid and weighty demeanor I had been wearing. I was unsure when it all became so serious, or when consequence became so grave. But clearly, there were miles between the mindsets.

I considered this particular conflict in my head and paid it some respect. Certainly there was the tallest of responsibilities which was assumed when raising kids. The management of their lives and schools and laundry and meals and interests was a huge feat. Couple that with meeting their budding emotional egos with love and faith and promise, every single day. It's a lot to get done, whether you were married or not.

But when you were flying solo, there was no one to reciprocally feed and replenish you. Yeah, *you*. Not the person standing over there, but actually *you*. These demands persist day in, day out, year in, year out, and we inevitably learn to meet our own needs last, if ever at all. Sometimes we haven't a clue how to meet them. Sometimes we forget what they are altogether.

Then there was the undeniable responsibility of the earning of money and the maintenance of a job or career. Few people I had yet to meet had such a steeped passion for their work that it was considered other than a necessary chore. There were, by design, sentimental rewards and recognition found in most jobs from which people did derive some fleeting satisfaction, teaser carrots suspended at roll call. But by and large, a job grew legs of its own and we were obliged to plod forward in its footsteps. Such was life. There was never a hiatus from financial responsibilities when I could invite extended reprieves from incessant obligations. Few things in life could be depended on with such certainty as the need to be present, somehow, every waking day.

Add to this equation the mundane, pedestrian tasks of simply processing life as it happens, year 2005, outside of the raising of children or the making of money. It was insanely chaotic. This pace of change was staggering, never a breather to be had to remain fully informed. I was continually jumping through someone's hoop in an effort to conform to the demands of life, including: household maintenance, which password went where, registration deadlines, health concerns, checkbook reconciliation, staying abreast of technology advances, wardrobe updates, travel constraints, and licensing affairs. I needed thirty minutes to get a live human being on the other end of the customer service phone line, then a keen ear to decipher their very broken, outsourced English. The turnstile never stopped. There was no reprieve from the hoops and obstacles presented to simply process a life, let alone six. On so many levels, this was not progress.

Between the wonderful and selfless and often thankless job of parenting, and the burdens to provide a decent enough life that seemed to be getting steeper by the year, I certainly was heavy. I weighed four hundred pounds dripping wet and saw no opportunity to lighten up. Even the earth itself seemed particularly grumpy with the recent onslaught of natural disasters spewn like nasty spitballs at our poor planet. Either global tragedy was particularly front and center these days or I had just started to wake up to the world that I lived in. I had assumed a painfully sober life since I inherited the role of adult and had somewhere been robbed of the passion for life that would have given me a far greater tolerance for the trials of any daily agenda. All of which, I surmised, was but petty minutia when one had passion and motive and partner in their sails.

Something was going to have to give. I wasn't clear about what actions needed to be taken, but adjustments had to be made. I could feel that my summer freedom was a good fit, and I wasn't sure why it took coming off of cancer for me to permit myself to relax and have some fun. Accordingly, I decided to find myself a social life. I needed to start drinking, at least once a week. I needed to dance when I could, because passion seemed to find me when I found a dance floor. Fleeting as it was, I would take what I could get.

But it was fall and I was nervous. It didn't seem possible that such random disaster could find me for a third straight year, yet I proceeded with a skeptical footing. I was feeling a comfortable degree of distance between me and cancer, noting that a year anniversary was tight under my belt. I welcomed the kids' return to school, as their book bags were retrieved with the same enthusiasm with which they had been cast away.

Most mothers tore a sentimental seam when putting their last child on the kindergarten school bus, but somehow I summoned the rush of no more day care burdens in Sophie's education. The big yellow bus would carry them all away, and I, the queen of nothing, could reign in the privacy of myself. I became determined to carve out windows of time that were about no one but me.

The plane still headed north once a month. I imagined Alex must have had a big vacancy for the kids and the daily antics of family, and that always strapped me with a grip of guilt that had peculiar physical manifestations that scared me slightly. I did all that I could to cook his favorite dinners and have plenty of Pellegrino flowing freely. I arranged tickets to ice shows or horseback riding or harvest festivals for him to step in and assume the role of *dad*. My psychotic efforts were employed to create as normal of a five-day likeness to a family as could be crafted in my brain.

Alex was still burdened with the tenuous bankruptcy reorganization affairs. His latest energies were directed toward solidifying commitments from a new set of investors who were relieving the old ones, helping him rise out of the ranks of default. There were lawyers and accountants and trustees and massage parlors that continued to crowd his busy days, while still tending to business as usual. Whenever I would bark about not getting enough of his attentions, his bark was louder and I would passively accept whatever I was offered, humbled by my own stunted voice. He did cosign my exit line, after all, a fact he was certain to never let me forget.

Our sex life was aching. Perhaps heightened by his disinterest in sleeping with me, I had an appetite for our intimacy that went largely unmet. Alex seemed to revere his visits as an opportunity to disengage from his chaos, sleep long hours, lay low with the kids, relax at a nearby casino, or visit with a dwindling pool of friends. Sometimes we fought, but sometimes we would manage to carve out a four-day connection that was fun and light and apparently enough to stave off discussions of our dissolution. But sex was a head trip. I had a particular pet peeve that I couldn't shake: If night one, or even night two if I felt flexible, didn't include his making or responding to my advances in bed, then I was Hell-bent that I would not accept the mercy fuck I might have been offered on that last night. I was clear on this quirk, and a total quirk it was. He knew how I ached for his affections, and I thought it was pathetic to have to plead for them. And I did plead, but I would never screw on the last night.

Any red-blooded mammal might conclude that his needs were being met elsewhere. He outright insisted they were not, which I wittingly bought because his interests never quite matched mine under normal circumstances, and now he was exhausted to boot. I assumed he met his needs privately, and that he occasionally would frequent strip clubs, but that he never engaged in monkey business with someone he might see twice. We talked on the phone five times a day, he always seemed accountable for his time, and he was still flying north to visit me. It was a very sellable argument, one which was far more convenient for me to buy, paying retail, than to foreclose on.

As I examined the scope of my social life, it became very obvious that I didn't really have one. I hadn't ever considered how neglected that facet of my life was in the ten years we had been together. It wasn't just Alex, it was also having children, a career, a house, and a husband whose circle of friends were never originally mine; I had adopted them all by proxy when I signed up for that program.

I started to get out more, sure that adventure lay beyond the rut of my routine. The movies advanced to one of my favorite escape valves. Laurie and I had a standing Sunday night date at one of our favorite art houses for independent films. I had another girlfriend who loved to drink wine; we would find quiet little restaurants offering acoustic musicians, Pinot Grigio, and always appetizers because we're always cheap and always on a diet. Roller blading called my name at least three times a week, and I met one of my friends as often as our schedules would permit while we caught up on our worlds while skating our thighs to an impressive tone I hadn't seen in years.

And, I had one naughty girlfriend who had a hearty appetite for circuiting some very fun bars. That was a scene I had not been in since college, I kid you not. We might find music, we might find shots, we might find people we knew, but we always found fun. It took some time to restore my tolerance for alcohol, but it followed suit like a bad habit. I started to run into people that I hadn't seen since high school and began to enjoy the art of being social that I hadn't known in years. Some people's company I enjoyed tremendously; others were just harmless barflies with intrinsic value for our shared desire in seeking a slice of an evening's diversion. I was often asked if I had just moved back to Buffalo, thinking the inquiry was regarding my return from Florida. Rather, it was regarding my return from college. My life had largely been relegated to the suburbs with demands from work and kids rarely calling me into the pulse of any nightlife.

It was a good groove for me. It brought some levity into my life that was sorely missing. Alex didn't welcome my branching out in this way, and wasn't shy about casting some judgment laced with attitude regarding my escapades. Movies and girlfriends he could marginally tolerate. Bars and shots he could not. I understood that this appeared threatening, but I was unsure how to process where this threat might take us. I was committed to keeping my marriage together, yet did not understand why my newly discovered social life needed to erode that union. I began to assert my voice, arguing that, if *he* wanted to protect that union, then maybe the continued investment in it shouldn't be all mine.

Ouch, it stung. This was a tenuous voice for me to exercise. I was certain that I wanted the marriage to prosper, as weird as the marriage was. I knew that this holding pattern we were in was not going to last forever, and that somehow we would figure a way out of it. We were almost halfway through the half-assed four-year plan. I didn't mind living my marriage in 4-day capsules; I had enough else going on that consumed me plenty. I respected that he had tremendous constraints on his time, but I was growing to wonder why it wasn't possible that he could just give a little more-a spontaneous weekend getaway, a romantic dinner, a promise that this would end soon, anything. Cancer and sex included, I was feeling like a permanent fixture on the back burner, simmering steadily without anyone checking to see if I was still even there.

Over the course of months, several friends, as well as my mother, approached me in the style of an intervention. They could plainly see that all else appeared to be going well in my life: My health was good, the kids were in a great space having reassimilated well, my job was almost fully restored. I was beginning to get out and do some things all about me. Yet, they said, I had assigned an unusual commitment to a man whose efforts and investment in the marriage did not appear to be reciprocal.

This is a very hard place for anyone to go, except maybe a mother. It is very difficult to assess the strength and value that one derives from something as private and personal as their marriage. It is a judgment that an outsider is reluctant to cast, understandably, as there are many furtive inspirations that reside behind closed doors. Their concern, however, was born in the seemingly blind case of denial I was swathed in. I don't believe their mission was to force my hand toward divorce. This was not merely a judgment about Alex. Rather, it was an effort to recover my stunted spirit whose demands for sanction had been sliced far too thin. Denial was a crime of nature, and its consequence would seek destruction in a relentless path of no mercy. No favors, no free rides.

I appreciated their concerns and I often answered them by going out more often, proving that I could assert the needs of ME and still protect the ring on my finger and the marriage in my mind. I stubbornly hesitated to read the cues on the wall, scripted in several languages, except for the one which my ego could discern. Damned if I was going to screw up this marriage thing. Twice, no less.

I had never had difficulty with monogamy. Be it boyfriends or husbands, my desires had never taken me outside of the covenant of that relationship. Certainly, relationships had eroded, and I had been capable of orchestrating exclusive, consecutive relations right on the heels of each other, but I had always drawn a definitive boundary in the overlapping of fluids. That notion of "consecutive" got me thinking about just how much time I had ever been able to tolerate without having a man at my side to validate my worth. Curious thought.

The lion's share of my experience with men was in high school and college. It was certainly a time of budding sexual curiosities and copious explorations of that power, yet it was stunted in its capacity to teach due to being relegated to a time when we were young and green and deaf to the knowing of our own voice. I began to suspect that this was an avenue for me to explore in hopes of better understanding why I had gotten most else in my life right except for this one critical mess that I had the proclivity to keep recreating for myself.

My serious and sober life was not solely paved in the sobriety of my husband. Naturally, our shared social life didn't include drinking, or even hanging out with drinking couples. I willingly forgave those behaviors with strangely no regard whatsoever. The demands on me were plenty; between kids, work, household affairs, who even had the time? My girlfriends, all mothers as well and *not* married to sober people, rarely went out for their share of fun, either. It just seemed a natural transgression from pregnancy forward. As mothers, we imagine our load will lessen when our children are grown. We sign up to meet the charge of raising children. We show up with everything we've got.

But it didn't seem as simple as committing to a twenty-year hiatus in sidelining fun and frolic. I probably had a taller order than most of my girlfriends, without a live-in husband to shoulder some of the burdens.

But maybe not. Some husbands, they declared, simply yielded more work than help. While I was obviously the architect of my mess and needed to assume this daunting task as the door prize, there was more at play than just the digestion of this daily charge. My strange deal seemed to make it no different. Most of them had complaints a mile long about meeting the demands of everyone in their lives but themselves.

The sentiment of feeling unappreciated by their spouses was usually front and center in their misery. The scant communication and intimacy ran a close second. Sex became less able to net the desired satisfactions when intimacy suffered, so the bedroom became another issue to manage. Tending to kids can be exhaustive, though most seemed able to receive enough rewards that offset the bustle, most of the time, anyway.

While I respected the shape of the bell curve and recognized there were a blessed and lucky few who had struck gold in their tremendous marriages, most women truly resonated in some degree of misery about their life. There was an overwhelming theme of dissatisfaction among women that I began to suspect was based in biology rather than circumstance.

It appeared that circumstance was trivial, irrelevant. Who did what, who didn't do what, who didn't applaud loudly enough for a particular feat, who didn't notice your hair was cut or the drapes were new, they all felt like empty answers to where the breakdown had occurred. Yes, on the rim of that bell curve there were some perfectly happy couples with the rare synergy they had struck, but the sentiment one can lift from any modern survey of mid-life busy women was that most were far more miserable than were the men in those very same marriages. There was an insidious estrogen chorus that continually resonated a theme of aggression as the musical score of my gender. By proxy I wore this burden. Biology was a much better answer.

Solutions weren't obvious, but certainly the state of those affairs were. Men seemed to engage a different set of gears when driving their life. They expected to leave an argument with a different version of closure than women demanded. Men usually didn't wear their outstanding marital discords like an angry headdress, hungry for validation. They didn't wantonly wade in their shallow quarters, preaching to the vaginal choir. No, they found distance. They retreated to hours of football or golf or spectating exotic dance, wearing little of the discord left behind, if any at all.

With no other agenda, they enlisted similar interests among their friends and showed up for the exact enjoyment they signed up for. It was very uncomplicated and it was very civilized. I admired their ease in engaging in the moment they were living in; there was nowhere else they needed to be. There were no suspended carcasses of forfeited battles, nor were there phantom delusions of tomorrow's promise and yesterday's mistakes that they were swatting away while making their point. They were watching football, appreciating the blitz of the tackle and the intellect of the quarterback with an equal respect. There was something to learn here.

This was the first kernel of wisdom for me that cast a meaningful light on the notion of futility. I had always had an unnaturally deep-rooted conviction that I had the power and savvy to make anything work, anything, from a blind date to a bad decision, regardless of the dead-ends that they may have pointed toward. It had always been about winning, never been about winning what. Utter, stupid, "I knew more than this when I was six" futility.

I had engaged the same measures of logic and reason and intellect to confront matters concerning kids and jobs and time management as I had in matters related to the men from whom I had assigned a single expectation. I had attempted to level a playing field and distribute a conforming set of rules to an opponent whose set of aptitudes and interests were geared for an entirely different game. It appeared that they knew this, and while I was busy talking and negotiating the distribution of handicap, they were all finding it very funny. Truly, it is very funny.

Feed them. Fuck them. Forgive them. Franchise them. They were indeed that flexible. It was really *almost* that simple. Men were gifted with impressive brains and extraordinary talents. They could practice a temperance that women would usually strive to achieve. They didn't seem to marinate in yesterday's pain in an attempt to shape a different tomorrow. Successfully, men invited more laughter into their lives and were better able to boycott obvious sources of pain and discomfort with the baseline instinct of any lowly animal. Women, I swear, invoke many of their own battles.

Yet, there were some key fundamental behaviors that would somehow short-circuit like a cheap toy. Simple efforts that men could execute would have alleviated the majority of their relationship complaints that they felt so burdened to consistently revisit. Very simple ones. Sensitivity and intimacy, I refused to believe, were the exclusive province of women. I had seen men in movies very convincingly appear to be compassionate, sensitive, and engaged. I'd even heard real-life depictions of tender male posture on more than one occasion. I needed to understand this better; these creatures were human, after all. There was a lot for me to learn if I was ever going to get this right.

Going to bars was the perfect venue. I had a couple of girlfriends who liked the scene as much as I did. One had gotten divorced a year earlier and only left her house for work or retail. The other was married, and reeling in active frustrations within her own marriage. She needed to spread her wings to see if she was still a bird.

I only went out with them separately, as they were not acquainted. Purposefully, this doubled my opportunity to explore this fit. Most of my other friends were married and rarely, if ever, would go out to play just for the fun of it. I picked Thursday as the opportune night, and managed to put this together almost every week. Friday or Saturday seemed more of a date night, and I wasn't there to observe men on dates.

My kids didn't mind this arrangement either. It had been the whole of their lives since they saw me doing something that was geared all about me. I thought at first there might be issues regarding my going out and not being there for a concern that might arise in my absence. Not at all. Mom was looking happy.

Leah enjoyed coming in to my room and playing like school girls while I dressed. She marveled at the prospect of her mother in make-up and trendy shoes and clothing that was purchased in this millennium. Peter, then 15, stood impressed, appreciating the music I was listening to and the fun I was permitting myself to have. He burned CDs of all of my favorite musicians. I found great pleasure in our shared respect for fine acoustic guitar, particularly enjoying his recognition of superior talent from the 70's & 80's as compared to the static that his era puts out. Sam enjoyed his mommy lightening her load, and found fervor in our silly new laughter that he would often push by pressing his desire to come out and play with me. Sophie didn't notice much, but she was doing all right managing the distance between her daddy's visits.

The time I spent with each of the kids, separately, in the private world of their bedrooms, absent my agenda for them to clean those rooms, became a great window of perspective into their lives. I surveyed their things, noted their favorite belongings, interviewed their wall posters and became curious about the depths of their displayed interests. I began to suspect that I was more of a hall monitor, way back when, when I would merely approach the door frame, motivate the resident, encourage a task, and move on with sketchy follow-through. Entering their space, sitting still with them in the gallery of their worlds, was a far better road to showing up.

There were two sultry bars that usually sported ample entertainment, with all the trendy sex appeal that any mid-life person could ever hope to find. My motive was not to be a tramp; it wasn't sex I was looking for. I still wore my wedding band, and never portrayed myself as being other than married and disinterested in extracurricular adventure. We would always sit at the bar, we would catch up on all matters girls were famous for exhausting. Cosmos were a favorite drink, and, invariably, we only bought the first one.

There was a never-ending choice of characters to choose from. Contrary to the scene I would have anticipated, there were always many more men than women. They sometimes came solo, sometimes in pairs, and sometimes they arrived in a small pack having just recreated on a golf course, ski slope, or strip club. They never appeared to have been coming from the world of big box retail where the fluorescent lighting and humming registers were still casting their chaotic, vibrational buzz with a half-life. I admired the radiance of men coming in from the outdoors.

I would always observe the entrance, finding great material in noting the initial saunter of men and women as they made their presence. Despite this clinical setting I am conveying, I did not take notes anywhere other than in my head. On the upside of all of this analysis, we were there to have fun, and fun was always to be had. It had been over fifteen years since I had been in such a scene where the bartender remembered my drink of choice, and, accordingly, I felt like I was partying with my parents, or at least an offbeat generation of people where fifty year olds never looked so young. My distance from this domain could best be summed up by how invisible I was to the twenty-somethings whom I might have cast an eye of interest on. Before too long, however, my mojo and I were reunited.

We engaged this setting from about six p.m. to almost ten p.m. I surmised the crowd would get sloppy as the night dragged on, and I knew my kids would appreciate knowing that I had landed safely from whatever mysterious life I seemed to craft out of nowhere. And the men that most interested me likely had lives that would have demanded their being in bed at a reasonable hour. Usually anyway.

Early on, my face wasn't a familiar one, which proved to further raise the integrity of the appraisal. I knew the rough template of man I was looking to observe: professional, educated, successful. I would push those boundaries a little each way, and discount all others that fell outside of it. I had this bizarre clarity about my mission that definitely startled me. I appreciated that clarity and kept moving forward.

There was equal value in being approached as there was in eavesdropping. Both were rife with distinct perspectives that operated in tandem for gaining that greater understanding. I found that when I would get hit on with an obvious slant toward sexual innuendo, that I felt rusty and awkward, not owning any sense of comfort or security within my own skin, and certainly not having the seductive charm I last knew in college. The ease of the conversational banter would change for me, and I might squirm in the fragments of its wake, rethinking the stupid things that seemed to fall out of my mouth like hay off a tractor.

There was nothing in my behavior that I found impressive regarding my talent to engage in dialogue that was initiated on a foundation of respect, rather than on my fee simple ownership of a potentially integrated body part. Some of these men I knew peripherally, and was well aware that many were married and apparently happy in those marriages. They seemed to find compartments for these isolated diversions, spirited in the pursuit of pleasure, while their wives were at home tucking in kids, finishing laundry, with day jobs to boot. I truly stood in no judgment, just in observation. Their interest seemed very simple, forged on a desire to satisfy themselves in an act that could take twenty minutes. Mine seemed very complicated, as the satisfaction I was seeking I hadn't found since, well, ever.

The dialogue between them was equally as simple. Sporting events, professional challenges, and hot women were perennial topics thrown around like a football. Few would burden these topics with obsessions of their personal drama, and rarely were they engaged in a particular concern for excessive lengths of time, especially if a group of provocative women crossed their path. There was abundant humor, which I grew to admire with a vein of envy for its absence on my calendar. They appealed to me as a fraternity of collegiates with the same passion for fun, but merely older, wiser, and wealthier.

Women would often pass them by with a private agenda to intrigue them, slowing their motions at an opportune vantage. Some carried the sashay in their saunter as though they were the lucky owner of the magic pussy. There was no magic about it; there was just pussy. Regrettably for those kittens, there was no threat of extinction either.

On a far lighter note, some silly observations:

- Men looked better with the streakings of gray hair and the character of wrinkles.
- Women took much more time assembling themselves for their evening out.
- Men surveyed the bar with their eyes, while women used their whole heads.
- Men were much more comfortable entering a bar alone, as evidenced in their body language.
- Men laughed using hearty facial muscles without regard for the consequence of stressing wrinkles.
- Women fingered their hair often; men rarely tended theirs.
- Men stayed put for longer periods of time, apparently owning more patience and contentment.

Indeed men had motive to fuck, and I imagined that those who excessively repressed that desire fostered an alternative deviance that wasn't so friendly. But they had other motives, other engagements, all of which contributed meaningfully to the whole of their lives and the levity of their ways. It seemed that women were granted access to a smaller part of the whole of their man than the part of their own whole that they wished to surrender to them. This was the distribution of handicap. It was vanity with its own agenda.

Pardon these sweeping generalizations; certainly there were plenty that fell out of this footprint. But after observing behaviors, be it in the scene of the smut, the lives of my friends, and the ways of my own, as well as years of trying to nail down what was often at the core of the division in our motives, this explanation carried some promise in identifying the tender nucleus of my pain.

I was not attempting to bridge any battlefield that men and women had navigated for eons, nor was I looking to become a man. But what I did discover was that the absence of a genuine, spirited passion, one for me and about me, was not simply the neutral void that I had considered it to be. The vacuum of its emptiness carried an invisible oppression allowing me to live the makings of a life without really having one at all.

Finding this passion, this painfully absent ingredient, was a luxury I couldn't afford to find. I was working as many hours as I could without inevitable household collapse if I gave any more. I knew I was spread as thin as veneer, my choices were few. I managed to make just the money I needed to meet the financial demands I had, but never before had there been so little fat. I became much smarter about how I allocated money, shifting priorities, and asserting new definition to the actual meaning of need. I must say, there was a strange satisfaction in trimming up on a fiscal diet.

I was pressed to make groceries, sneakers, haircuts, clothing stretch to their maximum yield, often beyond. Without much sacrifice, meeting this mandate was not nearly as depressing as one might think. There was an appeal in the art of conservation that spoke to me. I considered finding a different job but it would have been impossible to replicate my income when factored against my work hours and my inability to step that up. I had tenure, expertise, and a great reputation in my work, hardly the dust to discard in favor of starting something anew. I was leveraged perfectly. The balance was tough, but again, my choices were few. I had been doing this job since college and I couldn't even imagine what else I could do that someone would actually pay me for.

This thin line, though, did invoke my approaching Alex to lend some support my way. I recognized his pressures and constraints were many, and that the cost of living was higher with the palm trees, but I shouldn't have needed to assume the lion's share of responsibilities regarding the children. He did give money when I barked loudly enough, and it never came without the need to ask several times. I can't impart enough how much I hate to argue about or ask for money. With the lack of a structured, legal support obligation, the burden was on me to collect what I could, when I could, and this distasteful duty of collection was recycled month after month with no forward-thinking resolve.

My tolerance would further be taxed when Alex would come north and buy frivolous gadgets for the kids. I tried to respect that he received pleasure from buying them movies, video games, and other means of social seclusion, and the kids enjoyed them as any kids would. But this was an inverted allocation of priority as well as an erosion of the order I was seeking to keep. This was all a very gray area, because his money was not my money, nor did he share my decisions on how I felt he should be spend it. This was rendering me voiceless and powerless in feeling to be part of this very weird marriage, where necessary concerns became my burden and fluff became his.

It was late fall 2003, we had lived apart for a year and a half. I continued to clutch to, as evidence, the scraps of attention that were strewn about. Birthdays, anniversaries, weekend getaways, they all went by the wayside, rendered meaningless by way of our different zip codes. I knew he missed the kids. I imagined he missed me. But whenever we engaged in the kind of dialogue that escalated into manic threats of divorce, my heart sank to a place where my breathing became labored and my head became swamped with urgent fears. This was interpreted as a physical validation, one assuring me that divorce was not what I wanted, and subsequently I would lie low on whatever behavior it was that was the central crux of that particular argument.

The Intervention Club kept calling my number. They spoke in many tongues and urged many wake-up calls. People who were part of my inner circle were increasingly concerned about my denial of what appeared to look like, act like, and smell like a divorce on my near horizon. I attempted to stave off their concerns by jump-starting a social life I was growing to be proud of. I kept buying the Pellegrino and getting lost in the four-day delusions that proved to me that all was intact.

One excuse I often sold myself was founded in a truth that scared me. I knew that if I confronted the distasteful arena of the legal battle in the dissolve of our marriage that the fighting and coveting could have had the power to crumble me. Alex knew well how to play dirty pool; his eight ball I could have never been. My last experience with crumbling preceded my getting cancer. Connect the dots. It was just easier to deal with later and I could summon no urgent reason to confront it head on.

I rationalized that all else was working with a flair I was famous for. Then I might remind these friends of some of their own problems that should be up for examination. Go empty your own closet. Big deal that I didn't date. I knew I could get laid if I wanted to, but batteries were a better investment. I had all the satisfaction a mother of four could hope to find. I had a conjugal commitment, despite the fact that my marriage included no sex, only memories of love, and token offerings of inconsistent financial support, strewn at me like a whore receiving payment. (I should have known that nobody ever makes you feel that way without your permission). But I saw nothing.

I was a child of reason, though, and could see reasonable evidence to the validity of the argument. I appealed all efforts to understand why I had chosen to passively say this was good enough for me by permitting it to die its slow, sorry death, bearing witness to those desperate, final spasms before the flat line proved otherwise. Everything else I elected to live by was of an entirely different standard, one fortified with reciprocal respects and contributions. I had earned an impressive reputation in my profession; my expertise, work ethic, and success I was proud of. Concerns with raising children had been met with every ounce of love, responsibility, and commitment that one could show up with. I had a network of the best of friends with whom I shared relationships of resounding reward. My extended family was a bit more dispersed, distanced by way of both geography and temperament, though I did engage, when possible, and that was okay. Just this one monkey.

My lone answer to this quandary spoke to the pinnacle of the one pain I had known throughout my life, its harrowing face haunting me in alley ways and unconsciously shaping decisions that I made in its elusive, masked presence: *I was fearful of failing.* Namely here, a harsh branding of "D" stamped on my forehead, clobbered by gavel with scornful judgment, twice.

I didn't quite identify this gripping fear at that time, I just called it "the monkey" and knew that it needed to be off my back. I rationalized the day away by offering that: 1) This mess was my creation, 2) Big deal that my needs went largely unmet, 3) My kids would have been better off with the farce of our happy marriage in four-day capsules than to have us divorced. As smart as I thought I was, I must have thought my kids were that stupid that this seemed a sellable concept.

I was painfully aware that I would be swimming upstream to ever hope to find another man in my life, given the baggage I had in tow: four children, two ex-husbands, a dog that barks and sheds, some lovely stretch marks, and a bout with cancer. It seemed like a better percentage play to keep an outstanding marriage at bay in hopes of accidental change than to cut the loss, accept the failure, and fly it solo. This fear was manifested as my ass in the air, a sock in my mouth, an elbow at my back, accepting due recourse for failing to get this right on my second swing. It was definitely time for therapy.

With the supernatural knowing harnessed only in the best of friends, Daniela called. While it appeared to be a monthly catch-up call chock full of updates and exchanges, she read through the litany of my news on the grateful state of my affairs. While she may have been a charter member of the Mexican chapter of the Intervention Club, she didn't quite disclose it as such.

Daniela had lived in Mexico almost ten years. She was my college roommate and partner in many a crime. We had stayed close and enjoyed a relationship that continued to blossom year after year. Though raised in Manhattan and in boarding schools, finishing schools, and then party schools, and never too distanced from the life of privilege she was born into, Daniela was one of the most inspired and passionate people I had ever met. She was born with a compass that had never misguided her since she had learned how to interpret it.

When given opportunity to travel, which was always abundant, Daniela elected to journey to Nepal, India, Africa, as well as remote parts of eastern Europe rarely explored in commercialized travel markets. She was a student of culture and a keeper of many native faiths. Certainly her peripheral family wealth had supported her, lending the farce of hypocrisy to her modest, organic, self-made life, but only in the sense that she knew if she ever fell flat on her face that real risk was mitigated. She tapped into none of their resources to maintain the life she lived, but I suppose she knew that those resources were never far away. Unbridled absence of fear might make an inspired passionate soul out of anyone, but it certainly had out of her.

Daniela was in her mid-twenties when she traveled to Cuernavaca, Mexico to study Spanish at the University. She integrated seamlessly with the people, the culture, and the steep heritage of their mores. There she met a man, a Mexican by custom and upbringing, but French and Indian by native blood. They fell in love as young hearts are famous for, and married under a tree in the presence of God with no other licensed officiator.

They presently live in a little village named Tepoztlan, which is an ancient village set in the mountains with an elevation over 5500 feet, about an hour south of Mexico City. They had three beautiful children who were each a very interesting union between her blonde/blue Aryan blood lines and his dark, mystical tones of many nations. They owned a beautiful home just outside of this village, boasting inspired Spanish architecture, built with crafted detail, fine artisan tile work and building materials never sold by scanned barcode. They had lived there over eight years, and she was as integrated into this community as any native ever could be.

Her family fought her decision long and hard when they learned she had married in Mexico and planned on staying there. Her mother was immediately all over the truth that there was no actual license that bound their union in official definition, and remained hopeful for the first few years that her daughter might exercise this exit clause with the ease of a plane ticket when she tired of this phase. There was great distance between them in those early years, often threatened by financial extradition, which always fell on deaf ears. The distance was ultimately bridged when they met their grandchildren. Today they share a relationship that has been strengthened and enriched by the courage it takes to stand tall, stand still, and stand secure for what you believe in.

Daniela listened to my flighty updates on the ways in my world, happy to hear that the kids were well, work was good, Alex was okay, cancer was yesterday. I even bragged about my social life. She asked about tomorrow. She asked about me. I asked her what she was even talking about.

She suggested I come to visit for a week. It seemed a ludicrous proposition, given the fact that all just might disintegrate in my house if I weren't there to support it for that length of time. I got the same deaf ears that her mother apparently got. I told her I would seriously consider making it happen.

While it seemed like a journey I couldn't afford to put into motion, I also suspected it was one I couldn't afford to miss. I phoned Alex to see if he could extend his visit in November to one full week and hold down the fort while I went to visit a friend. He was in the throes of his chronic chaos, officially emerging from bankruptcy having lured some new partners to relieve his old partner's interests. His schedule was tight, his work demands were many, but I begged and he conceded. I gathered all 30,000 frequent flyer miles in my account and booked my flight to Mexico, leaving the following month, which would mark my first real journey without children since I had had children. I was grateful he agreed to spend the week, as I would have had inordinate worries had there been a hired hand trying to keep it all together. Alex's hand was awkward enough, but at least I knew nothing would fall to pieces. There would be plenty of order to restore on my return, but such was life. And I was off.

Daniela's husband was a big little man. His name was Allen and he spotted me immediately at the airport in Mexico City. I had heard much about him over the years, about his tenure with the Mexican army as a clandestine martial arts instructor. He was half sumo-warrior, trained for combat, half teddy bear with a heart of gold, all of 5'8" in shoes. I hugged this man as if I had known him since grade school.

I had only been to Mexico by way of resort or cruise ship, which is really never having been to Mexico at all. The Hyatt is the Hyatt is the Hyatt, only with different wares in their gift shops. I had heard about the danger that urban Mexico City was infamous for and I was wary in our exit from the airport through this massive, congested inner-city jungle that seemed much darker than it should have been at two o'clock in the afternoon. Daniela was at home, tied to some errands, and her husband was kind enough to tend to me in the hour-long drive. I was watching him cruise through the deep and vibrant urban pulse with a native air of comfort integrated with expert caution. He drove faster than I am comfortable moving.

With an hour to catch up with this perfect stranger, I stepped back from my usual seat of control and listened to him, watched him, as he went about his ways. His English was perfect, carrying enough of an accent to lend some mystery as to the origin of his native tongue. He shared stories of his kids, of his lovely wife, and of his four-year long study on the healing art of Polarity. I half-listened in a fashion I have become famous for, as I acclimated to the hum of the Jeep, the give of the road, the glorious sight of the mountains.

I was struck with an utter and breathless regard for the beauty of the whole of the landscape. The village of Tepoztlan was found by way of the Mexico-Cuernavaca highway, which meandered through some of the most beautiful countryside I had ever admired. What appealed most to my sense of astonishment took me a moment to gather. I had never been to such a high elevation, anywhere ever, which was not in a latitude where one might also ski. It was as though there were a symbiotic dependence that couldn't be separated. I had not known of a tropical climate and a mountainous topography existing in this particular harmony. Until here.

The massive cliffs and dramatic peaks and abundant bougainvillaea were all present as they may have been one thousand years ago. Nothing presented itself as though it were drafted as the blueprint of a brilliant landscape architect. More graciously, it originated from the inspired Mother of us all, with a gentle hand from the Divine, undisturbed by man and his elemental, transient notion of beauty.

As we approached the heart of the village of Tepoztlan, there was the usual hustle of people and produce and kids and markets. There were car horns and bike horns, of seemingly foreign variety. In as much as I don't read Spanish, I knew with complete certainty that there was not a franchised outfit on their Main Street. Traffic moved slowly, drivers waved to shopkeepers, kids crossed the street, wearing school uniforms and carrying armloads of books. There were many who opted for bicycles as their sole mode of transportation, weaving with flair in and around the orderly congestion.

The shops and streets appeared to be hundreds of years old, yet I learned this was not so. Rather, they were merely constructed out of raw building materials that were unrefined and naked in their beauty. They, indeed, were as old as the earth and abundant on their lands. Once refined by sun and time, they were then crafted by native artisans and humble laborers, building the roads and fences and bridges of this little village. And at least once in every journey through this charming downtown, traffic stood still for crossings of cows or pigs without any apparent irritation. It was anything but chaotic. It reeked of civilization.

Their home was on the outskirts of town. We approached their neighborhood, which I dare not call a subdivision, on a road that I was sure was older than dirt. The terrain was rugged and the road pocked with craters that looked like bunkers, yet this seemed to go unnoticed. When I asked how cars fared given these stressful conditions, I learned that one can only expect an automotive life span of about half of what we expect in the States. Interestingly, I noted that cars, on average, were much older there than the cars that crowded our streets, because people there actually kept their cars for the whole of that life span. The original VW Beetle was famous there for its optimal endurance.

We pulled onto their property, which was situated behind massive wooden gates that opened electronically. The drive was made from a crushed stone that was set in a fashion I wouldn't suspect needed paving or maintenance. There was abundant, mature foliage, all in vibrant, pregnant blossom, surrounding the perimeter of the property, well surpassing the stone fencing enclosing its boundary. Bouganvillea, hibiscus, and calla lilies all day long. Their colors and scents danced among themselves, mingled in a sensual tango married in the secret history of their soils.

There were the most beautiful terra-cotta tiles I had ever seen adorning the entry terrace that led directly into the home and throughout the first floor, fully integrating the outdoors with the in. The tiles looked imported, but they were actually made and fired about five miles from the house. The exterior fascia appeared to be an antiqued stucco with the weathered patina unique to time, yet impeccably preserved. Roofing was made from integrated clay tiles, desirable for their ability to withstand the weather, as well as for their local abundance. Windows were open, shutters were secured with genuine iron tiebacks. This Spanish-inspired house was perfectly at home in this reclusive setting.

We exited the Jeep and Daniela came to greet us in the drive. She truly radiated her joy to be exactly where she was. There is not language that can capture that sense of presence. We hugged, holding that embrace with a gratitude that transcended the years since our last time together. Simple joys have no greater destiny than the arms and heart of a great friend.

I spent much of the week doing nothing other than standing in as copilot to her life as it happened in any random week. Her children had school and activities, she had errands about town and markets to visit for items that were needed. Most staples were sold in simple wrappings, adequate to maintain freshness and quality, yet uninsulted by the inundation of hermetically sealed bullshit packaging showcasing marketing talents rather than the food therein. Cheese was cheese, nuts were nuts, the rest was fluff.

Her home was appointed with meaningful collections of paintings, furnishings, detailed accessories, all suggestive of an interesting life rather than an interesting decorator. There was not one PlayStation game to be found, no XBox, Super Duper Mario, or juiced-up electric scooters. Clearly, no surprise, her children were not suffering.

Daniela is an incredible chef, went to school at the Culinary Institute in San Francisco, post Boulder, and still continues to expand her art in culinary expression. We prepared meals for her family that were simple, inspired, organic reflections of the way in which she is presently living her life. Ingredients were retrieved daily, fresh from little shops owned by friends who knew a similar peace to hers.

I had a moderate paranoia of getting an intestinal plague while living high in the hills among the natives, absent the toxic chlorinating water filters utilized at the Hyatt. She met that concern with simple advice: Don't eat anything raw, drink only bottled water and lots of it, and end your day with a glass of red wine. Curious about the role of the wine in the squash of the parasite, she simply offered that it was as much for my head as for my digestive tract. God absolutely sends people to us with Divine reason.

The climate was room-temperature perfect. November marked the end of their rainy season, and the lands were ripe with nourishment and vitality and vibrant color. The days were seventy-five degrees, absent an ounce of humidity or wind, abundant with sunshine, and nights were fit for a favorite sweater. We shopped in the village, mingled in the markets, finding native pottery and crafts that were given their life through the hands of someone who was channeled with passion to create it.

We readied one of Daniela's kids for an upcoming seventh birthday party that she was hosting in her home the day after my departure. I observed her busyness as she gathered the games and treats and gifts for token festivities. I watched her son help make his cake with an ease and a tenor he appeared to have known during all of his seven years of life. When he cracked an egg with the stroke of an ace, it was impossible for me not to note that I would have never let my 6-year-old free with an egg, loose with all the possibility of disorder it held in its fragile shell. Nor was it possible not to regard the chaos that had surrounded the birthday parties that I had made myself, along with those that my children had attended, all inviting future landfill clutter while mainlining red dye #5 laced with refined sugar. Happy Birthday! Here's a gun.

Daniela started her business several years ago. She created a line of jewelry made from beads of sea glass, accented with sterling, and inspired with a refined celebration for the beauty of the female form. The inherent pores of the sea glass are rubbed with essential oils to individualize each piece with an aromatic signature. Visit her website, Aromaje.com. Very sensual, very beautiful, and very unique.

Her studio was in the den of her home, adorned with rich natural wood flooring and significant gum wood moldings. The room was flooded with expansive leaded windows and natural lighting and overhanging bougainvillaea sprays. There were simple wooden pegs along one wall for ropes of the raw gems, there were completed masterpieces along another, and there were vast compartments of trays housing accent beads, sterling silver, threads, and intricately detailed clasps on another. She was insane for the art of the clasp, assigning beauty and utility in the noble role of closure.

The studio abounded with the whimsical flair of passion not needing permission. Most of her clientele were from the States, though there were several spas in Mexico that she did business with. She came to the States four times a year to exhibit her jewelry, and was smart enough to know exactly where to go to tap a ripe market. She had cut no cords from her bloodlines. This girl absolutely got it right.

There were four local Mexican girls who helped her with the stranding and assembly, all under her keen directive. They were sweet and pleasant and dependable. One was named Aricelli, and she cared for the children as well. Her English was not much better than my Spanish, but I would often look for opportunity where I could communicate through language needing few words-maybe cooking, straightening, or playing with the kids. She was the eldest of four children, and her fourteen years had lended her a purity that was other than that which I was familiar with, either in the teens of today or the teen that I ever was. She attended school half the day and worked in Daniela's home the other half.

Often Daniela would drive Aricelli home if she arrived by bike and was leaving late. Her family lived central to the village, in an obviously less affluent setting. One afternoon, as we drove her home, she kindly invited me in to see her space. The neighborhood was very different than anything I had ever seen. There were perhaps a dozen homes, varying versions of clapboard huts, in no order or array whatsoever, strewn about like dice. The ground cover was hard-packed dirt in this one-acre parcel of land enclosed by modest fencing, deeming it a neighborhood. There were many heavy trees, several abandoned cars, and a few miscellaneous outdoor projects underway.

Nine children were playing outdoors in this little micro-village. They were engaged in games such as tag, tree climbing, orchestrating ramps for their twenty-year old bikes, and unearthing critters. There was not a bully among them, and not an adult to supervise them. The girls were busy with dolls or talking or straightening up after someone else's forgotten chore. Some might cross the threshold into the land of the boy warrior, but they seemed to return to their place with an instinct they were not ashamed of. Mothers were busy with meal preparations, while other people were delivering things or repairing things or just sitting at rest in a chair. The happiness of the children was most remarkable. The quiet and serenity ran a close second.

Inside of Aricelli's home, there was one large room. Areas were best discerned by the arrangement of furniture that suggested what type of activity might take place there. The far corner served as the kitchen, with a tremendous amount of creativity surrounding the meaning of the word *cabinetry*. Beds were arranged almost military style, though closer together and without tight turned corners, still more impressive than the corners that I turn.

There was a very peaceful order among all of the things owned by six people under one thatched roof. There didn't appear to be a grand chamber for private adult lovemaking, but apparently that had been figured out by the number of beds aligned on my left. I gave her mother a hug as if I knew her, sharing with her how much I had enjoyed getting to know her daughter, how beautiful their home was, how remarkably well all these children played, how blessed she truly was. All to be found in that embrace, that envious awareness of how much richer was her life than was mine.

On the eve of my departure, Daniela, Allen and I went into the village to explore the night life. There were a dozen cantinas with many people strolling casually, drawn by the same magnetic pull that any Main Street on the planet gets. We stopped at a few of the bars, had some tequila among a roomful of happy, easy people not urgent to get anywhere, wearing no regard for the workday ahead. Allen showed me some of the seductive footwork of Salsa dancing, and then I danced with a complete Mexican stranger who interrupted our layman's lesson. Music was played street-side by people who accepted no money, and kids walked around freely without fear for their well-being. Allen shared with me that Tepoztlan had almost no crime, none at all, whatsoever. He still maintained connections in the army, but he would not speculate on this issue. Thieves, vandals, murderers…they just didn't seem to go there.

I learned that evening that Tepoztlan had long been regarded as a retreat, an international haven, spanning many, many centuries, known for its cultural roots steeped in healing. All modes of healing. It was home to artists, musicians, writers, and spiritual seekers from all over the world, and well-known by those most esteemed in those disciplines. Some came for brief visits, some for their lifetime. There were more practitioners of Polarity, Reiki, Acupuncture, Spiritual Religion, and Yoga, located on that particular mountain, than concentrated anywhere else in the world. This heritage was accepted as an unchallenged truth among its residents. Allen offered some reasoning based upon a very clinical location of the polar axis integrated with a magnetic field, but I got lost somewhere in those words. I imagined that those who sought refuge there didn't need that clinical validation to underwrite their mission.

Standing still, a sad, rare luxury in the chaotic architecture of the life I was returning to, served me well in my journey to that high and human land. I wore a pumped-up pride that I had actually taken such initiatives to make it all happen. I resigned to adopt a few personal outlets of celebration into my micromanaged world. My energy stores had been completely replenished upon my return, and restoring all order to the house and kids proved a piece of cake. One dedicated day and the whole ship was back on track. Real estate catch-up proved just as seamless, and two of my listings had even sold while I was off being an international woman of mystery. Then came Christmas.

The holiday season sapped its usual degree of apathy from my life. It seemed the inundation of manic marketing geared at feeding a desperate hunger for newer and better and improved *stuff,* often with agendas of guilt and greed, reached a new pitch for me every year. There were so many opportunities throughout the year to express genuine, spirited recognition of gratitude, often amplified in its whimsical spontaneity, that I grew resentful of any marketing scheme that demanded I cram my love and appreciation into one particular day.

No affront to Jesus or any of His friends, this swamp of consumer gluttony was not a relative of His. My children have learned, at the foot of our many Christmas trees, never to expect anything other than items of maximum utility. I have no problem wrapping boring clothing, and the stocking is the perfect vessel to refuel their favorite toiletries. There will always be a few surprises, which may or may not carry veins of frivolous gratification, which is the extent of the material spirit I can summon. Perhaps I was beaten with a candy cane or molested by a Santa. Perhaps regression therapy might uncover the buried truth. I do know that I must make peace with Christmas sometime in my life.

January always brought a particular bounce in my step for that very reason. I had the maximum distance from the holidays I would know all year. Alex called needing some assistance in finding a new condo for himself, as he was burdened with moving to Miami when his new partners assumed their position in his company and they kindly demanded that headquarters be located under the close supervision of their own watchful roof.

I flew to Florida to help him explore housing possibilities, negotiate the sale, situate the financing. Miami was a huge urban metropolis that had been reinventing itself like no other city I had ever seen. There were trillions of dollars being invested by brilliant developers making tenfold their money in snapshots of time. The demand for housing, high-end retail, office, hotel, restaurants, civic recreation, and entertainment could not be answered quickly enough. If there were any strain or struggle in the economic climate in our country today, no one had shared this with the urban planners of Miami who could not seem to issue building permits or cranes fast enough.

There were droves of people relocating their retired souls, seeking their last ditch slice of happily-ever-after. Miami also attracted the self-made hedonists desiring an ocean, an airport, a city, a cruise ship, a Heat game, and the South Beach flat belly all within eight miles of each other, which could take eighty minutes to span at the wrong time of day. Bring your Spanish, your wallet, your knife, and your hurricane shutters, and you were good to go.

Alex was a classic metro-sexual. If he had suspicions of these budding tendencies when we lived together, they certainly had blossomed since we lived apart. He kept his space psychotically clean, but with one person to look after and a weekly cleaning lady, that feat impressed me none. His clothes, his nails, his affinity for sleek technology, his passion as a home-theatre audiophile, his alphabetized collection of 558 DVDs, most still in cellophane, his anally organized closet—all had an order that was a little more curious. His coffee maker had a litany of tricks it could do, well beyond coffee. If you are looking to spend three hundred dollars on a pair of jeans, check with him, he knows where to go. I understand he has company in the metro world, as there are many men who are very proud of their closet.

We found a European-inspired, new construction development in the heart of South Beach. The lobby reeked of tasteful simplicity, adorned with sleek art-deco chaise, sprays of steel and stone, and lighting suspended on tightropes. The condo boasted crushed glass sinks with cascade falls of water, stainless everything, granite counters, and a covered patio overlooking an infinity pool and several of those flat bellies.

I argued that perhaps it was too much money, unnecessary for a man who travelled often, worked insane hours, and could ever-so-barely afford it for starters. He asked that I figure the calculations, then he heard them, and decided I had very little business suggesting what he could and could not afford. Which was true. Or not. There was a lot of gray area.

He signed on board for the Euro condo. He opened whatever compartments money just seemed to come out of in such pinches. We piled on my fat three percent commission as credit and structured a three month closing, and he geared up for his new address in one of the hottest heartbeats in the country. Storm shutters and flat bellies both included.

I returned a little spent. There was a lot accomplished in three days, and still much to do to finalize arrangements for the financing and closing. It was the middle of a northeast winter, with unforgiving cold snaps and days where it seemed the sun was setting at 2 p.m. The kids were all locked in the inertia of their schedules with school, activities, and friends. Keeping up with the house and school and groceries and endless laundry, I felt as if I were on a treadmill of burden with a never-changing view. There was a pace in place, one which I had personally laid every stone for, well-knowing there was nowhere to look for a reprieve that lasted any longer than a Thursday night out with a girlfriend.

When things are not right in my body, it is first my breathing which shifts a gear. Sometimes there is an obvious alteration I can make which will lend some relief, and other times I am just aware that my kilter has been skewed. I have learned to pay close attention to the subtlest of nuances, to heed its quiet suggestions. There is language in that vibration as well as a message in an interruption. But there, winter 2004, things were simply not right.

My desire to sleep was an obvious shift in temperament. Sleep to me was the ultimate luxury. There was an art surrounding the entire activity, from the fabric on my body, to the loft of the comforter, to the give of the perfect pillow, even down to the wattage of the bedside lamp. Certain books needed to be handy. A couple of lotions, a notepad, a candle…almost nothing could compete. And the top prop, then and there, in that sole desire that I could privately celebrate, was the fucking door. "Close it," I barked, "I am tired."

But I wasn't tired. It was just the spot where I wanted to be. Nothing could descend on me that couldn't be better tolerated while I was in bed. I had the phone for matters that needed tending to, and for people that needed talking to, but that bar could be lowered at my own discretion. I recognized my required demands as needs surrounding the kids, and I would scrutinize all other superfluous obligations. I thought I could just sleep it off.

Fortunately, real estate had always been a steady for me, long before husbands, kids, or mortgages. I was grateful for that isolated compartment I could crawl into, operate with seamless proficiency, executing business absent the encumbered, emotional baggage that was weighing so heavy outside of that box. I had yet to confront a challenge related to my profession other than my shifting interest level in it, which added a new set of fears to the others I was gathering.

I began to take notice that my focus, when working with a client, was far more geared to their emotional psyche than usual. I might ask a different set of questions, listen to an answer with a different ear. Whenever a client would get off topic on some matter unrelated to the business between us, I normally would have immediately channeled it back on base. Not then. I listened. While this may seem like a lesson in compassion, it surely was not. It was a disaster lesson for sales. Still, on net, work was a necessary evil, and I would get the job done when I set out to do it. Sometimes just barely.

School was a whole different story. It was a daily burden to manage the book bags, the hands-on homework requiring that I locate some scissors, glue, and mustered enthusiasm, the tests to ready for, the snacks to fix, the papers to file. That one hour in the morning between wake-up and yellow bus was escalating to a chaos that I could marginally tolerate. Readying outfits and book bags and teeth and hair and breakfast, I felt like an angry zombie with four little masters making demands that I would scurry to meet.

Hired help without the hire. I felt like a walking free-for-all. The way in which one of them might engage me in dialogue through my closed bathroom door, or how my purse might get rifled through for something they needed, or the inane irritation of hearing a kid slurp the milk from an otherwise innocent cereal spoon—I was sprouting new pet peeves that could send me into a histrionic hormonal abyss. I summoned all I had to get through the disorder when it hit a fever pitch, knowing that I would find a valley soon enough. The still of silence served as my holy sedative, and it was a damn blessing that the fix wasn't for sale on any street corner.

The kids were not accustomed to my short temper. If ever I would bark something their way in an attempt to get them to do something, they might look at me as though I had whipped their bottom with a belt and a smile. I grew increasingly less tolerant of messes, and increasingly more resentful of the charge on my plate. Quiet moments, absent a television, bouncing ball, or sibling argument over who sat in the middle seat, I could not get enough of. I knew I couldn't afford to crumble, so I exercised every ounce of self-restraint to just move the muscles, get it done, and live by my mantra, *This too shall pass.*

My mother was the President of the Intervention Club. Each of the other members, all friends of mine and great women and men who stepped in when it seemed that I was stepping out, played an integral role in reminding me that I, indeed, did matter. A strange suggestion, one which should not need the tele-prompter. They would reach me, often in different ways, likely unaware of the efforts of the others. While I knew my mother supported my need to be at the seat of more prudent financial matters, and supported the efforts put forth on behalf of the kids, she was indignant with hatred, frothing with anger at the lack of support I was getting from Alex. She saw me scurrying to ready his shiny new condo, saw me disappear into the fantasy of my 4-day marriage, saw me disinterested in going out on dates. She also saw me struggling without getting adequate financial support that formal papers would have obliged. When she gets heavy on me, I go under covers.

My friends, as well, became increasingly curious as to why I would tolerate such scraps. There were no obvious answers, I just felt like I was paying the piper for past decisions. I could plod through each day, absent a passion, trained like a compliant scout. Who the hell was happy, anyway? This is a Prozac Nation we live in.

I knew I needed to stay steady in my social life. Thursday nights became my release, with the hissing relief of a pressure valve, for fun and drinks and desperate validation when I was flirted with. It felt excellent to be examined with an eye of interest. I began receiving that eye with a softened capacity to invite it. I tried on an integration of sex appeal and intellectual appeal when I was roped into dialogue with someone interesting, testing and pushing boundaries all the while. One Thursday night, riding high on the heels of two Cosmos, I slithered into a stall in the women's bathroom and got felt up by a slightly creepy guy named Joe just because it seemed so perfectly naughty. No last names or phone numbers exchanged, just monkey business. I suppose I created secret compartments for those pocket validations, just as men created them for their isolated diversions, hidden and protected from the field of their spouse. But I wear guilt like a bad dream; I just can't shake it.

When Alex would ask where I was, who I was with, casting condemning judgment on his notion of my behavior, I would cower behind the defense that there was nothing inappropriate in my actions. Sometimes I would lie about having been out with a girlfriend at a bar just to avert the ensuing argument. I owned the fallacy that as long as my clothes were on, no boundaries were crossed, and he could go fuck himself for these chains that I felt like I was wearing. I was chastised in a monogamous marriage with a man who wasn't even sleeping with me. This psychosis, I began to recognize, was more than a little disturbed.

My convenient defense was that he was still visiting me. It was two years since our return, and every season I would give back something without evaluating what was actually left. It was easier to disregard the sorely obvious truth that he had children here and would have visited anyway. My disturbed perception allowed me to accept the meager offerings as proof that I had not failed, and yet the wet blanket of my guilt for leaving negated my voice to demand more of what I needed. The ring on my finger, the noose on my neck, they felt one and the same. However, pressure and force might slide off that ring. Under that noose, there was no such wiggle room. It was my own personal purgatory.

Even with the sobriety of a life-threatening illness to awaken his love that was maybe just napping, I couldn't read the crop signs, no matter how obvious were the icons. It was an emotional and psychological holding pattern, absent an inalienable conviction on what I was even holding onto. The adage regarding why buy the cow when the milk is for free, more rightfully felt as though I was the cow and I was buying my own milk.

I could have filled my dance card, eight nights a week, with support groups in church basements offering a smorgasbord of possibility to whet my dysfunction. Welcome back to The Misfit Picnic.

Monday .... Single mothers run ragged
Tuesday .... Almost-twice divorced losers under age 40
Wednesday ..... Breast cancer survivors of today
Thursday ...... Alcoholics Anonymous of tomorrow
Friday .... Sexually hyper-frustrated monogamists
Saturday .... Figuring out what you really want (step I)
　　　　　　　　　Fear of getting what you really want (step II)
Sunday .... Battered wives who don't get hit
Anyday .... Can't seem to sleep enough

Rock-bottom hits hard. It seems there is always a last straw. For me, it was the feeling that I was playing with fire in allowing my kids to bear witness to what was acceptable in the expectation of marriage, both for my sons on how to treat women, and for my daughters on how they should expect to be treated. The consequence of my contributing to their perceptions of what should be sanctified within that holy union was burdening me with a guilt I couldn't bear, one which was steadily gaining ground on my guilt for leaving. Feeling emotionally and spiritually battered I could handle, but passing on that baton I could not.

This depression had no pharmaceutical antidote, nor would I have elected to merely bomb it into sedation. Medication might have served to perpetuate the reality of the mess of my life, one which I personally built with such calculating, deliberate precision. Rather, I needed solutions that offered promise to invoke real change.

Taking an honest inventory of the mess of one's life is perhaps the hardest thing one can ever do. It demands looking for answers that invite examination of beliefs we have owned so long that it is difficult to discern what is real and what we would like to be real. There comes a point, for those that enlist, where enough is enough. We can continue to recycle problems originating from the same root issue, rearing itself as a different animal, different day. Or not.

Then there is one day. For some reason, it becomes easier to stare in the face of the enemy and confront the veiled threat so dark but for its mystery. We stoically crawl into the deepest well in the core of our being. We resonate in the reality of what we are looking at. We challenge truths in a duel of discovery with no bias for convenient perception. We stand naked in the mirror, we study the warrior. Without defensive armor, we invite scrutiny and entice an appraisal. Through this journey, we ripen ourselves to embrace some truths that offer our freedom as reward for the confrontation.

Confronting Narcissus

I wrestled with where the hell to go with what was feeling obvious to me. I denied that I could ever put such a feat into motion and argued the dozens of reasons against such a journey. At first, it was easy to disregard as a fantastical solution in the great distance of my brain, but in its steady approach toward the crux of my quandary it became impossible to ignore.

I was a step child of my own world. Half-married, half-Jewish, half-employed, and half-battered, I was all of nothing. This was a time when I could least afford to take on new risk, yet it was a risk I could not afford to ignore. I needed to step out of my life, bear down to the nexus of profound simplicity, and reset my compass. I needed to return to Mexico for several months, with my children, in an effort to recover the hollow of my soul and restore it with some essential elements that had somehow been derailed.

Carving out such a window of time seemed almost impossible given the constraints on five busy lives. It did not seem that a brief vacation could own the possibility of inviting the awakening I was seeking. There needed to be a complete cultural integration into their esoteric customs if ever I was going to slow my speed enough to hop that train but not to miss it.

It only occurred to me, in my default defense on why this could not be structured, that in the course of my working life, I had never really taken any time off. I never elected to take a maternity leave after each of the kids was born. I was back to work as soon as I could walk without discomfort obvious to my clients. Most people stood a little more still during cancer confrontations and subsequent therapies, but I kept moving forward. It seemed that if I could string together all of these neglected time-outs that maybe I could rationalize this four-month breather as being due to me.

First step was funding it. Daniela applauded this decision and was eager to help orchestrate whatever was needed. While she did have a guest house on her property, lavishly appointed, I was not suspecting that this was the best road to the immersion this journey demanded. She offered to look out for a modest, furnished property in the heart of the village of Tepoztlan, walkable and bikeable to town, schools, markets, culture. Rentals were not scarce.

By stroke of good fortune which cheered for fate, there were some relocating clients in my office who were looking for a house rental while their new home was under construction. They would be arriving in July, needing housing until November, and were happy to pay twice my mortgage payment not to have to stay in a hotel.

Next step was orchestrating how to handle kids, schools, doctors, and the kids' fathers. Sam and Sophie were entering 3rd and 1st grades, certainly a curriculum I could handle for two months of home schooling. It was the best two months to be absent for, given the refresher work that usually began a school year. Leah was entering high school, not as easy a fit. She was never particularly tied to core friends or sports or malls that would have rendered her lifeless; rather I knew that the life she would be learning would be a very complimentary fit to the pulse of her. Last was Peter. He was entering his junior year, certainly not an academic year to miss a stroke of. That spring he was elected President of his Junior class, he was very entrenched in baseball, and his friends were an integral part of his balance. Peter shouldn't go.

Peter and Leah's dad is a great friend. I respect him immeasurably for his role as their father, and as well for the relationship we have shared, given some of the divided interests often paved by way of divorce. Peter had just gotten his driver's license and could live with Harry and his wife for our four-month absence. My car would be free, so the burdens of Peter's very crowded schedule would not have rested too heavily on them. They hadn't lived together since Peter was 3, and perhaps they could each take something valuable from that. I was sure that not seeing Leah for this period of time would be difficult on Harry, but in my appeal to peddle this program I assured him that she would take something with her that she would own the rest of her good long life. He had rarely stood in judgment of decisions that had been made on behalf of the kids, and he trusted that I was sincere about what I was conveying. Trust is the most valuable reciprocal asset one could ever own, and its dividends are priceless.

Dealing with Sam and Sophie's dad was not such an easy matter. Without question, Alex hated Buffalo, hated the burden of his visits here and the ghosts of his yesterday. The weather, the clouds, the depressed economy, all were enough to render him miserable for these trips. He wore them like they were a personal conspiracy against him. Though visits were shortening, they were still happening every month for a few days. But I knew him. He owned those days, and I was sure he would seek some twisted form of emotional compensation for having to surrender them.

I offered that he was welcome to join us, knowing that he would rather count rice in China than invite any form of spiritual awakening on a mountain in Mexico. I assured him that it was safe, that the kids would be under my constant supervision, and that there were many things for them to learn. He was never one to approach schooling with rigid respect, and still I added that I could cover the first two months of their school year. Last ditch effort, it was just a plane ride in a different direction, same distance, no need to pack a sweater.

He agreed that it would be okay. He was consumed with the transition into his resurrected company, with new partners, new administration, new egos to size up. While there would not be phone service that didn't cost a small fortune, we could e-mail whenever. I agreed to bring my satellite remote camera that connected each of our computers so that he could videoconference with the kids if he liked. I had that gripping hole in my gut when I got his approval.

School was my last area of concern. I approached the administration of their schools and shared with them my proposal. I offered to meet with each of their next-year teachers at the end of the school year to get a command of their curriculum, and gave my full commitment to meeting that charge. They didn't like it. I explained the difficulty I had had as a single-parent tending to demands that were overwhelming, that my friend had this short-term job opportunity that was hard to pass on given my present situation. Not much more interest. I explained that I had just finished processing my confrontation with cancer and its grueling chemotherapy regimens and needed this time to cleanse the whole of me. That interested them. I arranged to get each of their agendas by mid-June with the heartfelt reverence from one key administrator who helped me put it in motion. She had recently buried her mother, who fell victim to the same disease, but had not buried her faith in abetting small measures toward tall intentions.

Money would be tight. The rental I would get from my house would cover my mortgage as well as that of the the modest house that Daniela had located for July 1st, still leaving a few hundred dollars a month to spare. I had about thirteen thousand dollars in my life savings, which was a cushion smaller than I had ever known, but it was what it was.

My brother agreed to oversee mail, collect rent, pay the mortgage, and keep current some irritating revolving accounts. I left him with two thousand dollars to that end. Plane tickets cost sixteen hundred dollars. I withdrew four thousand dollars from my account, and mentally enjoyed converting it to Pesos. This left me with just over five thousand dollars to return to, a margin I had never known so narrow in all of my working years. On paper, this all looked very stupid.

Kids have an unwavering sense of adventure. Their enthusiasm and excitement was easier for me to grab hold of, riding shotgun, as though they were piloting this road to my recovery. I would breathe myself through any rushes of self-doubt regarding the stability of my faculties, which would come in waves, usually following an increasingly dependable argument with Alex. Our plan was to leave early July, having finished the school year and readied all final details.

There was clothing to pack, but not much other than that. I had utter relief that there was no burden to box a thing in the house. I removed many personal effects, emptied my closet, the refrigerator, and had the house professionally cleaned. Negligible effort next to what I was used to.

Goodbyes were in order to all those who had shown up for me in the biggest of ways. It is a shared edge that sustains the genius and the lunatic; often they share a final dance on the path toward their ultimate destiny. I imagine people were hedging bets on which side of that fence I might fall. To my surprise, that concerned me none.

My father called. It was a curious call, one which I did not see coming. I loved my dad, I had just never depended on him for very much from my adolescent life forward. Not for the reason that support wasn't present, but when it wasn't formally in my face I must have perceived that it was not there. We had maintained as meaningful a relationship as our twice-annual visits allowed for. He said he wanted to catch up, face-to-face, before his annual pilgrimage from Naples to Cape Cod. June would be fine, I agreed, and we carved out two days to visit with no other diversions on board. Except, of course, for my readying myself and the kids to depart the country in two weeks, for four months of something I couldn't quite find the language to explain.

He arrived unsure of the daughter he might find. He had almost never challenged me on the judgment calls I had made throughout my life. In the last few crazy years he was more present than ever, listening and supporting and rooting for the home team, albeit a background voice in the distant bleachers. It seemed as though he needed some tangible validation that I was still present and accounted for, as though roll call was his business and I was his onus. I was tenuous in sharing the full scope and breadth of the crisis that weighed so dark and heavy, it being so female and fragile and inconsistent with the pillar of strength he had always assumed was me.

Fearful of the ground to cover in bringing him up to speed, I eased into those waters, testing what he was willing to let in. He received the invitation into this foreign territory that he and I never did wade. I shared greater detail on my trials with Alex, on the color of Kool-Aid, on how Sophie's distance crushed me, on the big fat margin by which Peter was elected president of his class. I inserted some real-time engagement not possible via phone. We hung there, waiting. We skirted and skimmed and surpassed the dialogue that ought to have been spoken. Possibilities of relief were suspended everywhere, like lifelines I had not realized were missing. No lines were seized. I had this strange visual of moats retracting, summoned in rapid succession to insulate the island of me. That visual came with no effort whatsoever; it was frighteningly familiar.

Anger, rejection, guilt, the three flushed through me as strange impostors whose assault I could not rightfully assign. Free radicals whose mission remained a mystery. He was kind and sweet, my dad, yet this distance was never bridged for reasons that totally evaded me. I softened some; it seemed by default to be the only demeanor at my disposal, and I tried it on. It fit poorly, but there was nothing else to grab hold of, so I stood still with it. I just let it be.

Saying goodbye to Peter was bittersweet. He was my twin son, and I knew that he knew I should be doing this. He loaded my iPod with two hundred seasoned favorites, even loaded some new music he thought I might wake up to. We had always shared a knowing that rarely got challenged, a remarkable feat given the opposition teens were famous for. Aiding the cause, it didn't hurt that he would have my car at his disposal, the vessel of freedom for any sixteen-year old. We both saw some liberation on the horizon.

With surprisingly few things to nail down before leaving the country in the name of adventure and discovery, we were off. We left on Sunday, July 4th, which was the most spirited gesture of patriotism I had expressed in years.

At 35,000 feet, many insights crossed my mind that were apparently not available to me at lesser altitudes. As I was watching the ordinary airplane antics around me, noting the token crying baby, random pestilent passenger, and distant pressurized lavatory sounds, I stood still on the sight of my three kids in their private row of seats next to my lone seat across the aisle. Sam was befriending the older man in front of him, in hopes of getting his peanuts, which he had not immediately consumed. Leah was gracefully paging her "W" magazine, admiring the world of fashion with the same keen eye that will one day land her a high-ranking job in that industry.

Then Sophie. While she had crayons and paper and other tray top diversions to keep her occupied, I looked into her face, beyond the topography of her surface features, and saw how unhappy this little girl really was. She was six. What could have weighed so heavy on her heart that alienated her from the world she lived in? Why did laughter and levity bypass her spirit? Her passive anger emanated, even when she was merely talking, not upset about anything in particular. I considered how long it had really been this way, and with great grief I could see that it had been longer than I was proud of. I considered something that had not occurred to me before. She was two when my world turned upside down. Do the math. The haul had been long. No wonder she didn't smile much.

My resemblance to being a mother was feeling vague, surreal. I felt as though I were not almost turning forty. Maybe I was six and eight and thirteen and sixteen, operating with the fragmented wisdom in each of those ages rather than their sum total, which, when tallied, just narrowly surpassed that of my own. Gladly, I didn't hang there too long.

I reached over to Sophie and admired the clown she was coloring freehand. Clowns were her favorite character to color, a curious choice indeed. I told her I especially liked the emphatically happy smile he had on his face. She acknowledged that she heard me with a subtle nod, then returned to her artwork, almost covering his entire smile as she repositioned her forearm. This journey was none too soon.

The flight had only one change of planes and a negligible layover. We walked the retail scene on the concourse, which resembled more of a mall than an airport. The kids fueled up with some random overpriced, overpackaged activities, exhibiting abbreviated attention spans from one possible purchase to the next. I enjoyed thinking that this would be their last retail moment for a while, and that they would be required to shift their notion of play to a much different gear. I decided not to drive home this point with them. Instead, I threw thirty-four dollars at the excitement of being out of this groove for a welcome hiatus.

Daniela was at the airport with her son, André, and her youngest daughter, Anna. Anna was four, and spoke only Spanish. She was a proud little girl, and an interesting cross between both of her parents. She carried a confidence and security that she had inherited from her mother, both genetically and environmentally. Her hair was a deep chestnut, dark like her father's, with skin that tanned easily. Her eyes were a very stunning blue, radiant and peaceful, but not very native. The smile needed no language at all; it was that of a very happy little girl at the side of her mother.

André was seven. His hair was dark blond, in a wild mane of curls much like Sam's. His eyes were dark brown, with skin that was lighter than Anna's. André spoke fluent English and Spanish, and I understand he had bilingual dreams. He had a native look about him, but not to Mexico or the U.S. He looked like Tarzan. When we were all greeting each other in a big circle of hugs, Sophie whispered to me that André looked like the son of George of the Jungle. This softened her some, as that was one of her favorite movies.

The kids had never been in such mountainous topography, nor had they ever really left the insulated environments in the Hyatts of their travels. There was a comforting quiet in the drive to Tepoztlan. I was grateful that the kids seemed to assert a sense of presence regarding the scope of the journey that lay ahead. Sophie was seated next to Anna. Surprisingly, she was trying to capture her interests by showing her some random things from her travel backpack. She would offer a token something and Anna would hold it curiously, unsure of how to engage it, as though toys carried their own cultural cues. Sophie would then take it back, hoping to entice her more with something else. I did notice that the energy in the take-back was slightly kinder than the gestures I had seen her use before. Sam and André seemed to be making fast friends. There was only a year between them, and they were boys. Boys were born far less complicated creatures than were girls. There were no interviews.

Daniela had prepared a gorgeous feast for dinner. She created a salmon dish using herbs and citrus and soy that was incredible. Most meals are accompanied by an unusual rice dish, which was other than the rice I was familiar with. The kids pushed the food around their plates, wary to put past their lips something so unqualified as new food. But they were well-behaved. They were funny and quirky and still reeling with enthusiasm for the four-month summer vacation ahead. All of the kids got lost after the meal, off to size up the territory and the toys.

We kept peace at the table, enjoyed the quiet of the departed kids, and the balance of the two bottles of red wine. Allen had just purchased a massive, commercial pizza oven from a distressed business and was planning on making fresh bread for several of the stores in town. He had purchased all of the bowls, ingredients, and tools, setting up shop out on their rear terrace. It was a makeshift open-air kitchen covered by roofing, supported by pillars, and was thus protected from most of the elements. The niche he was bringing to his particular bread was live yeast.

There were very exacting measures of the temperature in the mixing and kneading of the dough that were necessary to insure that the yeast remained live. He had a tremendous respect for the value in consumption of live ingredients, believing that the life source was strengthened and supported accordingly. Live foods would include sprouts, wine, yeast, and other staples I was not familiar with. We sampled some of the bread he had made, and I was half-expecting it to be moving. It was not, but it was heavy and hearty, and not fit for a good bologna and cheese sandwich.

Leah stood in a state of sheer astonishment, speechless at the sight of Daniela's studio. There was an unusual illumination of the stones and the silver and the fabrics, cast by the the warmth of the sunlight as it bows come sunset. She admired the order, the semblance, the inspiration that flooded the full volume of the room. Daniela showed her some of the mechanics of what she did, how the gems on the rough hemp evolved into the unique expressions of finished art. They whimsically tried on a few scarves, wrapping the long necklaces in their signature fashion, like runway goddesses. They played for an hour in their fashion venue while Allen and I left for a walk.

Allen was a perennial student. It seemed as though there was not a window of time in his life where he was not engaged in the greater understanding of something. The particular interests had no obvious connection to each other, other than his curiosity about them. Some offered mastery in months, others he imagined might take several decades to fully command, if ever at all. His present passion was in the study of Polarity, an ancient healing art.

He had studied beneath a world-renowned Polarity Master for four years, and had achieved different levels of accomplishment within his study. His particular master was a man, almost sixty, who had spent nearly all his life studying and teaching and learning. He was a citizen of the world, spoke all over the globe, and was often in the States at conferences supported by far more mainstreamed, matriculated topics hosted by the American Medical Association, or similar boards of more universally accepted credibility. One feather in his cap happened to be a formal degree in medicine, but it was lost among the many. Allen said he was fortunate to be the apprentice of such a spiritual international leader, and that he was hopeful to be able to practice this healing discipline, officially, within a year or two. He shared with me that Ricardo, his master, had his home base in Tepoztlan, and he suggested that I meet him.

In a very crowded nutshell, Polarity supports the integration of the five physical elements of the universe into a particular manifestation within the body and mind. There is a condensing of each of these elements as they move from their universal presence into a physical being. Each of these five elements desires to achieve an integrated balance between them.

Air applies to the emotional and mental component, giving life throughout our circulatory system in the form of vapors. Water, present as two thirds of our body's mass, as well as two thirds of the earth's surface, is a common current that all humans share, and represents the changing fluidity in life, like the river of blood through veins. Earth represents the solid tissues within us, namely bones, teeth, organs, all grounded and rooted like the trees and dirt and rock. Fire represents the ignition of motive to forcefully propel heat and passion forward, certainly possessing a component of danger, but essential in its demand to maintain body temperature necessary to sustain life. Ether, considered space, involves magnetic and gravitational force, keeping in place the proper functioning of all the other elements, much like the earth stays put in its happy axis.

Should earth exist in abundance without adequate fire, or water, then this balance has been disturbed. Polarity supports this imbalance as being core to the root of illness or mental decline. There are infinite possibilities for disruption. Living a human life, with all of the inherent suffering as part of the journey, is destined for challenge when poised for triumph. The very spiritually elevated among us can discern disruption before threats become too grave. Threats may not present merely as life-threatening disease, but also as the dull, obtuse pain of living an unsung life.

Perhaps this sounds heavy, implausible even. Accordingly, if one were inclined to disregard any merit held in its philosophy, to write it off as hocus-pocus, then surely one would find no harm in having a session performed at the hands of an internationally recognized master. I might doubt that such a person hasn't wasted ninety minutes or ninety dollars on more frivolous concerns. Without a stitch of hesitation, I told Allen I would be grateful to have a session with Ricardo. He would be returning from India the following month, and we confirmed our intentions to invite some of the drama at the hands of the guru himself.

The kids and I spent the first night at Daniela's house. The house in the village would be available in the morning, at which time I was planning to meet with the owner and go over what was necessary. I wanted to go alone for this survey, in the event that affairs needed to be readied in a fashion other than how they were delivered. I anticipated needing some provisions in town, such as snacks found in familiar packaging and toiletries bearing cartoon characters. Perhaps, I thought, I would also need to situate sleeping arrangements in a fashion other than a straight line.

In the morning, I went to the rental property and met the daughter of the owners; she may have been twenty years old. She was very pleasant and beautiful, carrying a native air of tranquility in her fluid movements, her supple gestures. Her English was excellent. Daniela learned that the family often rented to people from the States seeking brief refuge, and I felt comfort in feeling that there were others before me. Her parents were busy, so she had stepped up in their absence.

She showed me the home, pointing out the kitchen, living, and sleeping areas, again all part of the same four unobstructed walls. There was indoor plumbing, and the bathroom was a separately dedicated room with a door, hot water, and now some very pink Barbie shampoo that looked, with strange alarm, far too much like the chemo Kool-Aid. The key she offered me was a comically exaggerated, metal-toothed rusty thing that could fit in no pocket, and seemed totally incapable of turning any tumbler. There were no leases to sign or credit reports to run. The referral from Daniela provided ample legitimacy. I gave her the Pesos she needed. She smiled, and left me with a piece of paper with very loose directions to the foot path to their home if we found any troubles.

No phone. Scant electric. No high-speed internet. No PlayStation. No dishwasher. Clothes got washed in the creek down the road. Clothes got dried by the sun in the sky. Should it get cold, there was wood. Should it get warm, there was wind, ergo the window. The stove was fueled with propane, and the ice box was filled with actual ice. That, of course, meant I would need to stay on top of that program.

The house was a wood and mud shanty, nicely maintained, and similar to the house in the neighborhood of Aricelli. It was not far from the downtown village, very walkable, even for the lazy. There were eight other huts in this little area. I walked into town to buy a few staples, 48 bottles of water, and my first supply of ice. I resigned to find a wagon before the day was up.

The afternoon was mine to ready our space. I arranged a few personal effects that the kids brought and dispersed them around the room. I created a small workspace for papers, records, my laptop, which was good for everything except for an internet connection and, accordingly, the streamlined video camera I had promised Alex we would regularly connect on. I knew there would be a decompression period for all of us. High-speed was my life line. PlayStation was Sam's. Daddy was Sophie's. And Leah had artfully perfected the state of negating any attachments, rendering her open and accessible, always. She brought nothing but her clothes.

As I arranged necessities in the bathroom, a sobering awareness crashed onto me hard. That outlet and my hair dryer were not compatible. Not only were they not going to be friends, but there wasn't an adapter to be found that could have accommodated the appliance, given the marginal electric supply to the house and the location of the one outlet. While I might not appear to be a high-maintenance woman to the onlooker, I must confess that I had a sick commitment to having perfect hair. I have mastered my talent with a round wooden brush, two of them, and my hairdryer. I have yet to meet a hairdresser that can improve the poker straight fullness that I can achieve myself. It's almost like masturbation.

If my hair dried naturally, it was just awful. Not quite straight, not quite naturally wavy, just limp and lifeless and absent a stitch of style. I wore my hair at a medium length, thus demanding maximum maintenance to get it right. It was not quite long enough to craft into a seductive braid or ponytail, nor was it short enough to shake out. And here I was, rainy season to boot, confronted with the management of my hair. I recognized these concerns didn't plague any of the far more humble people on this mountain. I knew I could get to Daniela's once in a while for a good blow-dry, but that it would be neither convenient nor routine.

I had one choice. It was time. This was one attachment that I needed to be free from, for reasons perhaps beyond my daily coifing ritual. I declared I could let my hair go, set it free, and see how it fit. With considerable determination, I visited the one barber in town. While he wasn't exactly instructed to shave my head, I shared my desire to have my hair as short as possible, but retaining enough hair so that it didn't stand straight up. I used the marginal distance made between my thumb and forefinger as a gauge, not trusting a Spanish syllable that crossed my lips. And my hair was gone.

I stood in the frame of the mirror, purposefully consuming nearly all of its reflection. I stood expressionless, as though the reflection might have offered a rebuttal to my crass violation. Nothing. Three minutes. Nothing. In realizing that I had not had this little hair since the day I was born, it all seemed very fitting that I should have so little today. I smiled; I looked like a boy of five without a concern for who in the Mexican barber shop was watching this strange woman please herself so very much in the presence of her reflection.

The barber had bad teeth, I had pretty bad hair, and the weather outdoors brought some very bad, torrential rains. There was a photograph above the check-out area of the shop, which was at least fifty years old, I guessed, judging from the texture and fray of its edges. There were three generations of men, humbly dressed in white buttoned shirts, arms crossed over their chests, proudly standing post at this very storefront. I admired their stoic stance, and the barber pointed to himself as a seven-year old boy with heritage a mile high. I paid my sixty Pesos, said *adios*, and walked through the village in a downpour that bothered my hair none. I shook it out like a dog, laughing at nothing, laughing at everything.

The kids returned from Daniela's just before dinner. My hair was hysterical to Sam. He thought it was the funniest thing I had ever done in my life. He sought a high five, and I gave him a big one that included a jump in the air. Leah was reserved; my haircut appeared to be the very last thing she might have ever expected. She appreciated my desire for liberation from my trusty appliance, but wasn't sure why I couldn't have captured a little bit of style by the same measure. I assured her that my hair would grow healthier and stronger and absent a single split end. Sophie assured me I looked perfectly stupid, but kindly told me that I looked better when I was stupid. *That* was an absolute compliment.

The kids spent an hour getting acquainted with the house, perusing their drawers, clothing, and bathroom. Sam went outdoors to find three boys playing games with polished stones. Sam had never been shy, but he wasn't sure how to approach them given the tall barrier of language. He and I walked outside and together we approached the little pack. I attempted to use all forty of the Spanish words I knew to say hello and see if Sam could join their play. At their polite amusement, hearing this grown-up, very short-haired lady stutter with this lame plea, they welcomed Sam, affirming the action by nods and a singular grunt, much like a roving pack of cubs. Children shared a universal language needing very few words. Perhaps as with many of our familiar attachments, the longer we owned them, the more they grew to own us.

The first few weeks we spent learning the lay of the land, appreciating summer in its casual spontaneity. There was much going on about town, and always there was an event that appeared to include the whole of the village. Daniela extended an invitation for us to attend the wedding of two of the young hearts who were marrying. They were in their early twenties, and Daniela knew the mother of the bride peripherally from her yoga group. It was a crime of nature to freeload a wedding where I came from, thus the thought of the crash was a violation to the decorum carved into my psyche. Daniela told me to get over it fast, that the entire town was invited when there was a marriage.

We all met at our house, with the intention of walking to the wedding. The ceremony and reception were held at one of the central village parks. Nearly all two hundred guests came on foot and gathered beneath a heavy canopy of trees, which covered much of the meadow where the service was being officiated. There was light rain that afternoon, yet this shrouded enclave, under a verdant parasol of mingling foliage, curiously remained protected from moisture while permitting sprays of sunlight and shadow to dance on the faces of the congregation.

People were dressed with no particular regard for their attire. They arrived in whatever they seemed to be wearing at the particular hour that the wedding had called their attention. Laborers came directly from work. Some women chose to wear elaborate, embroidered gowns of vibrant colors, while some were comfortable in simple peasant garb. Several children were dressed in smart, neatly tailored clothing, while others wore their play clothes.

The ceremony was officiated by a Roman Catholic priest, and interestingly, I could understand some of the service since it was held in Latin. Still sketchy on the details, I understood that God came down and blessed these two lovers for their shot at happily-ever-after. My money was on these two as compared to the last wedding I had attended, hosted at a country club with copious gossip surrounding an affair that the groom had just exited in time for his nuptials. Then I wondered if divorce still struck one in two on this particular mountain. Beyond the errata fleeting through my brain on that lovely afternoon, a chorus of children offered their pure, innocent vocal blessings, and there was a woman, big and bold in her late fifties, who sang solo the most eloquent and dramatic rendition of Amazing Grace I had ever heard. Then and there, standing still with her and her passion, I did hear the fat lady sing.

The reception area accommodated almost twenty long, simple tables, veiled with thin white linen. The tables were scattered around the grounds, positioned with regard for the massive trees and awkward roots crowding the lawns. Two-liter soda bottles were dispersed among the tables, along with an oversized plastic jug of water. Nothing fancy, maximum utility. Sprays of wildflowers adorned every surface, displayed in simple glass jars not competing with the whimsical floral arrangements.

Central to the park was a social casino, roofed with clay tile, serving as an open air kitchen. There, massive cauldrons simmered, stirred with utensils fit for the Flintstones. Women were mostly tending to the kitchen affairs, while the men were managing the rows of meat being cooked over an open fire. There were abundant paper goods at one end of the cantina and jugs of wine in burlap at the other. Between the posts, a feast was on display, a smorgasbord of preparations boasting fruits, beans, salads, salsas, and rice casseroles a plenty, all assembled potluck style by these cantina women.

One of the most unusual gestures of gratuity I had seen in my lifetime was the giving of the wedding gift to the bride and groom. This ritual was tradition, I was told, and speaks to the integrity of a village as it married its young. People greeted the newly married couple, similar to the procedure of a receiving line, carrying their gifts if they chose to present any, which was not a necessity. They shared their best wishes with the bride and groom, extended the wrapped gift as a token of their gratitude, then joined the reception.

The remarkable virtue in the ritual was that one did not include a card indicating from whom the gift came. As a collection, the gifts were all from everyone, a collective *adieu* as the couple began a life together. The gifts were not acquired with regard to the reciprocal attentions that the gift-giver might have been seeking, nor did they include private rivalry agendas, both of which were famous possibilities at the weddings I usually attended, as well as the gifts I usually bought. Simply, they were what they were, gifts to wish well to two people who loved each other.

Six groups of Mariachi musicians strolled through the crowded assembly, fully adorned in their ornamented Charro suit regalia. They approached tables, gathered crowds, sitting lovers. Little girls would rush to the feet of one of the musicians, take a brief curtsy, then enter a dance, which must have been a native custom judging by the way the others would flock into a circle as she shared her personal offering.

Sophie stood in the periphery of the formal circle, mimicking the rhythm with quiet hand gestures set to the beat of the music. It was engaging all of her. One of the young dancing girls was but four years old, with the confidence of forty years, and the soul of four hundred as she ushered her dance through to its climax. There was a wise and spirited grandmother among the crowd; she must have been watching Sophie admire the girl's talent by way of her tenuous hand gestures. "Hola," she said, smiling into the heart of my little girl. "Hola," said Sophie, respect-fully. With a coy and confident sidestep, the old woman swept Sophie into the center and showed her some very simple, emphatic steps, which they danced together. The crowd was crazy for this little American girl who was learning her own rhythm, and their bellows bolstered her focus on mastering the footwork of this native dance.

I watched Sophie. She was wearing a flowing cotton dress, embroi-dered with simple flowers of pinks and oranges that we had found at the Sunday bazaar. Her hair was the darkest of my kids, almost jet black, worn long and straight with no accessories ever. Her eyes were dark brown, wide-set, large like frying pans. We had been there almost a month, and her skin was deep and tan. She looked like a Native Ameri-can girl named Dancing Feet as she moved though the routine, finding her own steady step, cadence on cue, and inserting some personality to boot. I liked watching her very much. Her rhythm engaged me more than anything I had known in a dog's age, her age. When she finished her theatrical offering, having humbly accepted the ovation of the crowd's approval, she took a fabulous bow of rightful assent. Sophie then looked at me, into me, and found a place that she and I too rarely shared. It was her waking dance, and mine too. She rushed to my silent calling, into the circle of my longing arms. We hugged, I cried, as she held my heart cupped in her six-year-old hands, permitting us new territory to be explored from the vortex of that very moment.

I considered the chaos and congestion that surrounded the weddings in my repertoire, from shopping for the garment-rarely-to-be-worn-twice, to the excessive primping and the up-dos and the babysitters and the bold bridal registry. It was a feeling miles apart from the free-flowing inspiration present in that park, as the people heartily celebrated all that was genuine and divine and karmic in the magical integration of two lives.

It was September before I was able to meet with Ricardo. He was a man of many destinations, so fabulously elusive but for his lack of accountable presence. The afternoon of our meeting brought the storm of the season. People everywhere were buttoning down hatches, and I mean this literally. I took the kids to Daniela's house, feeling as though a more substantial house might have had lesser risk of floating downstream.

The rains were full and heavy, the skies unforgiving in their violent release. It was visual, audible, emotional, looming dark with the promise of a vicious collision between conflicting fronts. The gradient spectrum of grays found in that sky was without question the palette of the brilliant complexity found in the art of black and white. There was no reason to cancel my meeting with Ricardo on account of the weather; on the contrary, it felt as if the storm had been delivered on cue, supernaturally, as an enticement to invite the extraordinary and awaken the dormant.

His home was built of adobe. Its color and texture was the mosaic composite of ruddy earth and soil and clay, fired under solar directive. It rested high on a hill beyond all other houses, and the last two hundred feet were accessible only on foot. There was not a door to be found nor a key to unlock a single thing. His wife seemed to be in her mid-fifties. She was plump and happy and was stirring one fine tortilla soup when I arrived. She welcomed me with soft hospitality, then returned to her affairs in her open-air kitchen while her husband readied himself for our session.

I was observing the curious kitchen, which afforded no walls either. I wondered how the streaming rains were not finding their way into her space. It was illusionary. I pieced together a few words inquiring how this could be possible, and she directed my sight to the simple, mechanical eaves that raised and lowered as the climate demanded. Then she pointed to the candle lighting, to the solar energy panels on top of the roof (which I had completely missed in my approach) and to the fully composted gardening beds in the back. It was sustainable, low-impact living at its finest.

The reserved detail throughout the home could have placed it front and center on any page of *Architectural Digest*. It was breathtaking in its very refined and timeless simplicity. Toward the back of the home was the office of Ricardo, fully equipped with G5 Notebook, high-speed internet, and abundant bound resources. There was interesting furniture, maybe Asian, to enhance the contemplation of his reading materials.

The Polarity studio was wholly round. The floor was dirt, the walls were mud, and they climbed spherically where they met in the center. There were natural ribs along the ascension, which lended the feeling of being inside of the belly of the earth or the breast of a woman. A massage table stood in the center of the room, adorned as the sole token of furnishing inside of its boundary. I lay down on my back, clothed, hungry, ready.

For a man who spoke twelve languages, Ricardo was a reserved character of very few words. Though he may have been sixty, his body was fit like a twenty-year old's. He emanated peace, there was a palpable ease in the lucid light of his fine periphery. Merely as a voyeur to his self-content, I could tap a strange and radiant satisfaction. As he approached my body with a measured resignation, he welcomed me into the possibility that existed within his world. He walked full circle around my reclined body, slowly and with intent. Surveying his path, I mentally noted how remarkably this man moved within his own skin. His smile was easy, his heart was full. He began with my head.

The technical work included much of the handwork from my Reiki experience, though there were firm and isolated manipulations on many of my pressure points. I had never felt such shudders of sensitivity with even the suspicion of touch; it was emotionally very tantric. I breathed deeply when it peaked to an apex that seemed unbearable. The sensation was similar to the sensual shiver that precedes a sultry kiss in those nanoseconds before contact on longing lips. I could send that shiver across a room, up a spine, down through the tunnels of my hungry vacancy. That shiver and I were born together.

Curious if he might find a focus on my right breast, I lay tense and still in anticipation of his assessment. Gratefully, it offered him the same fluidity as the rest of my flesh. Then, without apology, he stopped and met my eyes with an insight. I awaited his words, hoping they would be offered in English. They came slowly.

Ricardo held his stance for several minutes, hands suspended directly above my female reproductive organs. I could feel his concerted effort to synthesize the congestion he was interpreting in the tender nucleus of my womanhood. He described the imbalance as a tangled web, encumbered by many closed circuits, having inadequate nourishment to sustain its ideal state of neutrality. He affected some physical manipulations, qualified by my understanding that they would provide only short-term relief.

He saw the war I had waged with myself. He asserted some energy toward elevating my awareness in meeting the very important charge of freeing myself from its grip. He also shared that sexual tensions were best relieved by sexual intercourse in its most banal expression, and that the resulting relief would serve me well beyond a fleeting climax. We are biology before we are brilliant, we are fearless children before we are fearful adults. It felt as though the conflict of my life, my successful assimilation in inviting the desired intimacies with a life partner, was having a battle of its own at the mercy of my very design.

Without prompt or suggestion, I lay still on my back, eyes closed, awaiting my share of something. I was flooded and flushed and breathless by the color blue. It was everywhere, suspended in a multidimensional landscape of the richest and deepest and darkest and lightest shades of blue, owning texture and scent and humidity. It encompassed the whole of my being, whirling with no respect for gravity. I told Ricardo of this intense vision. "Take it In. All of it," he offered, as though he knew it was coming, as if he had sent it for my consideration. And I breathed.

There were visible funnels of this powerful, brilliant blue that descended from my vision and entered my body through all of my air passages. These currents were tangible, swirling with temptations of all good things, choreographed by the draw of my breath. It took almost all of two minutes to vacate all of the color. After my final effort of ingestion, there was simply the void of black one expects to see when eyes are closed. It was intense and beyond my comprehension, and I was leaving with it.

When we said goodbye, he offered me some very unlikely words that struck me as most odd. He looked at me, held my eyes for a very long and pensive five seconds, then offered, "You are not your mother." Nothing he could have said would have caught my attention with a higher degree of curiosity. There was no discussion we shared even related to the topic of family, but that was his free advice for the afternoon. I left with that, too.

I thanked him, hugged him, and collected my respect for him. I was well aware that he did not want to fuck me. Perhaps if I went out into the world and fucked like a monkey let loose at a party, there might be unparalleled therapy in relieving my chastised soul of the chains of its boundary, he did not quite say. Perhaps intimacy and intercourse were not twin sisters. Perhaps they were barely related. He retreated to the civility in his office, and I went on my way.

I look far better clothed than I look naked. At 5'8," I had always been able to carry some excess weight on my frame, which so fortunately distributed itself with no bias for one particular area. Clothes, for me, had an illusionary effect. When I stood naked and examined my body, however, its curves and bumps and imperfections seemed magnified for the frank exposure. Men were far less self-conscious; I had yet to meet one who had any concern for how he looked in a bathing suit, let alone whether or not a particular pair of jeans cut his hips at that opportune angle.

It occurred to me what a very heavy burden vanity was, its weight being worn as baggage not calculated on any scale. Over recent years, I had bettered the respect that I showed to my body by way of diet and nourishment, but I fell short when it seemed I could slide under the bar on the count of the actual physical shape I was in. The tone of my muscle, the strength of my limbs, the endurance of my heart—all left very little to be impressed by, especially if this was the vehicle that would be escorting me through my next forty years. With no uncertainty, it was time to get in shape. No more bullshit.

I began by running. Actually, I began by thinking about running, which took an entire ten days to translate into an elevated pulse. The outdoors were a perfect fit. The steep terrain was most conducive to maximum benefit, cardiovascularly, muscularly, fiscally. Me and an open road, readying to meet the face of my maker.

I grabbed my iPod and my sneakers, no need for a scrunchie, and hit the dirt. In the mornings there was a casual gathering of neighborhood kids, supervised by mothers and grandmothers. They all mingled, camp-style, central to the homes. They asked no fee, but were willing to help me just the same. I left Daniela's phone number with them in case a problem arose and left my kids to learn some Spanish the hard way. I carved out about three hours for running, showering, shopping, and getting lost in the maze of myself.

I began by asking, Who the hell *am* I? I drive a fully loaded monster SUV fit to navigate backwoods terrain and I have never once been off road. My wristwatch is capable of intact precision at depths of three hundred feet and I am not a diver, nor am I ever on time. The cell phone I carry has fancy talents including realtime stats on things I couldn't care less about. As for our flat, wide-screen TV infused with far more channels than interest, check with Sam on how to activate its insanely capable functions; he is king of that domain. I have sat in its overwhelming presence, unable to make right the incorrect time flashing in the display box, dwarfed in the techno-talents of my 8-year-old. And at the foot of my FAX machine, I have impatiently awaited the transmission of twenty page contracts, wondering why the device didn't move at the rocket speed of email, still wondering how it even worked in the first place. I am Christmas, I am Hanukkah, and I am many miles and many moons away from the compass of any higher power.

I felt like a distant cousin to the year 2005, three times removed from myself. While I was absolutely sucked into the streamlined high efficiency it all afforded me, it seemed that these shortcuts had yielded the passive consequence of my numbing disengagement. I love what technology brings to me, I hate what technology takes from me. I cannot have it both ways.

When given unbridled room to roam, my brain usually visited the unconquered frontier of my mastery of men. The rhythm of my jog, however, began more as an elderly woman in smart shoes, affording little opportunity for any channeled focus. All energies were directed at an imploring plea to the Gods to make it another hundred feet, then another, and so on. Endurance does prevail; it's a remarkable thing. A body seems to recall where you last left it, and demands that you step it up a notch in return for the memory. Before long, the groove and I found each other, we made friends, and we had a forty-five minute date every morning in a measure to uncover the truths behind closed door number one: my obsession with men and me, and why I hadn't gotten it right.

I have profound respect for the complicated intricacies that wire most people, and have learned that genuine compatibility, regardless of gender, is no easy feat. People, as a model of acquisition, interest me very little. Too many variables, too little trust, too much energy to shape in a way that serves my end. We are blessed if we die with a dozen souls who knew us intimately. Those are some ugly returns if you're one to keep score on an investment.

Those elevated relationships, however, did ignite a passion for me that was the reigning triumph of my human experience. Those friendships owned a depth and an accessibility that ripened only with the passage of time. One could not truly engage, could not effectively align the intricate grooves of those dynamic gears, until one took genuine ownership of oneself. Absent this baseline ingredient, there were superfluous minutia, meaningless accumulation of bodies but for their eminent heat, hot breath, and consumption of time. I am mastering the art of friends, and I bow in humble gratitude for the dance we do share.

Beyond friends, however, there was that single appointment of one man who had become the object of my desire, a charge I had yet to meet with resounding success, if any at all. I feared that my attraction had been inspired by the mirage of all that I wished that I was but certainly was not. Perhaps I projected this phantom image in a competitive duel that I was fighting only with myself. It was destined for failure, as I had never assigned a victor other than myself. I had cowered in the fear that no one could assume the role of loving me as well as I could love myself. This was a huge piece of knowledge for me. And I kept running.

Leah spent her morning hours working in Daniela's studio. She and Aricelli assumed the tall task of creating the packaging for the finished pieces of jewelry. Presentation was Leah's forte. She rightfully appreciated the fine art of the first impression, ignoring no detail, including the quality of lettering on the address label. The girls communicated well. Leah's four years of academic Spanish gave her an initial footing, but once one was immersed in a culture with its quippy affectations, book knowledge ran dry.

They were very interesting to watch, these young women of different cultures, learning to temper hormonal surges that were neither invited nor understood. They learned their own voice as they readied themselves for a world that would not always be kind. They manipulated their octaves in a fine female art form when soliciting their needs, as they learned to keenly discern the subtlest of differences when electing which voice to carry where. There was so much that lay ahead of a young woman, inevitable pain and pleasure, and ensuing discovery. It was a journey whose lessons could not be forewarned with pitfalls conveniently marked. A destiny that took tremendous energies, many against the grain of convention, to align the core of one's desires with the God-given talents we were endowed with at birth.

We had a lot of downtime in the sanctuary of home. The rains would sometimes be heavy, so we would lie low within the four walls that encompassed our little world. Sam mastered some of the simple, preloaded computer games on my laptop, certainly nothing of the manic caliber he was usually sucked into. He exhibited an elevated engagement in those simpler games, much like the stoic challenge in the game of chess. Simple, uncluttered, highly cerebral. Sophie was a famous colorer, and she continued her missions with crayons and paper and staples and twine, crafting books out of her work, then making a library of her journey. She broadened her repertoire beyond the clown with his inverted suggestion of happiness. She graduated to houses and horses and happy little families holding hands. I wore great relief that the kids had assimilated to this slower speed, a pace that clearly incited more genuine creativity than the over-stimulating ignitions that usually fed their social appetites. Yes, we did a lot of nothing, but we did it very well.

The written word, for me, lended a back door access into the reality of Alex's and my connection, like an algorithmic query whose whispers were just proven but not yet publicly broadcast. For over two years, our communications were largely limited to our excessive phone conversations, masked by updates and kid progress and daily details. I hadn't realized how divided our feigned union really was until reading the black and white international e-mails that had replaced those phone calls. There wasn't the fallacy of his intimate connection to me in any of the mail, just news and weather and money. I tried to recall the last "I love you" or "I miss you" I had heard or read, then wondered why I hadn't noticed that obvious absence. I hadn't noticed a lot more than that.

These written renderings, of which there may have been twenty back and forth quips, all strung together from an original e-mail, were impossible to ignore. I printed the script, certain that I might find evidence of his intentions branded in toner, otherwise indiscernible in the mirage of computer screen. All tallied, they summed up the grand total of what we were not. I read it six times, nothing. Denying my failed marriage was no longer a neutral convenience. My silent vigil was spawning a hemorrhage of my spirit that could no longer be dismissed without consequence. I suspected it was time to embrace this defeat, to wear some of this grief and sorrow with the double 'D' branding of my personal stock. This was one battle that was clearly going to cost more than the war.

The story of Narcissus is a very interesting one. Like most things in life, I thought I knew the message behind the Greek myth of the young beautiful boy. I assumed in my peripheral lay knowledge of his story that he was a man who met his needs above all else, much like one might consider hedonism to be. In fact, I had speculated that I was married to Narcissus. Indeed, it is very much other than that.

Greek tragedy is rife with some of life's most vital lessons. Any course in self-examination should include reacquainting oneself as an adult, not as homework, through the many myths of the humbling journey of living a life not as a God but as a human.

Narcissus, indeed, is a young man. He is infatuated by the beauty of himself and has scorned many lovers along his whimsical journeys. The collection of these deluded hearts seek revenge from the Goddess Nemesis, to brand the self-love that Narcissus knows as the ultimate curse of self-destruction. By way of this curse, he forges a love in the mirage of his own reflection, and he is captured by the vision of his loveliness that is but a vacant, empty shadow of himself.

Narcissus is challenged by the frustrations that the reflection puts forward: his inability to hear, though when he speaks he sees the movement of his lips; his inability to touch, as he is frustrated, separated by the transparency of water; his inverted recognition that that which has made him beautiful has ironically made him inaccessible. His story concludes with his inability to truly know love, which climaxes in a tear of sorrow in the pool beneath him, which ultimately disturbs the reflection and it is there no more. In desperation, he reaches for it and drowns in his delusion. Efforts to resurrect his body yield nothing. It has been transformed into the beautiful narcissus flower.

I stood still. Narcissus was me. It did not seem possible that I was my own architect in the measure to settle my satisfactions with the promise of company that was but a vacant illusion. I wept beneath the angry skies that wept above the small of me. The rains beat upon my backside as I nestled into the the most compact human form, my face resting against the earth, my tears flooding in private baptism, salting all wounds I had ever known. I surrendered to the absurd irony of this duel. I recognized that the protective insulation from the vulnerability in intimacy had prompted me to barely lend credence to the selection of a life partner, as the job had been filled out of fear that no one better than me might show up. *Oh fuck*, I thought. *All on my watch.*

And I kept running. I found a steady groove in my aerobic stride, which whispered suggestions to me of the glorious depth of a life that I wanted to learn I was capable of living through the shattering of this shell. Life is learning, if it is ever worth living. Stagnation is the virulent cesspool of the small life married to the big ego. This knowledge was fostering in me a feeling of forward motion, of deliberate inertia fast-forwarding over past pitfalls, where clarity reigned with a bird's eye view.

Some of the most formative observations I made as the dedicated barfly and understudy to men, were steeped in the notion of attachment.

I did appreciate that attachment was, indeed, a necessity of the human condition, a byproduct of the nature of love, a tangent that elevated us from the monkey. However, it seemed that the collective level of happiness among men crested slightly higher than that of women. Perhaps this was because, on the whole, men did not attach to concerns out of fear of loss, motivated by the threat of its ensuing emptiness.

I admired the even temperance that most men seemed better able to assert in their life. I would work to exercise more in my own. I surrender that I am governed by a slightly different ruling policy, but I can borrow and lift where I am able. I teeter between what I am, and what I want. I am a woman who wants to be loved and seduced and owned by a man who I love and seduce and own in return. I want to make ravioli from scratch and raise children to be exceptionally human and grow tulips in spring and give a blow job that can take flight. I want to be respected for my ravioli and children and tulips and blow jobs alike. I had never formally engaged that mission, yet it had suspended itself like a dangling participle that had been unduly ignored.

And true to my gender, for reasons that I felt able to embrace with an honesty and humility that scared me sober, I had barely deviated from my ruling policy. I was a girl. Little had changed from when I was eleven, gabbing with girlfriends, or scribbling hearts on scented paper with the initials of one of us with a particular boy, and then penning the signature of our married name with this poor slob, who was totally unaware of our focused psychosis.

Today, we have grown-up versions of related behaviors. Women are nuts. They are loving and loyal and compassionate and strong, yes. They are capable of moving mountains on principle, and I wouldn't doubt that there are some who can part water. We can motivate the stubborn. We are the first to offer help and the last to feed ourselves. Martyr mothers steeped in the conviction of our beliefs, defenders to our habitat, trainers to our children, warriors to our offenders. Depraved psychotic social aberrations, including murderers, purveyors of dark perversions that teeter between illegal and just plain weird, filthy sanctimonious priests, mad teens with rifles, swindlers posing as God, crooks with smiles, even down to the buffoons of barroom brawls—they rarely set up camp in the circle of my sisters. I proudly sing in the chorus of my gender. Men can be pigs. Men can exhibit behaviors barely elevated from our cousin, the monkey. But yes, women can definitely be nuts.

And I suspected it was time that I took my tippy toe out of the circle of my brothers, resigned as the sideline voyeur so hungry for their play book, so desperate for the inside scoop, so determined to level that playing field, so discarded for my equipment.

Attachment, indeed, was spiked with sweet venom. Most men did much better than me at not investing in temporal, fleeting urges. I knew I must learn to do this better. One needed to believe that possibilities were abundant, never threatening to vanish, to own the courage to move forward and beyond, barely vesting in the trappings of the landscape. The irony of an attachment was that I could derive such comfort from its place in my world, yet I was rendered impotent with the threat of its absence. Not the actual absence, but the threat of it would suffice. A scorned woman seeking revenge is a lethal entity. Pay as much respect for the rush of that wrath as for the still of its wake.

As my pace was sustained in following weeks, the notion of attachment kept chiming its rabid agenda. I began to see that all things that I had assigned as privy and parcel to the web of my missions, my personal attachments, had been responses to polar fears that underwrote those very motives. I put forward example after example of behavior patterns I had exhibited and presented them in a petri dish before the jury of myself. No effort was needed to connect those dots.

Examine the mother of all attachments: The vanity of beauty. Ironically, this was a depreciating asset when surveyed by its outer shell. There was crowded company among the women of the Western world, lining up like Russian immigrants, desperately seeking to stave off the consequence of age and life as we visibly gained distance from the blossom of our youth. There was an urgent fury to drink from secret fountains to disguise the inevitable toll of life: botox injections, butt lifts, boob jobs, chemical sears, liposuction, toxic diets, a $100 1 oz. glass jar of an eye cream which might as well have been the sperm of an endangered whale with polka dots, all in the name of landing a man or keeping a man or moving on from a man. Aggressive. Invasive. Expensive. Risky. Negligible. Yes times five.

There was a huge market for all of this, with an appetite that could not be fed fast enough. It was frankly very sad to see the number of women who were slow to take inventory from the inside out. The gazillion dollars thrown at the futile task of ever-so-slightly, if ever at all, slowing the imminent was a testimony to the state of fear that surrounded my gender on this count. A fear of being overlooked for a newer model. A fear of being valued less as our resonating assets were forced to shift in their intrinsic values. Perhaps men aged better because fear was the masked culprit and the whale sperm was their ironic joke. I was in dire need of a better program, and felt open to explore these possibilities in advance of any deathbed awakening, emotionally excavated a little too late. It was time for some staying power.

I also realized that, while it felt convenient to align myself with all the women of the Western world, I was merely looking in the mirror, captivated yet impotent.

And I had attached to a marriage with someone that I had permitted to batter my psyche, which didn't necessarily mean that it was battered at all. That I loved him and that he loved me no longer seemed material to the ownership of the mess. This matrimonial fix had serrated twin blades: I feared wearing the failure of divorce, I feared the possibility of not having an intimate life partner. My reluctance to wake up and let go had been borne of that duo, hardwired in an empty promise, as I grasped each thinning sinew as a measure to negate that loss. The fear, in my desperate grip, did not make a better partner out of someone, nor did it make a saint out of me.

The illusion of what could have been, for me, was no longer a fight that had a prize which was worthy. Certainly, a different outcome could have been written of the fairy tale of my life. I would have loved nothing more than to pass to our children the legacy of our loving, intact, till-death-do-us-part union. But it did not work out that way. The closer I get to the pulse of my own fire, the better the maestro I make for my motive. That is a legacy I am honored to move forward. Denial and repression, otherwise, will only write the tale of someone other than me, and I will be buried in the grave of someone else.

Perhaps I had been threatened that someone would cast me off to the hungry fire-eating dragons as recrimination for failure on my watch. I realized that this was the tragic, recurring theme of my life: the shame of failure and disappointment, and the vicarious responsibility I had assumed in shouldering it. I had spent considerable energy defending people and things that were not worthy, and had accordingly discarded many that were. I had stepped in as if I were the personally appointed advocate for the devil himself, sporting both a vendetta to win and an agenda to surrender. It had been a zero sum game, save the step backwards for the sheer effort involved.

Any forensic analysis might conclude that I was branded with this phobia at a young age by a figure willing and eager to inflict pain, but no.

As best I can figure, it was a self-imposed battery I had apparently drafted as a measure to stunt my awareness and diffuse my awakening when it was summoned, as though such glory could not belong to me. Somewhere, I didn't get the memo or I cut school that day or I just simply got it wrong. To not answer a charge that called my name was worse than defeat; there was the added twist of the default, shaken and stirred, which stung even deeper. It was the classic, self-fulfilling prophecy: Assume no one can do the job of loving you as well as you can, and indeed, surprise, no one will.

This is a perfect example of how smart I am. I remembered having spent my eight HMO-allotted sessions in therapy with an excellent psychologist who undoubtedly loved her job. I first started seeing her on the tail end of chemotherapy and on the front end of my marital crumble. I recall having aired the big balloon of the grand minutia of my frustrating life. She had a knack for asking blind-siding questions, listening with an ear that heard beyond my words, just as an artist sees beyond the plane of color. I explained what the problems were, even offered obvious solutions as though my issues were the textbook protocol for the classic control freak, but she continued to listen, not noting any of my suggestions.

My life was a play. The characters had been depicted, the setting portrayed, the temperaments distinguished. Yes, I see how rich the art of my temporal existence can appear on a playbill. Yes, the performers are fantastic and complex and eccentric and sometimes wonderfully weird. Yes, there is so much I am blessed with and my gratitude shares no sun with my anger, therefore my anger does not exist. No, I have no idea why I won't offer more than eleven seconds to discuss my father. It is futile to discuss my father. I love him, but it is futile.

Perhaps, she offered, there was far more pathology in that nonchalance than I had considered, that his lack of presence was other than neutral. She swung a line drive straight between my eyes when she offered her opinion on the exacting similarities between the shared exponential degree in which both my husband and my father didn't show up for me. No-show or not invited, it didn't matter. I told her she was nuts.

But there, on that mountain in Mexico, I recalled this exchange between us with crystal clarity. I recalled the shoes I was wearing because I couldn't fully square her eyes with my validation. How ludicrous, it seemed, to have personally elected to perpetuate such pain and vacancy, an elementary pitfall that any ordinary mind would have had the instinct to avoid like a toxin. A lateral move from a father I expected little of to a husband I expected little of, or less. Clearly, I inherited something from my mother beyond her green eyes. And clearly, the toll has been sizeable if not utterly obvious, that darker side of the forward female movement that equal rights does not seem to address. I suppose I could crawl around, resonating in the elixirs from the womb of my creation and seek answers to these psychological acrobatics, but what was the point? The milk had been spilled. The mess was my own. At least now there was something to clean up that I could see.

October turned me forty. I never before owned the *birth* piece of the birthday, until this particular year. The whole of a decade. The half of a life, God willing. The fraction of the suffering whose remnants felt as inert as ash discarded but for the value in the vessel. I was silenced in gratitude for the turbulence in my life in these past four years, for I knew that I would have never been forced otherwise to demand my own accountability. These were some fundamental lessons on protecting myself that perhaps I had mastered by age ten, but then I became so smart and stood square in my own way, like a white elephant fast asleep. Indeed, I was proud of all else I did get right. My kids had been my richest resource in reclaiming some of the essential human rites of happiness. Seeking the obvious road to serving that end was easier as a child before fear could motivate a mission. They still had the treasure map, with all the X's and secret passageways and ability to recognize the pot of gold when they found it. If only I could show them how to never let it go.

And forty brought me Peter as a surprise guest at the dinner party Daniela hosted in her home. She and Peter had arranged details via e-mail, Harry bought him the ticket, and Allen transported him from Mexico City. We were returning to the States the first week in November, and Peter came to hang with us for the last two weeks of the journey and return on our flight home. I smiled with a flood of tears when I saw him enter the door frame, and we embraced with a connection that could melt rock. He stood in awe, surveying my place of peace and presence, and noting my hair, which by then was looking like the easy shag of an urban goddess needing only negligible maintenance. The whole of my fitness was far more calculable to me in the light of his presence. In a very fitting rite of passage, we shot some tequila and toasted the beautiful possibility that surrounded all spirited human endeavors. That was the happiest birthday, by a country mile, I had known in all of my years.

Perhaps the largest native holiday celebrated in Tepoztlan, one which engaged every living citizen, was the event of Halloween. I had never imagined that this holiday could have been steeped in ritual and custom of an almost religious order. There were parties, parades, vigils, sacrifices, all lasting over one week. Cemeteries were adorned with elaborate floral shrines and sculptures and gory reenactments, all surrounding the Day of The Dead, the rising of those who had passed on. Everyone was in costume. Commerce stood still. People paid their respects to the intricate, delicate balance that governed all, contributed by those before us and those who will follow. Kids went wild for the creepy rising of the saints and the spooky suggestions of the mysterious other world. We walked the parade, the five of us, silently, in utter respect for the sheer force that can be created by the collective voice of one united people. *Adieu Tepoztlan. Muchas gracias.*

And So It Is

And at the conclusion, there is always a beginning. At my present elevation of 35,000 feet, I do understand that the flight attendant was talking to me when she suggested I affix my own breathing supply.

I am watching the kids occupy themselves. The boys are playing cards, crazy 8's. Leah is reading, Sophie is writing a story. They are each, beyond fathom, my escort to humanity. I argue that they have given life to me.

So many lessons, always. We stop learning, we stop living. Just when it seems the trenches are overcome with the mundane and the ordinary, when greater purpose feels a distant mark, it's the clay in the muck, the grit and the silt through which no toes can thread, that keeps still the ground on which to calibrate. It's strange when you can view something with such lucid clarity just for gaining some distance, finding some focus that often only time and space can lend. I can suffocate a problem until it breathes no more, and still it is not clear whether my efforts abetted or aggravated the situation. I'd vote for the latter. At even odds it's a bad bet, unless time, as currency, has no value.

Today, I own these. Tomorrow, they may be for sale. This is okay.

My drive for efficiency needn't be disguised in the vessel of speed, and, for certain, my blinders have effectively done their job.

Plenty of battles, indeed, are well worth the loss that they yield. The temporal notion of loss is wholly subjective.

Figuring out what you actually want is much more difficult than getting what you want, unless, of course, you haven't hit puberty.

Some days just aren't as good as others, and there is nothing personal about it. This too shall pass, get over it.

Beneath every weed there is a root. Above grade, there is visual relief in the violent impulse of its extraction. Below grade, there is an intricate network of fragile capillaries, nursed as infants, still king of its DNA. Dig deeper, with feeling rather than sight, to shape your garden of tomorrow.

Feverish fun is not the exclusive province of children, nor is it confined to the magic of a laced vegetable. Be certain that fervent laughter lightens loads.

And with certainty, there is far less in this world that I am actually responsible for, which not only liberates some time, but should raise the integrity of the missions I take on.

With any hope, I have learned that together, men and women make that pendulum swing, that consonance does not fly solo. And I am a believer that when those gears are appropriately engaged, the resulting synergy exceeds well more than twice each individual contribution. Perhaps one of the differing motives that fuel the power struggle between men and women are actually gradients on the same continuum. Men's satisfactions are often answered in the apex of climax, whereas women's satisfactions graciously aspire to reach the ensuing intimacy that follows the flood of those swirling waters, both in the physical and emotional realms. And where there is a plane to be shared, there is a middle to be met.

And four years ago, back on that street corner in Manhattan, in the presence of the reflection of myself from a place in time where I was more free and more fun and more penetrable, I discovered that the powers lay within me to reclaim those essential elements that ignited the fire of me. My serious and urgent matriculation is not mandatory, the axis of this earth does not pivot for me. Rather, my presence in the days that I live, one after the next, is the charge I must wake to, dance to, play with, nourish on, and sleep next to. It can be just that simple.

Without question, there is a costly derivative in our accelerated, franchised, .com mentality of 1-800-fix me now. Unfortunately, our children will tailor their own gears for survival as escorted in the swift and seductive grip of this age of technology. It is a superhighway where speed reigns, e-speak is barely language, retail has no address, wordshavenospaces, ten-deep voice mail prompts into circular oblivion are maddening enough to make on mainline vodka, and hard research is so yesterday.

Dial-up is for dinosaurs. An attention span is fleeting. Identity is for sale. Accountability is sketchy. And privacy is no more.

It's a retail orgy where high-tech gadgets feed manic appetites, spawning an insatiable emptiness by way of their designed disposability. A mindset where genuine, real-time human interaction in conducting the business of our daily lives feels lethargic, archaic, and curiously suspect. In five minutes flat I can book a flight to Minneapolis and count the words on this manuscript and order live Maine lobsters for next-day delivery and view live web-cam photos of our planet Earth, but I can't always execute that lesson on how to tie those shoe laces. Yes, MapQuest can get me from my own driveway to the Empire State Building on a fifteen page tedious script, but ultimately an internal compass diffuses and Pavlov's dog no longer has instinct. Perhaps such progress is the most Trojan of all horses.

And it's time I bid farewell to my marriage. I have learned something I had known but did not choose to let in. Alex was an inveterate gambler, a craps player.   It fueled a passion for him that would forever subordinate all else. I was his dice. I got fondled under his control, then released in hopes of taking it the hard way. The come bet kept me on his table, near to the emission of his rushing fury. As his fine tossing talent got celebrated when his points were made, I was parlayed into a sum that was not me. Only if I still got fondled did I know that the game was not over. The snake eyes saw through and beyond me, as though I wasn't really there at all. Chances were slim that his shooting dice could turn me into the 20-year-old hard-body that I am not. Those dice they flew in hypnotic succession and the chips accrued in small mountains until the devil tainted a toss and poof, they were there no more. Craps has always come first. I am worth more to him married than divorced.   I am worth more to him dead than alive. Get me out of this forsaken Pit. Death by lightening offers better odds than winning this game.

Somewhere over the state of Georgia, I remove the band around my finger. It feels most fitting to leave it as a prize in the barf bag. Perhaps Sophie may want it for posterity some day. Perhaps not. The bag is better. I can only hope to slither out of this noose with such ease.

When I consider *my* passion, the one I knew as a child before I got tripped up in the currency of hormones, there is a love that I left behind. Undeniably, it was my motive in living. I was a writer, an uncomplicated little girl, always sporting a pen and paper, giving life to letters so hungry to dance, then moving words from thought into motion.

There is a book. It is impressively transcribed and illustrated by my talented aunt, and includes most of my writings from age five to age ten. Some are poems, some are stories, some are prayers of private possibility. This hardcover book was lovingly compiled by my mother, years ago, and rests high on her library bookshelf with a forgotten film of dust swathing its kernels of childhood wisdom. Writing was my road to reason, and I never got lost.

In the ironic inversion of the paradox of life, I am immersed in my laptop writing these last pages, first, of the book I am intending to write when I return home. This is my new trio, a happy hat trick in no strait jacket, respecting my present elevation, almost in outer space:

It will be a work of closure, an epiphany of the journey that has challenged me hard and made me far closer to being whole, far more fit to embrace life with respect for its tender and delicate and magnificent beauty. In the absence of a cure for cancer, one has no other choice but to let cancer cure you. This train only goes forward. And my indebtedness extends to the state of Florida. I hold no hostages.

It will be a potential job interview if I should be so bold as to give it flight in the commercial literary markets, a goal that I have always aspired to try, but was fearful of failing at. If you are reading this and you didn't get it from me for Christmas, this is a good sign. Whether or not this book puts me on the map, it matters none. It is the blueprint toward my own destiny that matters plenty.

Lastly, it will be my most humble and heartfelt token of gratitude to every person in this work, as well as those beyond, who have shown up for me with the most inconceivable gestures of love and reverence. They invoked their energy to insure that I showed up for my own recovery and didn't hire it out. Friends are, hands down, life's most valuable asset. And I am a sucker for love. I grow impassioned in my heart and weak in my knees at the prospect of finding the intimacy I have hungered for. I am sure the Intervention Club will be holding interviews if I should swing that bat again.

Acknowledgements

Timing is everything. The intricate and complex alignment of all living things, continually in motion, is neither random nor coincidental. I thank the mystical powers-that-be that founded my timing and launched my journey. Finding that fire took me many years to approach, many trials to understand, and many stumbled efforts to learn the shape of its prowess. To those in my periphery who kept me in such fine company, thank you.

For my Mother. For the steep and steadfast conscience that governs all that is you, there is no greater example I could have known. For those darkest of hours when there was *always* someone to call, I am eternally grateful. Your compassion and generosity know no boundary. Your love and commitment never saw a single day that was not met with your conviction to meet the charge of doing right by way of your three children. For that example, which I move forward, my children thank you. For the exceptional humor, the dead-on perspective, the unqualified understanding, and the wellspring of good judgement, I thank you. You will be with me forever, and we will *always* be laughing.

To Jon and Karen. For the dancing and the drama and the age-old dialogue which never needs a prelude, we are three very lucky ones. For every chapter we have lived together, for every memory we have made together, and for every sorrow we have nursed together, I am so grateful to be placed in the middle of you. Love knows no better home.

For Laurie, for thick and thin, for one through six, for that knowing you own that sets straight me and my wanders, I thank you. And I thank the mystical force that collided our worlds on that unlikely afternoon. We both found gold. Now, surrender to your clairvoyance already.

For Wendy, for the timeless tenure that surrounds our friendship. Your unwavering confidence in my ability to see anything through has served as a beacon at a time when I couldn't even see at all. What a safe haven, having a place where all fears and dreams have a forum to be expressed without a single dose of judgment. Thank you for being exactly as you are.

To Daniela, for sharing your compass and showing me how to calibrate mine. The strength and spirit of your first born will reside within you forever and you will sail with the grace in the light of his love. Thanks for everything.

For Shari, for September 12th, for the fire ants disguised as neighbors, for the bunkers below ground, and for all of the ground we have covered since then, thank you for helping diffuse my darkness.

To my girlfriends. The flame of our friendship burns with more brilliant radiance as life moves forward. While the circle may get smaller on the survey, it grows larger in the heart, deeper in the spirit, and eternal in the soul. Go there. You can take it with you, and you can leave it behind. It is the perfect arrangement. For Laurie, Wendy, Daniela, Shari, Debbie, Karen, Sarah & red-headed Ginger, I am so especially grateful.

For Jeff. No words can convey the depth of my gratitude for all you have been, all you have done in shaping two very incredible people. They are both blessed for your presence in their lives. There is much I've learned in the example of you. Thank you, and thanks to Teresa.

To Nancy, for the courage it takes to be straight with yourself, for balancing all of my kids equally, for living a strangely parallel life by my side, for your twin sister, for always knowing I had it in me, and especially for those 4 p.m. breathers, thank you.

With thanks, PG. He found me words, found me facts, and he helped me find the strength to find my voice. He enabled me to access my internal search engine to find the courage to look deeper if I was going to bother looking at all. The mentor in him, for me, showed me how to stand still, have faith, and dream big. He is a man of few words, but when two of those few were "keep writing," less is always more.

For Stuart, for the lesson learned in friendship first, thanks. Marketing and promotion took stellar strides under your wing, and it's a good thing you didn't quit your day job. What good fortune to have found you exactly when I did.

For Paul and the two hats one can never wear well. For the miles flown, the miles skated, the miles bridged, thank you for always being there for me and for my kids.

To my chemo angel, JFC, and her saint of a mother; my family has been shown the tallest of lessons. Your kindness and compassion and generosity are truly a window into the heart of a God I am learning to know. You have shown me that when Faith is blind, you can sometimes see more clearly.

To Wayne, the best of Braves well beyond baseball, thank you.

For MY, for your friendship, for your counsel, and for finding that woman who showed up on that unlikely Saturday morning. Thank you.

To Jenny, for having tall talents exactly where I have none, for your friendship beyond family, for your humor and confidence I so admire, and for your very likely shot at breaking the curse, you go girl.

For Mothers for Thursdays.

For Alex, for your role in bringing two beautiful children into this world, for some happy memories, and for what it was before it wasn't. The cardinal rule of the wheel is simple. Red or black, the house is the only sure winner.

To my Dad, for the passive guidance that demanded me to access that place where it hurts the most. Returning there, I was able to wake up, and that illumination cast a kinder, more loving light. I am learning to see things I hadn't seen and feel things I hadn't felt, and I am so grateful for that awakening. Thank you, thank you, thank you.

And always, all days, to those four little beings who help me return to that place of trust and love and wonder and purpose where spirits soar and magic always remains a possibility.

A portion of the proceeds from the sale of this book is gratefully being donated to two most-worthy causes whose missions strive to improve the world we live in:

THE AMHERST YOUTH FOUNDATION is a charitable, non-profit organization with a mission to raise funds for diverse programs and services for all youth and families in Amherst, New York, thereby increasing the quality of life by providing safe and healthy environments for the betterment of our children.

STEP UP WOMEN'S NETWORK is a national, nonprofit membership organization dedicated to strengthening community resources for women and girls. Through hands-on community service, mentoring and fundraising for women's health and critical issues, they educate and activate their membership to ensure that women and girls have the tools they need to create a better future.